MW00532702

Heartbreak City

Heartbreak City

SEATTLE SPORTS
AND THE UNMET PROMISE
OF URBAN PROGRESS

Shaun Scott

University of Washington Press | Seattle

4 CULTURE Heartbreak City *was made possible in part by a grant from the 4 Culture Heritage Special Projects Program.*

Composed in Garamond Premier Pro, Cooper Std Black, and Helvetica Neue Condensed Bold

27 26 25 24 23   5 4 3 2 1

Printed and bound in the United States of America

UNIVERSITY OF WASHINGTON PRESS *uwapress.uw.edu*

LIBRARY OF CONGRESS CONTROL NUMBER 2023941158
ISBN 9780295751993 (hardcover)
ISBN 9780295752006 (ebook)

♾ This paper meets the requirements of ANSI/NISO Z39.48-1992 (Permanence of Paper).

**This book
is dedicated
to Seattle's
working
classes.** As librarians,
baristas,
campaign workers,
nurses,
schoolteachers,
grocery store workers,
and more,
you power
what wouldn't
otherwise
move.

If you're going to go for something,
you're going to have some heartbreak.
But if you're not willing to go there,
you're never going to get there.

RUSSELL WILSON
Seattle Seahawks quarterback,
2012–2022

A good deal of our politics
is physiological.

RALPH WALDO EMERSON

CONTENTS

TRAIN RIDE
TO THE
BALLPARK

As steam from speeding locomotives wafted into the New
England ether in the summer of 1872, a heroic canine waged
a daily contest. Every day, the dog traced the railroad tracks
by the Connecticut River, trying to catch the train; every day, he came up
short. Undeterred, he kept after it. He refused to lose. His Sisyphean hustle
was immortalized in the July 18, 1872, edition of the Seattle newspaper the
Puget Sound Dispatch: "An ambitious dog sallies forth every day when the
train comes. He fails, but hope springs eternal in the canine breast, and
he continues, expecting with practice to beat the iron horse."[1] In the pup's
determination to track down a train, the *Dispatch* found a metaphor for
colonial Seattle.

The competition to secure railroad lines was a high-stakes contest, and
Seattle didn't want to be left behind. All around Puget Sound were feisty
settlements, each vying for the title of premier city of the Pacific Northwest.
One hundred eighty miles south of Seattle, the city of Portland emerged
an early contender for the Pacific coast crown, its situation along the Wil-
lamette River positioning it as a trade hub. Farther south, San Francisco
was the undisputed champion of the American West: it dwarfed Seattle
and its surrounding competitors, using the timber that Puget Sound towns
farmed and sent there to build a buzzing metropolis in the Bay Area. Before
upstart Seattle could breathe the rarified air of its superiors, it would have
to defeat its area siblings: Snohomish, Newcastle, Olympia, Victoria, and
above all, Tacoma.

Powerful railroad firms looked to place a train terminal somewhere
along Puget Sound. Allowing a rival town to take what Seattleites believed
to be theirs by dint of hard work and providence would constitute a grave

defeat of great material and psychological consequence. It couldn't happen. Seattle could not lose. But a year after the *Dispatch* chronicled the dog's railroad chase, devastating news came to Seattle's two thousand residents via telegram on July 14, 1873: the Northern Pacific Railway located the lusted-after train terminal thirty miles away—in Tacoma.[2] A year earlier, Seattle had entered a regional bidding war for the depot, offering Northern Pacific Railway three thousand acres of land and a big bucket of bonds and cash. The dowry was worth $17 million. The city's residents were confident this offer would lead to corporate commitment.[3] Poor Seattle had sold itself out, but was not selected.

How could this have happened?

Seattle was desirable. It had waterfront views. It had two sawmills. It had a fledgling real estate market, proximity to coal mines, and waterways for coastal trade. Seattle had more people than any Puget Sound city besides Olympia. But the attributes that made it a great locale for a railroad depot worked against it: the leviathan Northern Pacific Railway sought not just cheap labor to build their lines but also cheap land on which to build them. Railroad robber barons played the real estate market as a side hustle. So instead of putting more money in the hands of Seattle's already-established business class, Northern Pacific ran their rail through Tacoma—a tiny backwater of two hundred people that wouldn't even incorporate as a city until two years later.[4] Tacoma, not Seattle, would enjoy the spoils of victory: population growth, gluts of industry and national attention, a place on the actual map. In the cauldron of frontier capitalism, Seattle had done battle and lost.

Upon hearing the news, Seattleites cursed the businessmen who betrayed them. Many moved. But those who stayed didn't take the defeat lying down. Here was a city that prided itself on settler tenacity: "The pioneers of Puget Sound cut their trees and built their cabins and forced the wilderness back from a dozen beachheads," wrote Murray Morgan in his classic 1951 narrative of colonial Seattle, *Skid Road*.[5] "They had endured the damp and the mud, they had gone without salt and flour, they had left friends and relatives and comforts two thousand miles behind." If the ongoing frontier genocide they perpetrated against Puget Sound's Indigenous peoples was any indication, colonial Seattleites wouldn't be suffering the Tacoma defeat lightly.

When white settlers arrived in the Puget Sound area in November 1851 with the intent of establishing the colony that became Seattle, they accused the Indigenous people already living there of being lazy.[6] "Fish and berries give them an easy livelihood," a white land surveyor wrote of Puget Sound Natives in 1851.[7] "They float through life." Although white settlers depended on Coast Salish peoples for food and labor, lies about Native laziness provided a pretext for colonization. White Seattleites encroached upon Indigenous land, exploited the Indigenous to build their town with Native-farmed lumber and agricultural knowledge, sparked bloody conflagrations with the Coast Salish that bubbled over into open war, then named their settlement after the vanquished Duwamish statesman Chief Seattle in 1865—the same year the town's first city council passed a law banning Natives from the city. Colonial Seattleites were wanton. They'd fight any foe, scale any height, and sink to any depth to realize the fantasy of global prestige upon which their settlement had been founded.

Believing their town to be a great metropolis-in-the-making, the original name Seattle's colonists came up with for their town was "New York Alki," with *alki* meaning "eventually" in the Chinook language. In 1874, after the Northern Pacific Railway decided to run through Tacoma, Seattle's residents rallied, drunk with thoughts of revenge and eager to chart a course to becoming a world-class city. A preposterous idea emerged among aggrieved Seattleites in saloons and civic gatherings: Why couldn't they build a rail line themselves? "Let's quit fooling and get to work," said pioneer Henry Yesler, whose dinky lumber mill was supposed to attract the Northern Pacific Railway.[8] Connecting Seattle to railway depots hundreds of miles away in Eastern Washington would have entailed exceeding amounts of work and money. It was an absurd plan. Mercifully, it was aborted when an 1873 recession evaporated the funds needed to complete it. But while the self-made railroad was a short-lived pipe dream, the civic spirit it spawned survived. Many Seattleites began to believe that the key to becoming a great city was wanting it badly enough.

At about this time, baseball became a Seattle obsession that ran parallel to the railroad, the two tracks starting in the same place—civic ambition—and heading in a similar direction. In the spring of 1877, coal miners from the nearby town Newcastle challenged "any picked nine" from Seattle to a baseball game.[9] A Seattle logger and a business clerk teamed up to play pitcher and catcher, then fielded a team of elites and proletarians, capitalists and workaday laborers in Henry Yesler's mill. Wearing street clothes, Seattle vaporized Newcastle by a score of 51–0 in May 1877. Two hundred Seattleites accompanied the team on a boat to Canada for a game against Victoria, where the unnamed Seattle squad prevailed again. Winning felt good. Pioneer whites snubbed by the Northern Pacific healed their bruised egos by paying the pain forward on the field of play.

Baseball was a shortcut to the business clout the railroad would've brought. Before a July 4, 1877, rematch against Victoria, local businessmen raised $11,000 in hand-circulated financial contributions to the Seattle team. Wearing tailored uniforms and playing as the "Alkis"—the Indigenous name whites first gave their settlement—Seattle beat Victoria again in front of a thousand spectators on a playfield in the neighborhood Georgetown. When the Alkis notched another victory against Port Gamble later in 1877, the *Seattle Post-Intelligencer* praised the team for showing that Seattle was "good for something other than clams and timber."[10]

Seattle was a proud city. Its residents hadn't given up on the railroad. They named their first-ever baseball team the Alkis—the Eventualies—because they believed they'd one day live in a great city.[11] But before long, the city's lust for baseball glory and trains crashed at the same destination: abject failure.

Festival organizers slated Seattle's baseball team, now playing as the Reds, to play two games against Snohomish to celebrate railroad magnate Henry Villard's trip to the city in autumn 1883. Villard talked a good game. He promised to bring a railroad depot to Seattle a decade after the Tacoma defeat. Villard's visit prompted the most elaborate celebration in the young city's history; arches carved of evergreens adorned city streets above the parade route downtown. As part of the festivities, the Reds would play Snohomish in a doubleheader.[12]

Because the railroad and the baseball games both announced Seattle's intention to prevail over other Puget Sound towns, there was much at stake in these games in terms of civic pride. Consequently, residents were crushed to see Seattle drop both games by scores of 14–8 and 6–3, respectively. In a smoldering diatribe on October 6, 1883, the *Seattle Post-Intelligencer* lambasted the Reds for embarrassing the city: "For shame, boys! That you allowed yourself to be beaten, and then taunted and insulted over it, is humiliating to all in town. Disband your organization or get yourself in trim."[13] The *Post-Intelligencer* had absorbed the *Puget Sound Dispatch* that made a civic mascot of the railroad-obsessed dog in New England. The paper's sportswriters did no additional reporting to determine if the canine caught the train—Seattle sure didn't: after his promise to bring the city a train depot, Henry Villard went bankrupt. Bereft of investors, his company crumbled in January 1884. Seattle's train ambitions toppled with it. The city plunged into a localized recession.

When the railroad bubble busted, white Seattleites who had tolerated Chinese immigrants as a source of cheap labor (when they thought there were train tracks to lay) became hostile. In February 1886 a mob assisted by the city's cops expunged all but about a dozen of Seattle's estimated 350 Chinese from the city's Chinatown.[14] Losers in baseball and global commerce, Seattle had stooped to a new low.

* * *

For American cities, sports have never been just sports. Athletics are great vaults of fiscal and psychological investment, symbols of socioeconomic competition between groups that have more power and those that have less. Sports are an abstraction of the relationship that city dwellers have with other city dwellers, that cities have with other cities, and that urbanites have with their built and natural environments. How people do anything is how they do *everything*; the games people play say a lot about who they are.

Seattle's place on the far left coast of the United States puts it in the center of stories about hard work and self-reliance that Americans have been telling themselves since the age of westward expansion. In the same way that colonial Seattleites believed they could fashion a great city from thin air and willpower, many American city dwellers—even the urban poor—believe themselves to be momentarily defeated aristocrats who will one day become wealthy with just a little more effort. Just as sports fandom is subject to euphoric highs and devastating lows, politics in American cities sway from periods of progress to eras of retrenchment. The climax of collective action is often followed by a conservative crash. Progressives in America's cities experience their politics as they experience their sports: through a few ups and many downs, on the edge of failure, and at risk of heartbreak.

Heartbreak City tracks this contest between progressivism and conservatism in American cities through the medium of athletics in the late nineteenth, twentieth, and twenty-first centuries. I argue that historical iterations of the progressive movement succeeded inasmuch as they made the absolute most of opportunities for political transformation and failed to the extent that reactionaries countermobilized to undo progressive gains. Through the prism of Seattle and its sundry rivalries with other American cities, I show how progressive urbanites use athletics to solve persistent problems in American life: racism, gender inequity, and repression of sexual minorities; ableism, wealth inequality, and ruination of the environment. Concurrently, opponents of social progress have used sport to consolidate their power. Cities are open-air arenas where the forward winds of progress and gusts of regressivity swirl.

Tennis, swimming, golf, boxing, pickleball. Nearly every American sport appears in this book because every sport is politically significant. Basketball is the sport of forward-thinking urbanism, a game of grace and fluidity where divides of race and gender are confronted and reconciled: the SuperSonics modeled Black Seattle's fight for socioeconomic inclusion, while the Storm galvanized underrepresented women and LGBTQ+ fans. Conversely, hockey and football are rugged recreations that resurrect the survival-of-the-fittest frontier heritage that Seattle never truly left behind. As technological change proceeded at an unprecedented rate in the early twentieth and early twenty-first centuries, crowds cheered the hypermasculine exploits of the Seattle Metropolitans and Seahawks, respectively. Ultimately, though, this book's structure follows that of a baseball game. Its chapters unfurl as "innings" where progressives try to sustain momentum while stopping their opponents from doing the same.

If basketball is poetry—each possession an iambic stanza delivered quickly on the court's compressed lines—then baseball is a novel, with overlapping stories playing out across long swaths of space and time. Baseball and history both have payoffs, the former on full count pitches where sustained tension peaks, the latter in moments where mundane events are later revealed to have major consequences. In 1893 the Northern Pacific Railway that backstabbed the city sold forty acres of Seattle-area land to an enterprising German immigrant named Friedrich Trump, starting his family's fortune.[15]

In *Ballpark: Baseball in the American City*, architectural critic Paul Goldberger writes "in the ballpark, the two sides of the American character—the impulse toward rural expanse and the belief in the city and industrial infrastructure—cannot be torn apart."[16] The sport juxtaposes the dense crowd and the grassy field on which only an elite few may play. In many ways Seattle political history unfolds as the resolution of this tension.

Baseball has data for everything. The figure that relays heartbreak is "runners in scoring position," a stat that measures how well a team capitalizes on chances to score. The cruel pastime lets you know when potential runs are aboard the bases, making the sense of possibility more tangible, the expectations more tantalizing, and the failure to cash them in more tragic than in sports where potential is less palpable. Opportunities—seized and missed—decide our sports as they decide our politics.

* * *

Seattle and its people have long had a love-hate affair with sports; in *Heartbreak City*, I try to count the ways. Athletics are often at the center of raging debates over city space and public funds: in the early twentieth century, biking activists urged the city to tax itself to pave the city's first roads. In Seattle history sports have also typified competitions over resources between the city's ethnic groups: as segregation in Seattle housing, schools, and jobs endured, a 1957 title fight between a Black heavyweight champion of the world and a local white amateur became a charged racial spectacle. Examples of marginalized groups using sports as an instrument of greater sociopolitical inclusion are many. Seattle Japanese American baseball teams defeated military police in games played in incarceration camps in the

1940s, while women and LGBTQ+ bikers bucked retrograde gender norms after World War II. Popular games are also often deployed as a metaphor for politics, a simile of broader contests that find a microcosm in sport. While cracking down on organized labor during the Seattle General Strike of 1919, Mayor Ole Hanson wrote proudly of "[not allowing] anarchists to get to first base."[17] Through it all—strikes and ball games, swings at progressive change, and misses—sports are something like the soul of Seattle. Our games animate the values and aspirations of our city, in much the same way that love brings the best and worst out of the people in our lives.

The first part of *Heartbreak City* spans 1893 through 1942. It details the establishment of the initial progressive political framework in the United States, its subsequent iteration in the New Deal policies of the 1930s, and the impact this current of social change had on the intersection of sport and politics in Seattle. With the help of activists who encouraged the city to build inclusive bike paths and playgrounds, Seattle separated itself from its frontier past at the turn of the twentieth century; the roughneck sports of college football and professional hockey dragged it back, psychologically and socially, to the days of westward expansion. During the regressive 1920s, Seattleites built racially exclusive neighborhoods and golf courses that were accessible mostly by cars. Automobiles encroached on street baseball games and enabled exclusive mountain sports. This Seattle freeze of sociopolitical exclusion thawed in the 1930s. A new collectivist tide in local and national politics was reflected in the rising popularity of water sports, which brought Seattle the attention that Progressive Era parks activists sought a generation earlier.

The second part of the book (1945–69) is concerned with populations left out of the original progressive political framework of the earlier twentieth century. After World War II, women and LGBTQ+ Seattleites found social and physical liberation in park sports leagues and motorbiking in the latter 1940s. In the 1950s, Seattle University basketball star Elgin Baylor typified the resilience of Black Seattleites in the city's segregated Central Area. Ultimately the failure of progressive leaders to rally Asian American, disabled, and Indigenous Seattleites led to a defining heartbreak in the city's history: the 1968 transit elections which paved the way for the Seattle Mariners and Seattle Seahawks but failed to gift the city comprehensive mass transit.

The third part of the book (1970–99) deals with the commercialization of the progressive movement in Seattle. As Seattle gained widespread recognition as a postindustrial city of the future that would transcend the political divisions of the past, its sports teams bolstered its rising cultural cachet. Although the Seattle Sonics united the city in pursuit of the NBA Championship in 1978–79, many white fans were painfully slow to embrace the team because of the city's racial divide. The arrival of the Seahawks gave Seattle big-league status coveted by city boosters for decades, but progenitors of a pro-corporate streak in local politics criticized players for striking in 1987. Although Black superstars Ken Griffey Jr., Shawn Kemp, and Gary Payton shined brightly in the 1990s, Seattle was still a city where white supremacists burned churches, hoping to realize their vision for a racially exclusive society. Popular periodicals and mass media—*Sports Illustrated* and *Sleepless in Seattle*—elevated Seattle as the most livable US city in the late twentieth century. The hype was all hype. Seattle's reputation cratered, alongside the fortunes of many of its teams.

The fourth part of *Heartbreak City* (2000 thru the early 2020s) relays the conservative turn in American politics that led many across the country to look down upon the considerable achievements of the Seattle Storm in the WNBA as well as the popularity of soccer in the Pacific Northwest. The resurgence of political conservatism in the United States—the rise of "red" states like Oklahoma—led directly to the relocation of the Seattle SuperSonics. With the election of President Barack Obama in 2008, "blue" coastal cities like Seattle would get off the political canvas after the knockdowns of the Bush years. But the Obama administration turned out to be a missed opportunity for enduring progressive change—its failure mirrored in the national spectacle of the Seattle Seahawks' inability to become a football dynasty in a conservative sports league.

The final chapters of this book deal with manifestations of fake progressivism in Seattle sports in the 2010s and 2020s. At this time, area progressives used the widespread exploitation of college researchers as a reason to not allow college athletes to be compensated. Self-professed environmentalist politicians dismantled the construction of bike lanes. Others opposed plans to convert golf courses into affordable housing that could help reduce carbon emissions by shortening commutes. In

October 2022 the Seattle Mariners played a home playoff game in the dense fog of another summer beset by wildfire smoke; in the thick haze, little could be seen but the need to make the city the truly progressive city it had rarely been.

* * *

Historical scholarship is a contact sport that puts a writer on the contested discursive field of clashing perspectives about the past. In this colosseum of competing worldviews, those who come up short on the American social order's hierarchy—workers, the disabled, ethnic and sexual minorities, women—are seldom represented. In contrast to many liberal historians who see American politics as a consensus-driven enterprise characterized by broad agreement on core issues, Marxist historiography depicts the US social order as a competition between capital and labor, the potent and the less powerful. In the tradition of *A People's History of the United States*, Howard Zinn's landmark 1980 book, *Heartbreak City* is a people's history of Seattle—narrated not from the vantage point of capitalism's victors but from the standpoint of its discontents. Because they have one winner and many who were never supposed to win, sports demystify our politics by mirroring them.

To tell the story of the politicized relationship between Seattleites and their sports, I rely heavily on newspaper accounts. An early episode in the city's history illustrates why. In June 1913 the *Seattle Times* and *Seattle Post-Intelligencer* staffs played an exhibition baseball game against one another in Dugdale Park, located in the city's Mount Baker neighborhood. Afraid to lose, the "Times Terrors" used its considerable financial advantage to sign an actual major league ballplayer in its game against the "Post-Intelligencer Pirates." It was a slimy move. It sullied what was supposed to be an exhibition with the muck of big money and exposed the existential divide between the two publications. The *Post-Intelligencer* slammed the *Times* for "patching up their pitiful aggregation" by throwing cash at their hitting problems. The *Times* blamed crooked refs when the game ended in a tie. A few weeks after their baseball battle, the two papers brawled again—this time, over politics. In a rush to portray Seattle's rising left-wing political bloc negatively, the pro-capitalist *Times* falsely blamed anarchists for causing a fight at a civic festival in Pioneer Square in July 1913.[18] The *Post-Intelligencer* countered with accurate reporting showing that maligned leftists had nothing to do with the disturbance. The two papers duked it out all summer. Journalism being "the first draft of history," those drafts were steeped in disagreement in Seattle.

For generations before the advent of social media websites, newspapers were the most transparent gauge of public sentiment in American cities. News write-ups, recurring columns, and letters to the editor illustrate how Seattleites felt about the times they lived in and the games they watched. The city's competing political blocs—ethnic groups, labor unions, and organizations ranging from college leftists at the University of Washington to the Seattle chapter of the Ku Klux Klan—all had print media. Usually these publications had sports pages. Their coverage of working-class bowling teams, Asian American baseball leagues, women's hockey, and more showed how sports embodied Seattle's political struggles at the grassroots level. At the same time, national reporting about the city's professional sports teams indicated how Seattle was perceived by others. A 1926 edition of *The Nation* reveals that male Seattleites voted out the city's woman mayor because they felt she couldn't adequately represent a city of "mountain climbers and pioneering outdoorsmen."[19]

While trying to wrestle a clear narrative from a jumble of facts and events, I've found valuable teammates in a substantial body of secondary source material. I cite these sources in the text as well as in chapter endnotes but feel compelled to discuss works that were foundational to the completion of this book. The main inspiration for the scope of *Heartbreak City* is Arthur M. Schlesinger Jr.'s 1986 book *The Cycles of American History*. Schlesinger wrote that the motor of American political history is "that elemental human experience in which enthusiasm gives way to fatigue and disenchantment—the experience that characterizes the ebb and flow of the political cycle."[20] In describing shifts from liberal periods to more conservative ones—periods of public radicalization to those of rightward retrenchment—Schlesinger flexes an athletic subtext: "Sustained public action is exhausting. A nation's capacity for high-tension political commitment is limited. Nature insists on a respite. People can no longer gird themselves for heroic effort. They yearn to immerse themselves in the privacies of life. Worn out by the constant summons of battle, weary of ceaseless national activity, disillusioned by the results, they seek an interlude of rest and recuperation."[21]

Also central to *Heartbreak City* are three histories of Seattle: Roger Sale's *Seattle, Past to Present*, James Lyons's *Selling Seattle: Representing Contemporary Urban America,* and Fred Moody's *Seattle and the Demons of Ambition*.[22] In perhaps the most rigorous single-volume history of Seattle ever written, UW English professor and Sonics fan Roger Sale brought all the emotional peaks and lulls of sports fandom to the narrative of *Seattle, Past to Present.* Lyons's *Selling Seattle*, meanwhile, surveys how Seattle's glowing national reputation in the 1990s was a consequence of the declining esteem of its rival cities; his analysis advances a materialist interpretation of popular culture that implicates sports. Moody's *Seattle and the Demons of Ambition* is a darkly funny account of Seattle's rendezvous with cycles of overachievement and failure. Sale wrote: "I know no one who has been deeply touched by Seattle who has not felt the sense of it falling short of its potential."[23] Moody's text is an inspiration for taking this sentiment to satirical lengths, depicting a city that too often uses short-term fixes, business boosterism, and cheap pretentions to exhibit the kind of true progressivism that can only come from great public works.

Published fortuitously after I began work on the manuscript of *Heartbreak City* in the pandemic summer of 2020, scholar Terry Anne Scott's (no relation) essay anthology *Seattle Sports* is a valuable resource that contributes several fascinating episodes about the city's sporting history.[24] In overcast Seattle there are no "untold" stories—only those under more or less sunlight.

* * *

After failing in 1873 and 1884, Seattle finally got its railroad. Transit titan James J. Hill led the Great Northern Railway to the city in 1893. Hill partnered with timber mogul Frederick Weyerhaeuser to build a line that helped Northwest firs crack markets in the American Midwest and South.[25] It was a match made in capitalist heaven: the cross-continental railroad spurred new homestead settlements on the American frontier, while wood from Washington State forests formed the skeleton of millions of new domiciles in the American West.[26] Thanks to the partnership between rail and timber, Seattle flourished. It grew from 42,837 residents in 1890 to 315,312 in 1920, making it America's twentieth-largest town. Over the next century the Icarus city leaped at chances to climb even higher; it used sports to further inflate its civic ego like a lofty hot-air balloon.

The triumphs were many: the Seattle Metropolitans, SuperSonics, Storm, and Seahawks form the city's pantheon of championship squads, alongside the University of Washington football and rowing teams. Helene Madison, Marshawn Lynch, and Sue Bird brought the city the global buzz its settlers only dreamed of. And yet Seattle is defined as much by defeats and near-misses as by its many victories. Like the pioneer dog who tried and failed to catch the train car, the Seattle Seahawks' 2015 Super Bowl defeat reinforced a sense that the city felt doomed to fall shy of its full potential in the most excruciating ways.[27] More people watched Seattle fall three feet short to New England than watched anything else on television that year. Many piled on, joining the national chorus about Seattle's shortcoming. In our spectacular failure, urban America recognized some of its own.

Heartbreak City

1st Inning

"BEATING HEARTS OF GREAT CITIES," 1893–1919

Having secured a train terminal twenty years after it was humbled by Tacoma, Seattle set out to squash new rivals, meet new challenges, move new mountains. A national recession in 1893 almost sank the city's rise: suicides committed by tenants who couldn't afford rent made for grizzly reading in newspapers, contrasting starkly with giddy coverage of the coming transcontinental trains. During the business downturn, rail worker turned socialist agitator Eugene Debs eyed Washington, believing its state legislature to be prime territory for a leftist takeover.[1] But Seattle was a capitalist city—a big one, boosted by the railroad and by other turns of good fortune. When gold was discovered in the Klondike in 1896, merchants profited by milking miners who made their way to the Yukon through Seattle. A great fire in June 1889 gave developers an opportunity to rebuild the city's wood huts in sturdy brick. Everything was coming up Seattle.

The growing city mastered nature to become a major metropolitan area. In 1898, engineer R. H. Thomson began moving mountains to accommodate the city's population boom, sluicing dirt from buxom hills to ready them for new roads and homes.[2] In 1901, the Cedar River was dammed to create hydroelectric power for Seattle; and in 1902, Seattle voters approved bonds for the country's first public power utility. A year later, after West Seattle became the first US city to own its streetcar system, it folded the transit lines into Seattle's trolly network when Seattle annexed the neighborhood in 1907. Ballard, Columbia City, and Ravenna also joined city limits. Big and strong, there was nothing Seattle couldn't tackle.[3]

The next challenge was in the heart of the city. As Seattle sprawled, geographer G. W. Baist illustrated a map that bracketed the city's center in a

THE HEART of SEATTLE

Republished in a 1907 edition of the *Seattle Republican*, geographer G. W. Baist's illustration "The Heart of Seattle" predicted the future: the area eventually housed the Space Needle, Amazon's campus, and the arena where the Seattle Sonics, Storm, and Kraken played their home games. Library of Congress.

sketched heart, publishing his drawing in the 1905 *Real Estate Atlas Surveys of Seattle*. The message was clear: the area just south of Lake Union would be the new cardiac center of a town previously concentrated farther south, around Yesler Way. In July 1907 the *Seattle Republican* reprinted Baist's illustration, framing it atop a caption that read "THE HEART OF SEATTLE."[4] An accompanying article diagnosed the throbbing organ: "When [these blocks] will be the center of Seattle is only a question of time. The building boom plainly shows the drift of the city. The accompanying map will give the reader some idea of what sooner or later will be the heart of Seattle. As soon as Denny Hill will have been lowered, great blocks will be erected on the site that draw the city to it."[5]

Urban planner Virgil Bogue had a plan for the heart of Seattle. In 1910 the Seattle Municipal Plans Commission contracted the engineer to steer the city's explosive growth. Bogue focused on Seattle's coronary system. He thought the heart of the city could host a major subway terminal that hubbed ninety miles of Seattle transit veins. Bogue would build a new city hall for Seattle there, then place plenty of public playfields throughout the city, including a four-thousand-acre people's playground on nearby Mercer Island. Bogue's vision culminated in a grand park in the heart of the city. Presiding over the public lawn would be a monument to Chief Seattle, imagined by Bogue to be Seattle's answer to the Statue of Liberty.[6]

Public parks, transit, city streets, and sports stadiums are the four great chambers of urban connectivity, places where the private lives of city dwellers bleed into the public trust and the collective values of cities ooze out. Bogue's plan for the heart of Seattle resurrected the old "New York, eventually" ambition of its settlers. For it to materialize, Seattle voters had to approve it in a March 5, 1912, election.

* * *

Virgil Bogue was part of the national "City Beautiful" movement whose proponents urged that outdoor recreation could create a fitter, healthier populace.[7] In the place called Seattle, the body had always been an integral part of the body politic—and not just in the heart.

Collectively referred to as the Coast Salish, Indigenous nations in what became Seattle often named the land they stewarded after human anatomy. In the Lushootseed language of Northwest Natives, a knoll near contemporary Ballard was called k̓iɫalabəd ("ganging on the shoulder"). A slope in latter-day Interbay was siláqwucid ("mouth along the Side"). Seward Park was "high on the neck," Columbia City was "breast," and Northgate was "bald head."[8] As Indigenous languages made the human body a metaphor for natural terrain, the cultivation of Coast Salish territory meant the cultivation of the community on it. Conversely, to harm the land was in a sense to harm the self.

When the twenty-two white settlers known as the Denny Party landed on the landmass that became West Seattle on November 13, 1851, the Coast

Salish were in the middle of their annual harvest celebrations. The celebrations included archery, tug-of-war games, and early versions of track-and-field events. Sport and politics collided in shinny, an ancestor of lacrosse played to diffuse conflicts.[9] Before white capitalists struck it rich selling forest wood, the Coast Salish carved canoes from evergreens and raced them. Coast Salish cosmology had "career spirits" who helped individuals become canoeists, healers, and environmental stewards.[10] As it turned out, the white settlers who colonized Indigenous lands had a mythology of their own: in 1845, Washington, DC, writer John Louis O'Sullivan described America's "divine destiny" to conquer the Pacific Northwest. Settlers believed Charles Darwin's 1859 *On the Origin of the Species* handed them the scientific mandate of "survival of the fittest."

Though frontier Seattle had many business owners and real estate prospectors, most people had to labor for a living. Many men were blacksmiths, barley farmers, and butchers. Some women and LGBTQ+ Seattleites were service workers in saloons and sex workers in brothels. Teachers, cooks, caretakers, and seamstresses formed the literal and figurative fabric of life on the frontier. Seattle was an example of what labor historian Carlos Schwantes called "communities of migratory muscle" in the American West; scrappy cities of laboring settlers who survived with the same physical exertion they displayed during their free time.

When colonial Seattleites weren't working, they were into sports. They watched races between local runners and visiting speedsters from Portland. They hiked and boxed. When a pool table was placed in a hotel in 1865, it made news in the *Seattle Weekly Gazette*. A horse-racing track was built in 1872. In 1879 the *Puget Sound Argus* announced a walking contest as "A SPLENDID CHANCE TO WIN FAME!" among Seattle's thirty-five hundred residents.[11] If it weren't for these games, colonial Seattle seemed a monumental bore; it was sparsely populated and had many more men than women. "Our town is unusually quiet," read a report in an August 1875 edition of the *Puget Sound Dispatch*.[12] When word circulated in 1872 that townies planned to build a skating rink, the *Puget Sound Dispatch* advertised it as a chance to mingle: "The sexes can mingle freely at the rink. The awkward acquire grace of motion on rollers."[13]

As indicated by fervent support for baseball, love of spectacle ran deep

Lushootseed people in the early twentieth century piloted canoes in Puget Sound–area waterways, blending athletics and transit before the place that became Seattle existed. Courtesy of the Seattle Municipal Archives, item 101702.

in frontier Seattle. A traveling theater company introduced Seattle to the play *The Gilded Age*, a production adapted from the 1873 Mark Twain novel of the same name. The play inspired local thespians to start a troupe of their own.[14] In Twain's satire of politicians who let corrupt businessmen command great wealth and influence, some Seattleites saw their reflection.

Historians have called the generation from the end of the Civil War in 1865 until about 1890 the Gilded Age, an era where the fortunes of Cornelius Vanderbilt, Andrew Carnegie, John D. Rockefeller, and other capitalist titans were built on the backs of workers in extractive industries: dredging, mining, and especially logging. The Gilded Age was all about competition, pitting businessmen against businessmen, capital against organized labor, and cities against other cities. Ruthless self-reliance was seen as a virtue. When lumber workers suggested limiting the Seattle workday to eight hours, city founder Arthur Denny blasted them as "degenerate scrubs, too lazy to perform an honest day's work."

While trying to beat its railroad rivals, Seattle's social fabric was badly tattered. After Denny's Party arrived in 1851, Seattle's white settlers didn't build a hospital until 1877. They didn't number many addresses and didn't pave roads. Many street names merely reflected their economic function: at the lumber mill on the corner of "Commercial Street," laborers ran themselves ragged for cash. When Seattle City Council enacted a municipal tax in 1867, angry residents dissolved the government, not allowing reincorporation until 1869.[15] Imagine the shame when the city nearly burned down in 1889, and—with no fire department of its own—had to call for help from Portland, Victoria, and Tacoma. In contrast to the holistic civic vision later advanced by Virgil Bogue's generation of progressives, Gilded Age adherents to Darwin's dog-eat-dog narrative of natural selection resisted public action that wasn't about business activity.

Seattle railroad savior James J. Hill once said that "the fortunes of railroad companies are determined by the survival of the fittest."[16] Sports embodied norms of competition and self-reliance that frontier capitalists celebrated (ironically, all the while receiving public subsidies for mining and railroads). The first American football game was played between Princeton and Rutgers in 1869. Settlers founded Seattle's YMCA chapter in 1876, with a club official calling it a "storehouse of Virility" that complemented "the great enterprise of commerce."[17] The National League of Professional Baseball Clubs started in 1876; organizers later formed a separate "Players' League" of athletes who objected to the National League's restrictive labor practices. At this time, boxing matches were often opened by the "battle royale," an ugly melee in which Black males brawled for pennies before white audiences.[18]

Gilded Age crowds were hungry for barbarism. In Chicago spectators took tours of slaughterhouses and meatpacking plants, gawking at overworked laborers and suffering animals. A terrible 1882 spectacle shows what Seattle fans saw in their sports: on January 18 two hundred vigilantes searched the town for two men who robbed a businessman the night before. Upon discovering the perpetrators hiding in a haystack near Puget Sound harbor, the crowd turned them over to the police, but vigilantes decided that jailhouse justice wasn't enough.[19] At the arraignment of the robbers, the vigilantes surged forward with a noose. They took the men into custody, then hung them to a chorus of rave applause on a wooden gallows built for the occasion. Five hundred strong, the mob then stormed the King County jail. They nabbed a prisoner who had been charged with killing a Seattle police officer. "Hang me, and you hang an innocent man," said the prisoner. Before two thousand onlookers, he was strung up.

The *Seattle Times* described the incident as "a day of lynching for sport."[20] In politics and in play, Seattle spectators weren't innocent.

* * *

After a Seattle crowd exiled more than three hundred of the town's Chinese Americans in 1886, city records point to a single bicyclist of color: a small business owner of Chinese ancestry named Mark Ten Suie, who donated to the Queen City Cycle Club to help create bike paths in the city. As anti-Chinese expulsions occurred throughout the American West during the Gilded Age, Suie risked ostracization by being a visible champion of biking.[21] Suie was joined by Seattle women riders who, it was reported in 1896, "believed in the extension of suffrage to their sex, in cancelling the word 'obey' from marital affairs, in hopping off their bicycles in muddy roads."[22] At the turn of the century, the spinning spokes of change took Seattle out of its frontier period.

Bikers saw where Seattle needed to go, and suggested how to get there. A cycling boom began in 1893 with the introduction of "safety bikes," so named because they were more accessible than earlier contraptions that had cartoonishly large front wheels and required great strength and balance to ride.[23] In 1892 there were two dozen bikes in Seattle; by 1900 there were ten thousand riders in a city of eighty thousand people. Throughout the 1890s cyclists lobbied local government to create smooth bike paths that became the stencil for the Seattle's first paved streets. The Queen City Good Roads Club built fresh bikeways with the blessing of city government, which assessed a tax to further subsidize new trails—a novel and revolutionary idea. Seattle was on its way from midcentury settlement to modern city; the trip took place on a two-wheeler. The Queen City Good Roads Club prosecuted Seattle cattle owners when their bovines violated bike lanes. Ferocious wild bears may have terrified riders on the Lake Washington bike path, but many Seattleites couldn't have it said that they lived in a cow town.[24]

Lake Washington Boulevard bike path, circa 1900. At the turn of the century, Seattle was at a fork in the road: more Gilded Age inequities or a progressive turn? Courtesy of the Seattle Municipal Archives, item 29658.

The competition with rival cities was constant, and Seattle needed a niche. Hilly San Francisco created the country's first cable cars in 1873. New York had the most marvelous pedestrian path in the Western world: the immaculate Brooklyn Bridge, whose iconic brick arches opened in 1883. In 1897, Boston built the first subway tunnel in North America. Cities were on the move; Seattle had to keep up and it found a winning edge in bikes. In *The Cycling City: Bicycles and Urban America in the 1890s*, historian Evan Friss writes that "Seattle's twelve miles of attractive bicycle paths made it the envy of city engineers from Oakland."[25] A Bay Area street superintendent wrote to Seattle officials for advice on how to build bike paths. Seattle finally had something on another major city.

When safety bikes and train transit came to Seattle in 1893, Chicago was already a behemoth. Though the "Windy City" and the rainy one were very different, they had doppelgänger histories: Chicago had grown exponentially because of the railroad in 1848 and almost burned down in 1871. It was the ultimate cow town—because of the cattle trade, it outpaced its rivals and became the capital city of the old "Northwestern" states near the Great Lakes. With 1.1 million people in 1893, a world's fair showed Chicago off to the world. Seattle officials grew jealous. What did flat, chilly Chicago have that their city's climes didn't? Seattle needed a showcase of its own.

The city had established a Parks Department in 1887 but didn't fund or grow it much.[26] Most of its playfields had been donated by Gilded Age landholders. If the city wanted to grow up, it couldn't keep depending on the kindness of millionaires. It had to proactively acquire outdoor play spaces. In an 1894 survey of potential playground locales, Seattle's leading parks superintendent wrote that "parks are the beating hearts of great cities."[27] The bureaucrat believed in the democratizing influence of public playfields, calling them "pulsating life-centers where rich and poor mingle." The doubling of Seattle's population between 1890 and 1900 forced the issue. Activists urged Seattle to spend more money on playgrounds, publishing their plea in a *Post-Intelligencer* spread in 1902: "Other cities give the boys a place to play ball. Why shouldn't Seattle?"[28]

Over the next decade the city partnered with the famed Olmsted Brothers architectural firm to design dozens of new parks, many of them superimposed on bike trails that had been established in the 1890s. This was a competitive move, made by a city that meant business: the Olmsted Brothers' father had designed Central Park. The Olmsteds themselves were responsible for the Golden Gate Bridge in San Francisco. In Seattle the Olmsted reforms peaked with the Alaska-Yukon-Pacific Exposition of 1909, a world's fair that took place on the University of Washington campus in northeast Seattle. Then, in 1910, Seattle's Plans Commission recruited Olmsted disciple Virgil Bogue.

Before the vote on Bogue's plan to bring plush playgrounds and mass transit to Seattle, a preeminent architect said: "America's awakening of civic spirit may be traced to the Chicago World's Fair. Cities are watching Seattle's effort to adopt a plan that will mean greater beauty for the city of tomorrow."[29] If playfields were "the beating hearts of great cities," the March 1912 election was a referendum on Seattle's standing in the league of great American urban areas.

* * *

The votes ticked in. Seattle voters had to decide whether to
build the Bogue Plan or stay in the nineteenth century; whether to elect a
moral reformer to the mayor's seat, or stick with Hiram Gil, who two years
earlier collaborated with area pimps and the Seattle Police Department
to construct, in Beacon Hill, what would have been one of the largest
brothels in the world.[30] Gil's opponent—George Cotterill, the progressive
pick—had been instrumental in paving twenty-five miles of biking trails
throughout the city. Seattle voters elected him mayor on March 5, 1912.[31]
The "open town" days of wanton drinking and police graft in the city's
Pioneer Square appeared to be dwindling, with downtown business interests who had supported it all on the defensive during a new era of public
morality.

The Progressive Era, deemed by historians as an "age of reform," saw a
flurry of federal and local laws that created public schools and utilities,
advanced environmental conservation measures like public parks and
trash pickup, and sought to rid big cities of vice and corruption. Though
they often went to great lengths to distinguish themselves from socialists,
progressives generally supported an end to child labor and overly long
workdays. They cared about the country's collective situation in ways their
frontier forebears did not. In *The Upswing: How America Came Together a
Century Ago*, political scientist Robert Putnam wrote: "It is hard to name
a major civic institution in American life that was not invented [during
the Progressive Era]."[32] The Red Cross, the NAACP, the Boy Scouts, the
American Bar Association, the Sierra Club, and the League of Women
Voters were among the associations founded at this time. All had Seattle
chapters. "We're passing from an age of individualism to one of association,"
wrote Chicago progressive Jane Addams in 1902. "Our thoughts cannot
be too much directed from mutual relationships and responsibilities."[33]

A by-product of Judeo-Christian theology, adherents to the idea of
progress understood world history to be a linear path of civilizational improvement, a straight line from wrongdoing to reformation. The priestly
aura of judgment and shame was never far from progressives who stoked
moral panics about sex, jazz, and modern entertainments such as telephones

Spectators watch a ball game in 1909 at the playfield eventually named Cal Anderson Park. The intersection of outdoor space with urban density defines both baseball and the city of Seattle. Courtesy of the Seattle Municipal Archives, item 76255.

and movies. In 1909 a lawmaker from the 43rd Legislative District representing Seattle in the Washington State Legislature agitated against horse racing, believing racetracks facilitated sex trafficking and craven behavior in addition to gambling. The rep said a Seattle track "caused more crime than any in the county."[34] After his bill curtailing gambling at racetracks became law, this crusading rep earned the nickname Holy Ole (rhymes with "goalie") Hanson.

Progressive social engineering could be quite regressive. In residential boarding schools, Coast Salish Natives were abused and made to do forced labor. Although Washington State voters approved women's suffrage in November 1910, the law disenfranchised Indigenous women and non-English speakers. That President Teddy Roosevelt was a proud capitalist, an unrepentant warmonger, and the face of the progressive movement encapsulated the contradictions at the heart of American progressivism. "Progressivism is a strange compound of compassion and contempt," historian Thomas C. Leonard has summarized.[35]

City historian Taha Ebrahimi has illustrated the severe limits of progressivism in Seattle by uncovering how a baseball diamond in Capitol Hill was the site of a charged crackdown on youth sports. In 1902, near a high school on Capitol Hill, Black, Asian American, and immigrant European students played spirited baseball games. Some Seattleites complained, as upset by integrated sports as by petty mischief from the kids. Seattle's Board of Public Works instructed police to arrest kids who threw debris at a nearby reservoir. Community leaders argued that building more playgrounds—not criminalizing Seattle youth—could help occupy idle hands. "Children need recreation," printed the *Seattle Republican*, a Black-owned and -circulated newspaper in the city. "Force them to find it in the streets and their moral standing is lowered."[36]

After the Seattle Parks Department recruited the Olmsted Brothers to turn the Capitol Hill greenway into a park in 1904, the firm suggested the city put a permanent patrolman there. Mayor Richard Ballinger supported the proposal, whether it actually prevented crime or not: "I don't feel it necessary to furnish any data regarding enlarging the police force in this city." Unfortunately for the mayor, Seattle police were in a spate of ugly stories during the Progressive Era. In 1901 the police chief came under fire for rampant bribe-taking. In 1904 city officers were criticized for using racial slurs. A year later, drunken police bullied bartenders into giving them free booze. The bad publicity hurt attempts to expand police presence in Seattle parks; Broadway residents argued that a police station in the Capitol Hill playground would "have a bad effect on high school students." The mayor relented. Seattle's new playfield would be cop-free. It opened in 1909 and was later named Cal Anderson.[37]

Elected in 1912 on the same ballot containing the Bogue Plan, Mayor George Cotterill steered Seattle police to make seventeen thousand warrantless arrests to crack down on rowdy bars and brothels.[38] Seattle had a self-proclaimed "progressive" mayor, but that didn't make it a progressive city. Bike lanes and a few parks were fine. Public power and streetcars were steps in the right direction. But a nice city isn't a great one—and all great cities had two things in common: expansive gathering spaces and mass transit to get people there. If the Bogue Plan had been approved when Cotterill was elected, it would have announced that Seattle was ready to be progressive in fact, not as a façade.

Virgil Bogue decried what he called "the American mind [which] attaches more importance to individual property rights than community interest."[39] With trains and free play in public playgrounds, Bogue wished to link white-collar students in the University District with the blue-collar Ballard neighborhood, the blocks of Black and Japanese Americans in Central Seattle with the ritzy mansions of "Millionaire's Row" in Capitol Hill. An upstart city chased railroads to connect itself to other cities; a mature one built trains to connect the city to itself. Otherwise, one had less of a city and more of a *town*—a town where disconnected neighborhoods reinforced a sense of separate destiny between elites and everyday people, where downtrodden populations frittered away in distant margins, where opportunity was always elsewhere. Because of the progressive ideals that inspired it, this vision motivated a conservative response. Bogue's plan was a political third rail.

On the same day Seattle voters made Cotterill mayor, they emphatically rejected Bogue's vision for subways, an expansive parks network, and a great civic playground in the heart of Seattle. If this was a progressive city in a Progressive Era, elites who spent big to block Bogue's plan weren't notified: the plot to shift the city center slightly northward out of downtown—and therefore slightly out of their hands—was a threat that couldn't stand. The town gentry decided that if they couldn't control the pace of progress, progress wouldn't happen.[40] Seattle's business class found allies in neighborhood cranks who decried the plan to build trains and parks as a scary unknown. Reactionary Seattleites had grown tired of change—tired of public utilities, tired of calls to tax the wealthy to build new parks, tired ultimately of Progressive Era attempts to make urban America slightly more inclusive.

Had Bogue's plan passed, its public lawn, playfields, and ninety miles of transit would have been civic riches enjoyed for generations to come. Instead, the failure to realize these reforms highlighted the shortcomings of the progressive movement. Many progressives intended their movement to be a "golden mean" between the radicalism of desperate masses after the 1893 depression and the inequalities of the Gilded Age.[41] Progressive urban planners focused their efforts on increasing urban inclusivity with mass transit but were largely silent on the fight of Seattle streetcar workers who went on strike in 1903 and 1917; Seattle technocrats wanted more public playfields but also asked for more police to restrict access to them. Absent an additional commitment to the fair redistribution of wealth and political power, Bogue's plan to simply increase proximity between the rich and the poor in parks and public transit was a defanged reform.

Sketched broadly, "progressivism" and "reform" had become watered-down umbrella terms under which law-and-order politicians like George Cotterill could comfortably fit. Supporters of Bogue's plan learned a bitter lesson: if everyone is progressive, no one is.

* * *

The Progressive Era had its perks: new playgrounds, paved streets and bike paths, public power utilities. But the problem with the age of reform was that it made men soft. "What would you give to have the same energy you did a few years ago?" asked a Seattle physician in city newspapers in 1905. "The manly man [has] courage and strong heart." The quack doctor prescribed an "Electric Belt for Puny Men" that zapped groins to help them recover their buried virility, harnessing the modern accoutrement of invisible power to cure the age-old issue of impotency.[42] It was a charlatan's treatment for changing times.

As the hearty Gilded Age gave way to the Progressive Era, brainy city bureaucrats and recalcitrant labor leaders replaced the brawny pioneers of yesteryear. Seattle founder Arthur Denny was disgusted. "If people possessed more of the spirit of the old settlers," he wrote near the turn of the century, "we would hear less about a conflict between labor and capital. We had no eight, or even ten hour days, and I never heard of anyone striking. Every man who was worthy of that name struck at whatever obstacle stood in the way of his success."

If masculinity was in a crisis in the Progressive Era, many believed the full extent of the problem could be seen in the sorry state of University of Washington football. Established in 1889, the University of Washington's football team had some success at the turn of the century, typified by a smashmouth 2–0 win against Nevada that clinched the Pacific Coast Championship in November 1903. Chief Joseph of the Nez Perce went to the game and was galled by the violence: "I saw white men almost fight today."[43] The boys played home games on a shabby First Hill yard which overlapped with a coal bike track that caused awful contusions when players hit the ground. Students called it "the Swamp."[44] As far as many Seattle football fans were concerned, those were the days.

Seattle became a more mature city as the 1900s progressed, separating itself from its wild past with manicured parks and new rules regulating violent sports. UW football moved from the brutal "Swamp" to a field on the college's pristine northeast Seattle campus. In the process, the team lost its edge. In 1906, Washington football went 4–1–4, content to tie as many games as it won; a year later, it had a perfectly mediocre record of 4–4–2. What was going on at UW?

After the subpar 1907 season, an article in the college's alumni publication titled "What's the Matter with Washington Athletics?" argued that the school was too preoccupied with contemporary distractions: "Too much society. Too many social stunts. Too many young men and women wasting energy 'queening.' Too much competition among the sororities and fraternities as to which can give the biggest social affair."[45] Too much, too many, too much. Too many dandyish late-Victorian sartorial stylings, the men in cutesy Edwardian bathing suits, the women in bloomer dresses riding bikes. Too much chatter on newly invented telephones: it was estimated that 30 percent of all calls in Seattle were unnecessary dials between bored friends. That time and energy could've been spent training and turning out to games. It was time to get tough again.[46]

In 1908, Washington searched for a new coach to reinvigorate its football program. School officials decided on Gilmour Dobie, who hadn't lost a game in four years as head honcho at a Minneapolis high school and at North Dakota State. Upon arriving in Seattle, Dobie laid down the gauntlet to players and fans alike. He challenged Washington students to come out and support a winner and inadvertently coined the mascot name the team would be known by in the coming years: "The huskies must come out, and if they do not, the rest of you must get them out."

Born January 21, 1878, Robert Gilmour Dobie was a hard-boiled product

Coach Gil Dobie, 1915. From 1908 to 1916 his team went 58–0–3. Dobie inspired fear in his players and admiration from Seattle fans. Museum of History and Industry, Seattle, 1983.10.10125.2.

of the Gilded Age who had worked as an indentured child laborer after his destitute parents orphaned him in the 1880s. A rail-thin man, Dobie donned a black trench coat to look tough. He wore sweaters made from animal skins. He chewed cigars on the sidelines and cursed out referees. He liked to remind Washington players of his personal motto: "I'm always right, and you're always wrong."[47] Gil Dobie challenged the whole team to a fight, but had no takers. He made them run twenty laps after they won a game by 70 points—why wasn't it 100? Football was figurative war. In his nine seasons as Washington's head coach, Dobie's team never lost: from 1908 to 1916, it went 58–0–3, decimating rivals, earning Seattle national press attention, and setting a standard for competitive excellence that was utterly unmatched.[48]

In anticipation of a November 1915 game between Washington and California, a Washington alum penned the fight song "Bow Down to Washington," which remained a fixture at Husky football games. Washington creamed rival California, 72–0. After the game, the *New York Times* confessed the best in the West was the best bar-none: "Turn the spotlight so it may shine upon the most remarkable coach in college football—Gilmour Dobie, pilot of the football destiny of the University of Washington in Seattle."[49] The winning spirit spread to the city's other sports, radiating outward from UW to the rest of the city.

Seattle had gotten its first taste of sports dominance since its baseball team romped with rival towns in railroad days of the 1870s. At "the Swamp" where UW football played some of their games, tiny crowds still turned out to watch the Pacific Northwest League team descended from those old Seattle Alkis. The field was a dump. The city had to do better.

A rotund man with equally wide ambition, real estate prospector Robert Dugdale had the cash to build Seattle a new stadium, and the ego to name it after himself. He opened Dugdale Park in 1913 in Seattle's Mount Baker neighborhood. The *Seattle Times* called it "one of the nicest ball parks, as far as ballyards outside big league towns."[50] The facility seated ten thousand in double-decker stands—but they were made of wood.[51] And wooden parks fell out of fashion when scores of them burned down at the turn of the century. Shortly after Seattle's arena opened, Chicago debuted timeless Wrigley Field in resplendent brick and mortar. Seattle had been outclassed.[52] Dugdale Park incinerated in a mysterious fire, a fallen minor league monument in a city trying to make it to the majors.

Seattle's wooden arena burned because lumber reigned. An 1890 promotional pamphlet gave Washington the nickname "Evergreen State" for its fulsome conifers—the original skyscrapers.[53] As American cities grew in the waning years of the nineteenth century, doctors recommended time spent in expansive forests, seeing fresh air and space to roam freely as an antidote to congestion and pollution in fledgling urban areas.[54] The need for new housing throughout American cities expanded the lumber market. Seattle industry capitalized. Ballard became the world's largest exporter of wooden shingles in the last decade of the nineteenth century. By 1910, two-thirds of all Washington State workers were loggers, their labor the root of great wealth amassed by timber barons who brought Seattle its next great sports triumph.[55]

In 1911, Northwest timberman Joseph Patrick eyed a new hockey league to build the family fortune with his sons. The Patrick brothers started the Pacific Coast Hockey Association (PCHA), placing Canadian teams in Victoria and Vancouver, and another in Portland. Seattle was awarded a franchise in 1915.[56] Because the winner of the PCHA playoffs played the National Hockey Association champ for the Stanley Cup, Seattle was suddenly a big-league city. Named the Metropolitans after the company that financed the team's brick Ice Arena just inside the southern boundary of the "heart of Seattle" on Fifth Avenue, the Seattle PCHA squad defeated Victoria in front of a packed home crowd in its first game ever on December 7, 1915.[57]

After a promising inaugural season, Seattle ripped through the 1916–17 PCHA campaign, its eye-catching red-and-green-striped sweaters appearing as a blur because of the team's speed. Hap Holmes gave up the fewest goals in the league, and Bernie Morris led the PCHA in points. The Mets were all white men of North Atlantic heritage, with Iceland, Canada, and the United States represented on the roster. The buzz around the Mets reflected Seattle's complex racial politics. The Seattle Ice Arena, where hundreds skated recreationally when the Mets weren't playing there, discriminated against Black attendees.[58]

In *Seattle from the Margins*, historian Megan Asaka describes how elites and politicians colluded to elevate white Northwest loggers over their Japanese, Indigenous, and "less desirable" immigrant counterparts.[59] A 1911 federal labor report praised Scandinavians as "well-adapted to the Northwest, industrious, and progressive."[60] Logging companies offered these workers skilled positions denied to others; Weyerhaeuser built them company housing and gave them wage boosts to keep them from joining unions. As upwardly mobile white workers joined the Seattle bourgeoisie, an all-white hockey team conquering cold and competition reanimated the city's settler heritage, profiting from nostalgia for the perilous pioneer period. Something of the old settler spirit survived in Seattle sports; fans were galvanized by a squad from North Atlantic lands where daring mariners warred with mythic kraken.

First played by the Mi'kmaq people in what became Nova Scotia, hockey spread west on the Great Plains of Canada and the United States.[61] By the time it reached Seattle, the game simulated the dangers of the North

As shown in this 1916 scorecard, the arena where the Seattle Mets played their home games doubled as a community iceplex for recreational skating. Because the facility was racially segregated, the Mets' red-and-green jerseys were the only color seen there. Museum of History and Industry, Seattle, 2018.3.3.47.

American wilderness for big city crowds in search of bread and circuses. The modern marvel of indoor electricity reproduced the frozen frontier that spawned hockey, enabling a game where fights and broken bones were simply part of the barbarous charm. The Mets began play as Progressive Era reformers tried making American sports safer. The forward pass was created in 1906 to make football less violent, to the chagrin of barbarism-purist Gil Dobie.[62] In the 1910s it became customary to cap boxing matches at fifteen rounds, curtailing lengthy bouts that formerly lasted until someone quit or was knocked unconscious. Before its 1915–16 season the PCHA allowed managers to rest hockey players with line shifts. By advocating for this change in their league, the Patrick brothers might have seemed like responsible corporate stewards who looked after labor's well-being.[63] But reformers treated sports like they treated politics: just as progressives sought to regulate capitalism without overthrowing it, they wanted sports less lethal but not necessarily less violent.

Most progressives weren't revolutionaries but referees. "I believe in manly sports," said President Roosevelt in 1903. "I don't feel sympathy for the person who gets battered, so long as it isn't fatal."[64]

When fans settled into their seats at the Seattle Ice Arena, they expected a theater of sadism. As the Mets took a 2–1 lead in the best-of-five Stanley Cup Finals in March 1917, Montreal's frustration showed in petty skirmishes. A Mets fan complained—not about the fights but about the referee's policing of them: "A fight is just a fight. A player who doesn't defend himself deserves more punishment than the silly ass who starts the scrap."[65] Underneath it all—underneath the wealthy neighborhoods and pretty parks, the pristine UW campus and uptight city bureaucrats—Seattle was still a frontier outpost. Its fans were out for scalps. Raucous Seattle spectators lifted the Metropolitans to the Stanley Cup, cheering as they mauled Montreal 9–1 to clinch the championship on March 26, 1917. Readers of the *Boston Globe* and *Vancouver World* learned Seattle existed because of its hockey conquest.[66] "Seattle has shaken the dust of small town sport," wrote Royal Brougham in the *Post-Intelligencer*.

On downtown street corners, newsboys sung the Mets' praises to the tune of thousands of dollars of print sales per day. Before long, geopolitical strife knocked sports from the headlines: a day after the United States entered World War I in April 1917, fifty thousand hawkish Seattleites attended a pro-war rally that ended at the arena where the Mets had become the first US team to win the Stanley Cup weeks earlier.[67] An ambitious town with a competitive streak, Seattle won its hockey struggle against other cities; it would soon lose a more important struggle to itself, in the process showing the promise of the Progressive Era to be short-lived.

When World War I helped spread a deadly influenza (nicknamed the "Spanish flu"), Seattle officials mobilized to stop its spread. The October 1918 discovery of seven hundred cases at the University of Washington launched the city into full-on pandemic prevention. Gatherings in restaurants, theaters, and poolrooms were forbidden. Stores adopted erratic hours to socially distance customers. Schools closed. Cops enforced an anti-spitting ordinance, and Seattleites put on masks. Public health officials briefly handed down a stay-at-home order. At first, Seattleites abided by the pandemic restrictions, hoping civic collaboration would make their city safer. Gradually, though, they grew stir-crazy. When America signed the World War I armistice on November 11, 1918, rallies celebrating the end of the war were superspreader events. Roughly as many Seattleites died of the pandemic (1,513) as Seattle-area soldiers perished in World War I (approximately 1,600); still, the civic consensus required to stop the spread dissipated.[68]

Unfazed by the pandemic death toll, the PCHA started its season in January 1919. Seattleites packed the hockey arena to cheer the juggernaut Mets on another Stanley Cup run. On March 29, 1919, three thousand fans exited Seattle Ice Arena wearing frowns instead of face-coverings after the Mets dropped Game Five of the Stanley Cup Finals to the Montreal Canadiens.[69] With the series tied 2–2–1, a Game Six was scheduled to decide the series. It was never played: on April 1, 1919, five Montreal players and their coach caught the influenza. One of them died. After the stress of war and quarantine, Seattle fans went to the Ice Arena for a good time. Their cheering mouths spread the disease that denied Seattle a second title. On April 2 the *Seattle Post-Intelligencer* solemnly wrote that "the ice has been taken out of the arena."[70] The paper's front-page story that day was about Seattle parents refusing to quarantine kids with smallpox.

Seattle's bid to win the 1919 Stanley Cup ended at the same time as the Progressive Era, and for the same reasons. Progressives aimed to create a culture of association that moderated the individualism of the frontier period with civic cohesion. During the pandemic, social reform was replaced by survival of the fittest: As the Spanish flu pandemic wore on, Seattle's public health commissioner said tightened restrictions around face-covering and social distancing were "caused by people who seem to feel they're individually immune from influenza."[71] After the age of reform's last gasp was taken without a mask, progressives had a lot to be proud of: its lackluster pandemic response notwithstanding, paved roads, playgrounds, and sports arenas made Seattle more metropolitan. But because the Gilded Age was left largely intact, Seattle entered the 1920s asunder—a city divided between labor and capital, landholding aristocracy and urban poor, white city dwellers and people of color. Though progressives had only intended to referee these fights, they still managed to lose them.

2nd Inning

"MOVED BEYOND ENDURANCE," 1920–1929

Although it's unclear who played third base for the Seattle Ku Klux Klan baseball team, history hasn't masked the team's origins. Leaders of the Seattle Shipbuilders' League met in April 1918 to discuss their upcoming baseball season. When a rival shipyard proposed disallowing teams from improving their rosters with new players, Skinner & Eddy abandoned the league. Workers there produced more World War I vessels than any other in the country; they had the right to do what they wanted. Insulted by an adversary trying to tell them what to do, the Skinner boys formed their own tournament of cohorts within the company: the Boilermakers, the Timekeepers, the Professionals, and the "Ku-Klux," led by pitcher Kid Hurley and catcher B. S. Smith.[1]

Baseball historian Amanda Cummings first uncovered Seattle's Ku Klux baseball club, noting that "the city's shipyard teams were entirely white." Skinner teams played their tournament in May 1918, with the *Seattle Times* commenting briefly on the "chatty" nature of the Klan's team manager.[2] The KKK had been the talk of the town. D. W. Griffith's 1915 film *Birth of a Nation* was a smash, gripping white filmgoers with its three-hour saga of a teetering American republic rescued by the Klan. An ugly spectacle with white actors in blackface, the movie made its Seattle premier in June 1915.[3] Following progressive President Woodrow Wilson's celebration of *Birth of a Nation* as "history writ with lightning," the *Seattle Times* proclaimed the film a "marvelous tribute to the patriotism of the American people."[4] Though the movie projected dreadful stereotypes of white innocence and Black criminality, the only words of caution about *Birth of a Nation* in Seattle media pertained to its colossal cultural impact: critics feared that cinema had the potential to replace theater, leaving sports as the country's last great live drama.[5]

After the release of *Birth of a Nation*, the Ku Klux Klan used the movie as a recruitment tool.[6] Like fans buying their favorite team's merchandise, moviegoers purchased Klan-themed costumes, aprons, and other apparel.[7] By 1918 the group celebrating the ghosts of dead Confederate soldiers with white sheets was mainstream enough for a Seattleite to remark that mask-wearers during the influenza pandemic "resembled the famous Ku Klux Klan."[8] The hate group had a full-blown renaissance in the ensuing decade.

At its peak in the 1920s the Klan had between two million and five million members nationally, with clandestine members in local police departments, state legislatures, and school districts across the country. In the Washington State Legislature in March 1923, a bill to illegalize public Klan gatherings failed in the House of Representatives. Days later, the Ku Klux held a rally in the heart of the city, at Crystal Pool on Second Ave and Lenora.[9] In 1924, Seattle's Klan numbered 8,000 in a city of 350,000 people, nearly double the size of Seattle's Black population. When the Grand Wizard of the KKK visited Seattle that year, he was warmly received at a banquet by the Seattle Chamber of Commerce.[10] Seattleite congressman Albert Johnson was elected with broad support from the KKK, then scribed the 1924 Immigration Act, which established strict racial quotas on who could enter the country.[11] Far from fringe, Klan politics were popular.

The year 1920 was the first in US history when more Americans lived in major urban areas than not. In cities there was noise, crowded blocks, and strong ethnic communities; in response, reactionary whites embraced both the slow-paced allure of baseball and the racism of the KKK.[12] In 1920 the Imperial Wizard of the Klan complained that "overgrown cities are a menace" and claimed that "the great city corrodes American life."[13] For many white people in urban America, the only thing worse than living in a big city was sharing it: Seattle was one of scores of metropolitan areas to establish segregated neighborhoods, institutions, and sports after World War I.

As historian Linda Gordon explained, "baseball was the white, Protestant, game that represented the small town, homogenous society that the Klan idealized."[14] At the same time, big diverse cities were the only place where a large enough base of athletes and audiences could be organized

Seattle Police Department baseball team, 1915. Rampant corruption among the city's cops prompted the first woman mayor, Bertha Knight Landes, to advocate defunding the department in 1924. Courtesy of the Seattle Municipal Archives, item 64763.

into sustainable leagues. The Los Angeles Ku Klux Klan's baseball team debuted in July 1924, with the *Los Angeles Times* praising them for playing "good consistent baseball."[15] That year in Atlanta, a Klan team participated in a citywide sandlot league. Klan baseball teams played against Black and Jewish clubs in Wichita (1925) and Washington, DC (1927), using sport to perform their white supremacist worldview in games against minority city dwellers.

Thousands of African Americans moved to Seattle to work in the city's shipyards during World War I. The casual racism of the 1918 Klan baseball matinee was one more indignity in a city where Black people were segregated into Seattle's Central Area. Night baseball wasn't played regularly in America until the 1930s; the Seattle KKK team appeared in broad daylight.[16] Yet despite the Klan's visibility, Seattle's Ku Klux baseball squad is still cloaked in mystery.

We can only speculate as to the on-field performance of the team. No sports coverage can be found in the Seattle KKK newspaper, bolstering historian Felix Harcourt's finding that "sports were never prominently featured in Klan publications."[17] In 1925 the Wichita Ku Klux Klan played a Black baseball squad in front of five thousand fans; they lost, 10–8. History concedes no indication that Seattle's Ku-Kluxers could've done better.

Alas, not much else is known about the Seattle KKK baseball team, besides the fact that it existed. But perhaps not much else needs to be known.

* * *

Had "Holy Ole" retired from the state legislature after his bill curtailing horse-race betting became law in 1909, history might have remembered him as just another progressive. A freshman lawmaker with fiery red hair representing Seattle's 43rd Legislative District, Ole Hanson's missionary zeal for social engineering was typical of his peers in the age of reform. For most politicians scaling the summit of public life, authoring signature legislation weeks into one's first term might have been a career apex. But the rep from the 43rd was a man of great ambition. The day Hanson moved to Seattle in 1902, he told locals he'd become mayor.[18] He was right: after declining to run for reelection to the state house, he worked on Teddy Roosevelt's "Progressive Party" presidential bid in 1912, was a candidate for US Senate in 1914, and was elected Seattle mayor in 1918.

Born Ole Thorsteinsson Hanson on January 6, 1874, near Milwaukee, doctors once believed Seattle's new mayor would never walk again after he was badly injured in a trainwreck in 1900. As the frontier ideal of the survival of the fittest endured, disability was looked down upon at the turn of the century. Seattleites who couldn't cut down trees for work or play sports for recreation were punished with social exclusion. Practically no public accommodations existed for paraplegics during the Progressive Era, a time when Washington State law made relatives "of sufficient ability" solely responsible for people who couldn't work because of disabilities.[19]

In the state legislature Hanson himself cast a vote for a forced sterilization law that was later expanded to include people "who produce children with a tendency to feeble-mindedness."[20] By the time Hanson was elected mayor in 1918, people with disabilities in Seattle were either presented as sympathetic "cripples" in need of charity or superheroes who overcame the odds society put in their way.[21] Defying doctor's predictions, Hanson stayed on his feet through extensive exercise and physical conditioning.[22] He described his win as a triumph of willpower: "I've always believed that if one wants to do anything bad enough, he can do it."[23]

The football domination of Gil Dobie's UW teams and the Stanley Cup conquests of the Metropolitans united the city in celebration of physical specimens and manly men. The ableist spectacles had political implications. The adjective "weak" appears twenty-one times in Mayor Hanson's memoir, indicating a cruel worldview that saw government support and worker associations as betrayals of America's rugged frontier heritage.[24] The mayor decried the "weakness" of Seattle labor bureaucrats who, in his view, allowed militant unions to influence impressionable workers. He insulted the "mental and physical weaklings" in Seattle unions who were radicalized by low wages and soaring costs of living in the post–World War I period. Hanson hated socialists: "America believes in strength; Bolshevism teaches weakness." In championing what he called the "America first" policies of war, capitalism, and anti-communism, Hanson's political career bridged the more quietly intolerant Progressive Era with the openly hostile 1920s.

After the Russian Revolution of 1917 and the influenza epidemic of 1918 stoked fears of the big scary world beyond American shores, socialism infected Seattle's shipyards. On February 6, 1919, thirty-five thousand pier workers struck for higher wages, joined in solidarity by thirty thousand laborers in other industries. For a week Seattle was silent. Streetcars stopped rattling and newsboys didn't sing the headlines. The Seattle Mets' 1919 season stalled, prompting the *Post-Intelligencer* to note that the labor stoppage gave injured players time to heal. Workers provided one another childcare, groceries, and utilities during the General Strike. Mayor Hanson co-opted their work, writing in the *Seattle Star*, "We'll see to it that you have all necessities."[25]

Holy Ole got the fight he wanted. He had campaigned for mayor on a

Seattle mayor Ole Hanson operates a streetcar over the University Bridge at opening ceremonies for the new transit line in 1919. Husky Stadium debuted nearby a year later, causing chronic traffic jams, which made mass transit seem more appealing than ever. Courtesy of the Seattle Municipal Archives, 12660.

platform of stern "Americanism," framing socialists, anarchists, and militant unions as an existential threat to the United States.[26] The message was a hit. The same day that Hanson was elected, Seattle voters recalled socialist public parks advocate and Seattle School Board member Anna Louise Strong. Making good on his promise to stamp out left-wing activity, Hanson martialed thousands of police officers and federal troops to patrol Seattle's silent streets during the General Strike. An anarchist jurisdiction Seattle was not; but the mayor's show of force—with police stationed next to storefronts that striking schoolteachers and barbers had no intention of sacking—made it appear to outside observers that a socialist mob had taken siege.

The Seattle General Strike quietly petered out in six days; Hanson loudly claimed credit for ending it. Not content to read his press clippings, Hanson also wrote them, scribing anti-socialist editorials in the *New York Times* and

McClure's to complement his positive coverage in the *Los Angeles Times* and *Atlanta Constitution*.[27] "HERE'S A MAYOR!" announced a *Chicago Tribune* headline atop a Hanson diatribe against anarchism.[28] During the Progressive Era, Seattle sought sports triumphs and public works to raise its national profile; Holy Ole showed that leading a reactionary political climate could be an equally effective way of getting attention. Seattle's mayor became an icon of the 1919–20 Red Scare, when American politicians and law enforcement cracked down on unions and civil rights demonstrators. In this series of competitions against the nascent American left, the Seattle General Strike was an opening contest; Ole Hanson pitched. His belligerent *New York Times* editorial "Anarchists Tried Revolution, but Never Got to First Base" announced "law and order are supreme in Seattle," positioning the city as a capital of America's capitalist backlash.[29]

Something about this city—its remoteness from East Coast power centers, its proximity to West Coast rivals—seemed to breed a civic inferiority complex that encouraged some of its politicians to express themselves in cringeworthy displays of delusional grandiosity. Because a mayor is the biggest fish in a small pond, Hanson appeared bored with the job, perhaps becoming more interested in capitalizing on his celebrity than in fixing potholes. He commanded more in speaker fees than he made as mayor. He tired himself out responding to every reporter in need of anti-communist comment, every magazine in search of a screed against socialism, every college looking for a lecture on the villainy of Vladimir Lenin. The incessant pro-capitalist cheerleading of Seattle's mayor was briefly silenced when, after the General Strike, neuritis in Hanson's teeth caused him great pain. His hyperactive mouth had finally done him in. While recovering, the man who detested "weakness" was unable to leave his bed. Still mayor of Seattle, he summoned the strength to move to California.[30]

Hanson resigned in August 1919, wrote his 1920 memoir *Americanism versus Bolshevism*, and established the city of San Clemente in 1925. The town was a civic resort, with luxury real estate and golf courses. But its founder was never able to build a platform as large as the one he had in Seattle. In short, Holy Ole had been the most popular mayor in the country, the biggest bullhorn of the American Red Scare, and a bellwether of a coming conservative era.

* * *

Sports and cars caused Seattle's first traffic jam, and man was it a doozy. University of Washington athletics director Darwin Meisnest had sold Seattle businessmen and students on the idea of a new football stadium on campus, pleading that "such a bowl constitutes a civic necessity."[31] He identified vacant land near Union Bay as the perfect spot to put the arena, and rallied investors for money. Construction broke ground in May 1920. On November 27, Washington played its first game in the arena that came to be known as "Husky Stadium" after the team adopted the mascot in 1922. An estimated forty-five hundred drivers made the trip to see Washington lose 28–7 to Dartmouth, clogging Seattle's arteries. Swiftly and surely, the Progressive Era's appreciation for shared civic spaces was being replaced by automobile-licensed individualism.

Like sports and playgrounds before them, town boosters believed new car infrastructure could help Seattle become a world-class city. Tourists came for the seafood, stayed for the late-evening spring sunsets, and couldn't be sent home complaining about the city's roads. Pro-automobile activists pushed officials to build a new car bridge connecting Husky Stadium to nearby Montlake. More improvements couldn't come soon enough. "Seattle is not a frontier outpost," thundered the *Seattle Times* in November 1920. "She is a great city. We cannot afford to have globetrotters and wealthy businessmen leaving with a painful memory of our thoroughfares."[32]

The regrades that began in the 1890s were supposed to make Seattle's hilltop districts climbable for trolleys.[33] The real winners were cars and rich people. Scalable hills enabled the creation of suburbanesque neighborhoods in lofty neighborhoods like Queen Anne and Madrona. Seattle became a truly stratified city, and socioeconomic climbers didn't stop at the hills. Some white Seattleites with race and class privilege joined the city's Mountaineer Club in the 1920s. They drove their cars to area peaks, ate dinner in downpours of snow, and called the domestic servants they dragged with them anti-Black slurs.[34] Back on solid ground in the city, they took tee time at area nines.

When golf's popularity soared after World War I, enthusiasts convinced Seattle leaders to build huge courses that gobbled up valuable territory in

Jefferson Park Golf Course, 1925, benefited from exclusionary post–World War I policies that cordoned off huge swaths of land in an increasingly crowded city. Unlike public playgrounds, golf courses brush aside actual ecosystems and put a hollow simulacrum of nature in their place. Courtesy of the Seattle Municipal Archives, item 31449.

an increasingly crowded city. In September 1918 housing activists had embarked on a "Build More Homes" campaign to turn idle urban lots into five thousand new dwellings of housing for shipyard workers; by 1920, Seattle parks commissioners created a sixty-acre addition to the Jefferson Park Golf Course on Beacon Hill. Progressive pretenses and wartime sacrifice were a thing of the past.[35]

Seattle golf courses were as exactly as exclusionary as the city's growing neighborhoods. Jackson Park, where a course opened in 1928, was a whites-only subdivision: property holders signed a deed that excluded "any race other than white."[36] A similar stricture existed in the northeast Seattle neighborhood Sand Point, where a course opened in 1927. An ad ran in area newspapers that year touting Broadmoor as "The Country Club Within the City"; buyers were welcome to "inspect its perfect golf course and fine residential district."[37] In language typical of racially exclusive covenants in Seattle, the neighborhood banned racial minorities: "No part of said property shall be occupied by any Hebrew or person of the Ethiopian, Malay or any Asiatic Race, excepting only domestic service employees."[38]

After World War I the capitalist ideal of homeownership was encouraged by federal officials in the United States to defray socialist influence in American cities.[39] Exclusionary housing deeds existed in virtually every 1920s Seattle neighborhood. From Ballard to Beacon Hill and Magnuson to Magnolia, they forbade nonwhites from residing outside of the Central Area and Chinatown.[40] After consulting with segregationist Harlan Bartholomew in 1920, Seattle's Plans Commission zoned the city to illegalize apartment buildings in most of the city in 1923. Bartholomew—who helped design similar zoning regimes in Saint Louis, Kansas City, and Pittsburgh—opined that restrictive zoning would "preserve desirable residential neighborhoods" and restrict the movement of "colored people into finer neighborhoods."[41]

While people of color were frozen out of Seattle's white neighborhoods, segregated sports were the cultural icing atop socioeconomic exclusion. The Mountaineer Club opened a nine-hole golf course on Nisqually Glacier.[42]

* * *

How do city dwellers make themselves at home in unfriendly places? In *Who Set You Flowin'?: The African-American Migration Narrative*, scholar Farah Jasmine Griffin invokes the notion of the "safe space" to describe strategies used by Black city dwellers to cope with hostile urban environments.[43] Building on the work of Black feminist author Patricia Hill Collins, Griffin writes "at their most progressive, safe spaces are spaces of retreat, healing, resistance." Baseball was such a space for Black Seattleites. In athletic contests against police officers and prison guards, Black Seattleites defied the white city that had moved on from the inclusive aspirations of the Progressive Era after World War I.

Black Seattle grew substantially during and after the war, as migrants sought employment in area shipyards. The community numbered 406 in 1900, swelled to 2,894 in 1920, and reached a peak of about 5,000 in 1926.[44] The Great Migration away from racial oppression in the rural South led to a political and cultural flowering of Black life in northern cities. One of the most prominent figures of the 1920s Harlem Renaissance, poet Langston Hughes, lauded trains as a conduit of liberation, identifying Seattle as a destination point for African Americans fleeing the postbellum South in his poem "One-Way Ticket."[45]

Unfortunately, Jim Crow North mimicked the Jim Crow South. Black Seattleites didn't have the luxury of passing unimpeded through the city, driving to and from golf courses and area mountain ranges. Seattle was an American "sundown town," where Black residents were subject to police harassment for showing face after dark in white neighborhoods.[46] Segregation was the silent rule in many establishments; the Seattle NAACP found that the city's Ice Arena discriminated against Black attendees. Although they were confined to a few dozen blocks in the Central Area, Black Seattleites didn't allow exclusion to define them. Sports were instrumental to the forging of a vibrant community.

Black Seattle formed its first baseball team in 1911, a squad called the Gophers that competed against other Black, white, and Japanese clubs, wowing spectators with circus catches in a May 1911 defeat of a Black team from Tacoma.[47] On June 1, 1919, the *Seattle Post-Intelligencer* reported that Black Seattle baseball "[had] been strengthened by players who have returned from overseas service."[48] The next day, on June 2, anarchists sent explosives to American leaders who supported the deportation of left-wing immigrants.[49] Earlier mail bombs had targeted New York City's police commissioner, John D. Rockefeller, and Seattle mayor Ole Hanson. The ensuing escalation of the Red Scare coincided with the arrival of Black migrants to northern cities like Seattle: in the Red Summer of 1919, mob violence and police brutality targeting Black Americans who petitioned for desegregation became commonplace. A tone was set for the new decade: in the 1920s a Black person was lynched roughly every ten days in the United States.[50] In his 1926 autobiography *Confessions of a Chief of Police*, Seattle Police head William Severyns relayed how the city's cops tortured suspects of all races by hanging an iron ball and chain around their necks.[51] Baseball simulated a broader struggle for equality.

Renamed the Giants, Black Seattle's baseball team traveled to nearby Cle Elum for a match against a white team in 1923; the opposing manager threatened to "knock the tar off the tar babies."[52] In another game in this period, the Giants beat the Seattle Police Department baseball team, only to have the cops retaliate by ticketing Black fans who came to the game. Later, when the Giants played a game against Monroe Reformatory inmates that was umpired by white guards, they suffered obvious racist discrepancies in officiating.[53] Much of white Seattle had been moved beyond endurance after the Progressive Era, largely abandoning activism after the age of reform. Black Seattle didn't have the luxury of rest.

"In a better world, there wouldn't have been a story to tell," wrote Lyle Kenai Wilson in his history of Seattle's black baseball teams; "we would have lived together, played on the same teams together, without distinction of color."[54] That better world wasn't urban America. The 1926 Supreme Court decision *Corrigan vs. Buckley* validated the use of racially exclusive housing covenants in neighborhoods established after the war.[55] While many white Seattleites drove great distances to get away from the ethnic communities and urban confines of big cities, Black Seattleites bucked the trend. A child of the Central Area once reflected on her upbringing in the 1920s, showing how the absence of cars facilitated Black reclamation of urban space: "When I was a girl, we used to play baseball in the middle of the street," she remembered. "Everyone didn't have a Model-T, so you could have a game going."[56]

* * *

In 1920 the president of the Seattle Chamber of Commerce proposed a "Speak to Your Neighbor Campaign" because Seattleites were in need of a thaw.[57] He was desperate. He begged the city to become more outgoing, saying "talk costs nothing, and thousands [can be] made to feel at home."[58] It was reported that year that strangers tried to make small talk on Seattle streetcars about rising costs of living in the city but got the cold shoulder. A Michigan transplant complained "people in Seattle act as if you're going to steal their pocketbooks if you remark about the weather."[59] It seemed that Seattle was populated by settlers who wanted to get as far away from everybody else while still remaining in the United States. This "social freeze" was a barometer for the rest of the country. The age of reform had incessant calls to public action, new ordinances to abide by, and constant moral panics. World War I depopulated and disturbed urban America, pummeling people on the home front with the daily trauma of gory war details. Ending the flu pandemic had required great collective sacrifice. The anxiety was overwhelming and people were tired. "We are at the dead season of our fortunes," wrote economist John Maynard Keynes in late 1919. "Our power of caring beyond our direct experience cannot move us. We have been moved beyond endurance and need rest."[60]

If the years spanning 1893–1918 were America's Progressive Era—Jane Addams's "age of association"—then the 1920s were its era of escapism, a decade of withdrawal. The institution of housing segregation and anti-Asian immigration quotas showed that the progressive urge toward social admixture in playgrounds and transit was a faded ambition.[61] Culturally the country became more reclusive, more privatized; cars replaced streetcars. Radios domesticated the relationship of city dwellers to sports, making people less likely to go to the ballpark.[62] Something of the Gilded Age survived in every-person-for-themselves cities where affluent communities self-isolated, took up socially exclusive hobbies like golf and mountain climbing, and flaunted great wealth. "Public values evolved into a private vision of individual well-being," wrote Roger Sale of the post–World War I years. "The possibility of politics as the expression of something more than personal desires was lost."[63]

Small-town Seattle was a place of the past after World War I, replaced by a big city with movie theaters, jazz clubs, stuff to buy. To stock their homes with the latest tech, shoppers in ostentatious new downtown retail outlets purchased new radios and phonographs using the new tactic of installment buying. New Husky Stadium was the site of President Warren Harding's final public appearance: after giving an address there in July 1923, he died of food poisoning brought on by bad seafood.[64] Harding's laissez-faire economic policies lived on through Presidents Calvin Coolidge and Herbert Hoover. Seattle real estate ratcheted up, reaching all-time highs in 1926,

1927, and 1928. Construction cranes loomed over evergreens. The city's post–Progressive Era rate of growth impressed even Ole Hanson: "The waterfront was ablaze with thousands of lights. Some of the great hills were gone, washed away. And where were the forests? Cut down, sawed up, and in their places stood thousands of homes."[65]

When the Malloy Apartments overlooking the University District opened in August 1928, realtors touted its proximity "to the shops of the fast-growing University business district," its subterranean parking lot, its wild Washington pine fashioned into French doors and parquet floors.[66] The building had every convenience: a range stove, Frigidaire, and electrical outlets for radios, all designed to "attract the discriminating apartment-seeker." Conservatism followed consumerism: Americans achieved elevated class standing after World War I, while left-wing associations, unions, and civil rights groups were criminalized. As Richard Rothstein, a historian of housing segregation in American cities, has argued: "We like to think of American history as a march of progress toward greater equality. Sometimes we move backward."[67] The 1920s were such a time—but some held the line.

In 1924, Seattle City Councilmember Bertha Knight Landes was an old-school reformer who took on playground preservation, police corruption, and the institution of reasonable hours in the city's raucous bowling allies. When Seattle mayor Edwin Brown briefly left office to attend the June 1924 Democratic National Convention, Landes became acting mayor and delivered a scathing letter to Seattle Police chief William Severyns: "Either there is collusion between the police and criminals, or the police department is so inefficient that law violators neither fear nor respect its power."[68]

Councilmember Landes proposed defunding the Seattle Police. To curb corruption, she suggested removing at least a hundred crooked cops from the force and argued in her letter that no additional taxpayer funds should go to more police "until there has been a house-cleaning in the department."[69] Biographer Sandra Haarsager discovered that in drafts of Landes's letter to Seattle's top cop, she edited her language to be "direct, clear, and forceful. 'Housecleaning' took on a masculine quality."[70] Others have noted Landes's use of sports metaphors to sell her image as a tough, able politician: she won a "two-fisted fight" over dancehall regulation and

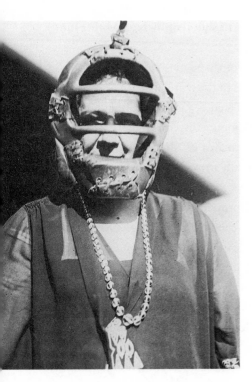

The first woman mayor of a major US city, Bertha Knight Landes used sports to appeal to voters who didn't believe she had the stamina to lead the city. Wearing an ump's mask, she officiated a Pacific Coast League baseball game in April 1927. University of Washington Libraries, Special Collections (POR2388).

"wrestled" with park cleanup.[71] After sparring with the police chief, Landes fired him. Two years later, she came for the mayor's job. In March 1926, Seattle voters elected Landes mayor, making her the first woman to ever hold the job in a major US city.

Born Bertha Ethel Landes on October 19, 1868, Seattle's new mayor lived in the Wilsonian Apartment Hotel in the University District. From her residence she could see the buzzing intersection at Forty-Seventh Street and University Way, the Model-Ts that whizzed by Seattleites on foot and in wheelchairs. Mayor Landes pondered her city's problems. She identified pedestrian deaths as a major problem in a city where there was one car for every four people, saying "lives are lost to carelessness and love of speed."[72] She proposed pedestrian subways. She funded a renovation of Green Lake playfield. She participated in sports to buck backward expectations of women in the public eye. In April 1927, she put on a catcher's mask and officiated a baseball game at Dugdale Park.[73] She blasted a gun at a firing range for flashing cameras: "I threaten to shoot, on sight, anyone calling me 'mayoress' instead of mayor," she joked.[74]

People took note of the audacious woman up in Seattle. In July 1926 the *New York Times* profiled Bertha Landes in the write-up "Seattle Ably Run by Woman Mayor." America's paper of record was shocked that Seattle—that rugged city of industrious settlers, mountain climbers, and pioneering outdoorsmen—had elected a woman to lead it: "To the country, it came as a surprise that this hustling, essentially masculine city should put into its Mayor's chair a woman."[75] The *Times* was impressed with Landes's seriousness, particularly her attempt to reform the Seattle Police Department, which it called "the citadel of entrenched evils."[76] Where Ole Hanson brought national recognition to Seattle for captaining a new conservative era, Landes did the same by defying it. Her record as a progressive was flawed because progressivism was flawed. Although she took inspiration from the Bogue Plan and bolstered Seattle's playgrounds, she also helped implement the zoning code that made apartments illegal to build in most of the city.

Although her participation in technocratic segregation was in step with the exclusionary 1920s, *The Nation* reported in 1928 that Seattle men were tired of being teased about their woman mayor. Journalist Julia Budlong argued that frontier Seattle's worst instincts had gotten hold of it during Landes's reelection campaign. Proud men who skied and watched baseball could no longer suffer petticoat rule: "The chivalry of great open spaces sustains itself by occasional reversion to more primitive social attitudes. In no other light can we view the refusal of Seattle to return to office its progressive woman mayor." Sensitive to its reputation, Seattle was irritated by the taunt "Haven't you got any men in Seattle that you have a woman mayor?"[77] Landes lost reelection in 1928 to a fiscal conservative with ties to the KKK.[78]

Had progressives been moved beyond endurance, or had they just moved on? After the disappointments of the latter 1910s—the social trauma of world war in 1917, the election of local reactionary Ole Hanson in 1918, the implosion of the Seattle General Strike in 1919—Seattleites en masse scaled new heights of consumerism, leaving behind the collectivism of the age of reform. The sunset of the Progressive Era was visible from Seattle-area mountaintops: after being recalled from the Seattle School Board in the same election cycle where Ole Hanson became mayor, leftist journalist Anna Louise Strong exchanged the lows of politics for the highs of strenuous hikes—"my new form of opium," as she called mountain climbing.[79] "I turned like a wounded beast to the hills for shelter," wrote Strong, who earned international notoriety for her pro-worker reporting on the smothered Seattle General Strike. "Few newspapers reached me; I did not read them. On the high slopes of Rainier, I drugged myself with cliffs and glaciers. I exhausted myself with twenty-four-hour climbs. It was the end of youth, the end of belief."[80]

3rd Inning

FIRE VERSUS WATER, 1930–1942

Shortly after midnight on July 5, 1932, thousands of Seattleites gathered beneath a smoky red-orange sky to watch
one last spectacle at Dugdale Park: the stadium's fiery funeral. Flames had
broken out in the Seattle Indians clubhouse and devoured the wooden
arena's ten thousand seats. Cops dropped guns, exchanging them for water
hoses to help overmatched firefighters. Mount Baker residents evacuated
their homes. Fanned by northerly winds, smoke rose high in the southeast
Seattle heavens and drifted over the rest of the city. A fireman discovered a
can of oil in the ashes—perhaps used by baseball players to break in their
gloves. After initial speculation that July Fourth fireworks were to blame,
it was determined that team programs given to fans were the kindle that
kick-started the blaze. Incinerated Seattle Indians baseball uniforms hanging in the clubhouse were among the $691,000 worth of property damage
caused by the apparent arson.[1]

Seattle had a problem. Extravagant torchings had become a regular
occurrence. Arson on the city's waterfront on June 9, 1931, decimated the
city's industrial tract, causing damages worth $4.7 million to Northern Pa-
cific Railway and other company mills. Fires in lumber yards, construction
manufactories, and public institutions continued. In a torrid ten-day stretch
beginning March 7, 1932, fifteen arsons caused $1.6 million in damage. A
government dock charred on April 12, followed by fire at a West Seattle
apartment complex. By this time, Seattle papers had taken to calling the
lone arsonist the "Firebug."

Handwritten notes the fire starter left behind pointed to a grievance
against capitalism as well as prejudice against racial minorities: "IT'S A
SAD TRAVESTY ON AMERICANA THAT TO GET JUSTICE, BUMS

MUST PRESSURE LARGE CORPORATIONS." In another note the Firebug threatened "LONG AS I LIVE IN BREADLINES, HEARING NEGROES AND ALIENS INSULT WHITE PEOPLE, I CONTINUE FIRES. WHEN YOU GIVE ME A DECENT SALARY JOB, I'LL BECOME A FRIEND OF CAPITAL." Some of these notes were signed "WHITE CITIZEN." Several told employers to fire minorities to end the arson. A Black janitor who worked at the city library downtown angered Firebug just because he had a job, as did a public aid assistant who, the arsonist claimed, "INSULTS WHITES WHO ASK FOR CLOTHES."

Fueled by bigotry, Firebug didn't relent. For years following the Dugdale Park inferno in 1932, the kindler laid waste to dozens of machinery depots, manufacturing complexes, and especially train boxcars, torching rail containers and industrial plants while settling for smaller rubbish fires to bide time until bigger burns. Firebug rested slightly during Seattle's rainiest months, then restarted in spring and summer. Like befuddled batters trying to solve a dominant starting pitcher, hapless Seattle authorities could only hope the pyro made a mistake.

* * *

November 8, 1932, was a watershed Election Day for American progressivism, when voters swam against the conservative current of the 1920s. Locally, Washington State voters approved an income tax on the wealthy; they voted down Prohibition and had a drink.[2] Nationally the Evergreen State was one of forty-two in the Union to pledge its electoral votes to Franklin D. Roosevelt, who defeated Herbert Hoover to become the thirty-second president of the United States. His son a member of Harvard's rowing team in college, Roosevelt heralded a new reformist wave for a country sunk in a Great Depression.

The long business boom of the 1920s came to an end in October 1929 when the stock market plummeted and the debts of unhinged real estate speculation came due. The economy cratered. In Seattle, women scrambled for food in refuse piles at Pike Place Market; a journalist visiting the city during the Great Depression described arsons committed by aggrieved timber workers who couldn't find jobs.[3] Smoke from the man-made forest fires smothered Seattleites in a haze similar to the one blanketing East Coast urban areas during the Dust Bowl of the early 1930s. For a country besieged by capitalist crash and environmental calamity, there was relief in the water.

President Roosevelt rejuvenated rural America with irrigation projects; buckets of public money opened new public swimming pools in New York City, creating construction jobs and providing city dwellers spirit-boosting recreation during tough times.[4] On a trip through Washington State in 1934, Roosevelt announced his plan for public dams: "The power we are developing here is going to be controlled for all time by the government."[5] Seattle park officials waded into the tide of collective action in 1932 by allocating funds to construct shower stations and lockers for public park-goers, built by laborers in search of work.[6] In 1935, Roosevelt's economic recovery program funded bridge projects for construction jobs at nearby Deception Pass and Canoe Pass. Concurrently, New Deal funds cleared two acres of public beachfront by Golden Gardens Park in Ballard.[7] The Panic of 1893 had initiated a Progressive Era where American cities built great parks and took utilities into public control; the Great Depression prompted a repeat of the age of reform.

Whatever the extent of this progressive revival, Seattle business elites wouldn't suffer it without a fight. Washington State's new income tax targeted the big businesses, financial firms, stockholdings, and personal estates of the wealthy. The tax was "progressive" in the technical sense of the term, meaning those with more paid more. Campaign organizers drove hundreds of miles a day between big cities and small towns to spread the word about what the new revenue would mean for struggling communities: better roads that everybody drove on, financial aid for the homeless and unemployed, improved schools, and a break from property taxes for struggling farmers. After the Washington electorate voted the wealth tax into law on November 8, 1932, however, it would be washed away by a business backlash.[8]

An officer in the Seattle Junior Chamber of Commerce, William Culliton was a man of good standing in Seattle business circles in 1932. He cofounded the Washington Athletic Club (WAC) in 1930, its imposing brick confines built on a classic 1920s real estate pyramid scheme that targeted grieving widows to finance its twenty-one-story tower on Sixth

Avenue downtown.[9] Exercise facilities were open to paying members; a pool was placed on the sixth floor. A capitalist socialite, Culliton spent many hours cavorting with aristocrats in the Athletic Club's bowling alley.[10] Seattle's elite were all in agreement: the income tax had to die. Culliton led a campaign to revoke it, becoming the lead plaintiff in a suit arguing that the levy was illegal. Insurance agents and car dealers applied public pressure, penning anti-tax editorials in area newspapers. In September 1933, Washington's Supreme Court repealed the income tax, arguing that income was a form of property that had to be taxed uniformly (per state law) and not progressively (per common sense).[11]

The point of having an income tax was to pay for things that everybody used. If a poor log worker paid the same rate as lumber tycoon Frederick Weyerhaeuser, tons of money would be left on the table, leaving Washington more prone to budget crunches caused by business slowdowns. Most knew what was at stake: fourteen US states already had income taxes before the 1929 stock market crash. Sixteen more enacted them in the 1930s. Washington had been among them. But that was history now.

In "Of Rain and Revenue: The Politics of Income Taxation in the State of Washington," historian Phil Roberts describes how a steady spigot of temporary sales taxes were introduced in the 1935 Washington State legislative session to help the government keep running; they were supposed to be temporary stopgaps.[12] Most state legislators believed it was only a matter of time before a new levy on wealth became law. The rain never came. A revenue dike blocking cities in Washington State from taxing the rich to pay for public services, the 1933 Supreme Court decision stayed on the books for longer than anybody thought it could: for generations.

* * *

What would possess Seattleites to congregate in the middle of the night and watch their wooden baseball stadium burn to the ground? During slavery, enslaved African Americans were made to race, box, and wrestle one another for plantation entertainment.[13] When the Civil War broke out in Virginia battlefields in July 1861, throngs gathered with picnic baskets to watch.[14] Into the twentieth century, white audiences organized civic gatherings around lynchings. When they weren't watching baseball, Seattle crowds gathered in the 1880s to hang prisoners and evict the city's Chinese community. In 1900 a Seattle store scored a hit with city listeners when it sold a phonograph recording of a southern Black man crying in pain as he was burned alive by a white mob.[15] America's values put on fine clothes in science books, in political speechifying, in the stocks and bonds section of the *Wall Street Journal*—in spectacles, the values appear nakedly.

Poet Rudyard Kipling happened to be visiting Seattle in June 1889 when the city was ravaged by fire. He described a "horrible black smudge in the heart of the business quarters."[16] Seattleites stood by the docks to see if their waterfront would survive. Some watched on First Avenue as firefighters flailed. In the coming years, staged demolitions of crashing locomotives would captivate audiences in the American West. Seattleites didn't have a train terminal yet—but they did have a dream of becoming a great city, a dream that many of them couldn't wait to watch go up in smoke. The night of the fire, they sat on surrounding hills and looked down on ninety acres of debris and dancing flame. As the sun set behind the Olympic Mountains, Seattle showed itself to be a town where one-third of the city would watch as one-third of the city burned and one-third of the city tried to help. When Firebug torched a tract belonging to the Northern Pacific Railway in June 1931, Seattle police had to put up barricades to keep the crowds away.

Were the Seattle Indians not part of the spectacle of total annihilation? The Minor League Baseball team descended from the Gilded Age squad that captivated frontier Seattleites. For many years their uniforms flaunted a red face in a headdress. After seizing Coast Salish lands and relegating many Indigenous children to cruel residential boarding schools—after criminalizing the presence of Lushootseed peoples in Seattle in an ordinance that was never repealed—white Seattle turned Native people into entertainment. They watched as the Seattle Indians unraveled.

Seattle team owners scrambled to find a new baseball stadium after Dugdale Park burned in 1932. Civic Stadium in Queen Anne was secured on a short-term lease, with the City of Seattle offering to help pay the team's electrical bill in exchange for a cut of its ticketing revenue. In part because of this arrangement, the Seattle Indians went bankrupt. On September 19,

1937, federal and local tax agents descended on Civic Stadium and seized everything they could to settle the team's delinquent tax bills.[17]

Government couldn't afford to be gracious to a tax-evading baseball team. The New Deal and new bureaucracies like Social Security and the National Labor Relations Board cost money. The day of the tax raid, Roosevelt announced a visit to Washington and Oregon's Bonneville Dam, which cost $1.7 billion (in 2023 dollars) to build. Washington's income tax had been repealed, leaving the state cash-strapped. The public had bills to pay, so during Seattle's September 19, 1937, doubleheader against the visiting Sacramento Solons, local and federal tax collectors collided in Civic Stadium, flashing badges and forcing ticket stand attendants to hand over whatever cabbage they had. Agents reached into cash registers and took what they wanted; Civic Stadium's manager absconded with $3,932 in unpaid Seattle City Light fees.[18] A Seattle Indians official stuffed greenbacks in the pockets of the team's first-base coach during the game, trying to hide them from the taxmen. More money was hidden in the outfield, under bases, in the infield dirt. Civic Stadium threatened to evict the team. It was a trainwreck. The Indians took both games of the doubleheader.

Still on the loose from city authorities, Firebug nearly ended professional baseball in Seattle. A more primeval competition was put in its place. In an article detailing one of the arsonist's major blazes, the *Seattle Times* said: "Fire and water fought while spectators gaped in amusement. It was a duel to the death."[19]

* * *

Once the holder of twenty-three world swimming records, it is difficult to exaggerate Helene Madison's historical significance to Seattle.[20] The city had had championship teams before: during the Progressive Era, Gil Dobie's Huskies and the Seattle Mets galvanized local support and made Seattle more visible to East Coast media. However, Seattle never had an individual superstar. Bernie Morris of the Mets came closest, but he was a mercenary free agent, signed from Canada in 1915, years before sports became a mass spectacle with the advent of radio, film, and increased commercialization. And by 1919, Morris's reputation was in tatters after he was convicted of draft-dodging during World War I. In homegrown, wholesome Helene Madison, Seattle had a dominant competitor, the best athlete alive in her sport, and a proud Seattleite who knew what it meant to represent the city on a global stage. When asked whether the rumors were true—that she would be abandoning Seattle and joining the Los Angeles Athletic Club—Madison shut them down: "That's bosh. If I can't represent Seattle, I won't swim."[21]

Born June 19, 1913, Helene Gemma Madison graduated from Seattle's Lincoln High School in Wallingford. She learned her way around the water in Seattle's Parks Department swimming program. In 1929 she broke the Washington State record for the women's 100-yard freestyle, then won every freestyle competition she entered at the US Women's Nationals from 1930 to 1932. At the 1930 US championships in Miami, the *Seattle Times* described "a tall, thin girl, who didn't possess the flowing beach robes of the New Yorkers. She strode awkwardly and looked out of place."[22]

When businessmen incorporated the Washington Athletic Club (WAC) in 1930, the group's bylaws proclaimed their intent "to support amateur athletics in the Seattle area."[23] Sports were brand maintenance, putting a positive shine on Seattle corporations after capitalists had driven the country to economic collapse. Three months after the WAC opened, boosters partnered with William Culliton's Junior Chamber of Commerce to sponsor its first athlete: Olympic hopeful Helene Madison. The WAC castle was made headquarters of the swimmer's fundraising surge, with Depression-era fans contributing whatever they could to send her to international competitions.

Madison's Olympic hopes became a cause célèbre in Seattle, as corporations and small donors pitched in to fund the training expenses of the athlete deemed "Seattle's First Sports Hero" by historian Maureen Smith.[24] When the 1932 Summer Olympics began in Los Angeles, Madison owned every women's swimming record in existence, impressing observers by beating top swimmers from bigger cities.

The LA Olympics were a star-studded affair, with international media swooning as matinee idols made appearances at sporting events. Charlie Chaplin entertained crowds; cameras filmed newsreels seen by millions. Propelled by community support, Madison won gold medals in the 100-

meter freestyle, the 400-meter freestyle, and the 400-meter relay. She knew just what to say: "Tell Seattle how glad I was that I was able to win after they made it possible for me to come. I feel I have compensated them for their generosity."[25] Madison gracefully navigated the murky waters of sports celebrity as a young woman: meddlesome reporters with repetitive questions, invasive fans looking for autographs, the galling sexism of a Parks Department coach who claimed total credit for her success. Seattle officials planned a massive reception for Madison's return from Los Angeles, with Seattle mayor John Dore exalting "the maid who has brought honor to our city."[26]

The swimming pool exploits of Helene Madison were but another way Seattle owed its identity—natural, economic, cultural—to the water. When they created the country's first public power utility in 1902, Seattle City Light engineers dammed the Skagit River, one of several streams that fed into the expansive estuary known as Puget Sound. Beneficiaries of this body of water's biodiversity, the Coast Salish built their civilization on the accessible abundance of life near lakes, rivers, and an ocean.[27] In ceremonies and drum circles, they paid tribute to the local life force; they rode canoes for war and sport. Lushootseed-speaking peoples called the great mountain at the southern tip of Puget Sound "Tahoma," which translates to "mother of waters."[28] White settlers renamed it "Rainier," echoing a defining trait that Seattle owed to its maritime situation; on his maiden expedition to the Pacific Northwest in May 1792, explorer Peter Puget and his crew bemoaned a "perfect deluge of rain."[29] Though grungy weather became something of a demerit on Seattle's reputation, damp air and dank skies furnished the Douglas fir trade that sustained the city. Into the twenty-first century, sundry Seattle sports teams would adopt aquatic mascots, buoying civic ambition with the local symbolism of raging storms and swooping sea hawks, intrepid mariners and dangerous kraken. From sports to socioeconomics, it wouldn't be an overstatement to say that water was the source of everything that made Seattle Seattle.

Back in town from the Los Angeles Olympics, Helene Madison became one more Seattleite struggling to stay afloat during the Depression. When she couldn't teach swimming lessons in Seattle pools because the city's Parks Department reserved those jobs for men, she made ends meet by selling hot dogs at the Green Lake park where she learned to swim. "Seattle's First Sports Hero" tried parlaying her celebrity into acting, making her cinematic debut in *The Human Fish* (1932). All the films flopped.[30] Once the most famous person in the city, Madison became a spectacle of fallen celebrity. Newspaper articles detailed her money problems, her battles with diabetes and later cancer, her lightless Green Lake basement apartment where her gold medals collected dust.[31] She didn't have the money to travel to Florida for her induction into the National Swimming Hall of Fame.[32] As Madison tailspun publicly, the Washington Athletic Club sponsors who had capitalized on her talent were nowhere to be found. The money had moved on.

The University of Washington's rowing team picked up steam in the early 1930s when its coach learned that the red cedarwood the Swinomish used in their canoes made for exceptional racing shell material.[33] With the UW rowing team practicing on a site in the Montlake neighborhood where the Duwamish once congregated to ride canoes, Coach George Pocock's manufacturing breakthrough was grifted upon the older wisdom of the Coast Salish.[34] The new racing shells torpedoed the Washington team representing the United States in the 1936 Olympics to a gold medal victory in Berlin. The WAC threw its fundraising apparatus behind the Washington rowers, whose defeat of Nazi Germany at the "Hitler Olympics" was immortalized in Daniel James Brown's bestseller *Boys in the Boat* as well as the PBS documentary *The Boys of '36*. Neither the book nor the film so much as mentioned Helene Madison, whose talent first created the fundraising apparatus that UW rowing rode to prestige. Though a 1941 exhibition later pitted Husky boaters against a Swinomish racing team, popular recitations of the greater glories of UW crew also tend to exclude the Coast Salish contribution to Seattle sports. In the canoe clash between the Coast Salish and the University of Washington, historian Bruce Miller described a competition between "an aboriginal Swinomish worldview where canoes represented a sacred connection to the land and the water," and the settler society where "rowers represented the vigor of a community based on fishing, logging, and [an intimate] connection with the sea."[35]

The UW crew benefited from the support of cash-strapped Seattleites who contributed small donations to help them cover the cost of competing

Beachgoers in the segregated Madison Park neighborhood, 1930. Area waters spawned the city's first international sports stars: Olympic swimmer Helene Madison in 1932 and the UW rowing team that defeated Germany for a gold medal at the 1936 "Hitler Olympics" in Berlin. Courtesy of the Seattle Municipal Archives, item 29786.

during the Great Depression. Madison did so with the added headwind of sexism, which scrubbed her from a history she started.

* * *

After four years, Firebug faltered. On the evening of May 4, 1935, he tried to ignite a Russian Orthodox Church in the heart of the city, near South Lake Union. His bungling prompted a heroic neighborhood dog to begin barking, at which point two proprietors of a Russian restaurant went outside to see what the commotion was, taking a meat hammer with them for self-defense. They chased and tackled a stocky five-foot-five

SEATTLE FIRE DEPARTMENT

DEPARTMENT BUSINESS ONLY

May 5 193 5

FROM:

TO:

Statement of Robert Bruce Driscoll, taken at Fire Headquarters
at 1:30 A.M. May 5, 1935.

I Robert Bruce Driscoll, of my own free will and accord and without
promise of any kind make the following statement:

That on the night of May 4th I gathered papers and kindling at
the rear of the church building at 753 Lake View Boulevard and places them
under the northwest corner of the building and set them on fire with the
intent of the distruction of the property.
I done this because of my destitute circumstances and because I
was sore at the world in general.

Signed:

Robert Bruce Driscoll

Witnesses:

Frank H. Hartfield

E. L. Smith.

James V. Harrison

Marion W. McCutoch.

Bigoted arsonist Robert "Firebug" Driscoll burned down the city's main ballpark
in 1932. The Seattle Fire Department extracted this confession from him in May 1935.
Courtesy of the Seattle Municipal Archives, Box 96, Folder 3.

man, subduing him until police arrived. In a statement transcribed by the Seattle Fire Department, signed and dated May 5, 1935, at 1:30 a.m., the forty-three-year-old Firebug incriminated himself: "I, Robert Bruce Driscoll, of my own free will, make the following statement: on the night of May 4, I gathered kindling at the church at 753 Lakeview Boulevard with the intent of the destruction of the property. I done this because of my destitute circumstances and because I was sore at the world in general."

In police custody, Driscoll confessed the extent of his crimes: between March 1931 and May 1935, he lit 140 blazes in Seattle—one every eleven or so days—causing $15.1 million total in damages. The Northern Pacific Railway wrote to the Seattle Fire Department, thanking them for catching the man who had done so much damage to their property. Details about Driscoll's life emerged when Seattle authorities corresponded with West Coast public safety officials.

Driscoll was born in Spokane, Washington, in 1893 and was briefly a professional boxer. From 1916 to 1918 he was a firefighter in Oregon; a former supervisor of his in the Oregon State Legislature, where Driscoll worked as a stenographer, noted he "seems to feel the world owed him more than he was getting." Driscoll served in World War I, racked up misdemeanors and domestic violence charges, and committed extensive arsons in San Jose, rural Oregon, and possibly Canada. When he migrated to Seattle in 1931 after a brief stint as a logger in Tacoma, Driscoll slept in vacant train cars when he wasn't lighting them on fire.

On the same day that Driscoll was apprehended, the *Seattle Post-Intelligencer* warned that westward migrants who moved to Seattle because of the Dust Bowl would struggle to find adequate housing. Named "Hoovervilles" after President Herbert Hoover's failed conservative economic policies, waterfront shacks sprouted up in Seattle during the Depression, attracting mostly middle-aged men like Firebug who were experiencing houselessness. Firebug took up residence at an integrated Seattle homeless encampment in 1933, where destitute men of all races fraternized by listening to Seattle baseball games on the radio. Camp residents played sports at the nearby recreational center built by the city to keep them occupied.[36] After white women in the North End Progressive Club complained of the encampments, Seattle police were authorized to set fire to them, condemning Seattleites experiencing houselessness to no shelter at all.[37]

11548-2
2-7-33

Seattle "Hooverville" homeless encampment, 1933, situated on the grounds later occupied by the city's major sports arenas. Courtesy of the Seattle Municipal Archives,
item 191876.

Progressive white bureaucrats saw Robert Driscoll as a troubled soul
who merely made the mistake of setting fire after fire after fire. After his
arrest a Seattle Fire Department functionary said: "His case may be taken
as an argument against a social system that condemns a man for human
frailties and errors." Yet when Seattle police murdered an unarmed Black
waiter a few years later in 1938, accusing him of loitering in the hotel where
he worked, no condemnation of unfair "social systems" was ever issued by
the city's public safety authorities.

During the interrogation that led to Driscoll's confession, a Seattle fireman saw fit to ask him about "the n—— who worked at the library." Years

later, when a state fire marshal reflected on Firebug, he mused: "I grew to like this fellow. He never set fires to buildings occupied by people."[38] The marshal was perhaps unconcerned that the arsonist damaged three homes in the Dugdale Park fire, burned down a Beacon Hill elementary school, and destroyed a service center for the disabled. For all the wreckage he caused, Driscoll drew only second-degree arson charges, a sentence that came with five to ten years' imprisonment. Firebug's impressive career as one of the most accomplished arsonists in American history revealed racial discrepancies in New Deal Seattle, highlighting a long-running distance between who progressives said they were and what they did.

Just as the rugged individualism of the frontier period and Gilded Age spawned the Progressive Era, the capitalist excess of the 1920s motivated a New Deal. If history wasn't repeating, it appeared to be rhyming. Yet if the Progressive Era had been resurrected, then so had its prejudices. The earlier President Roosevelt curtailed Japanese immigration with a 1907 gentleman's agreement. The later President Roosevelt forcibly removed Japanese Americans to concentration camps.

The Issei generation of Japanese immigrants formed the Seattle Nippon and Seattle Mikado baseball clubs at the turn of the century, and hosted cross-continental contests between clubs from Japan and America.[39] While the skill of Japanese American farmers prompted some of Seattle's white farmers to have them banned from Pike Place Market after it opened in 1907, Issei baseball was also met with hostility and suspicion. In June 1905 the *Seattle Times* cast Japanese Americans as cultural outsiders because they tended to be quiet during baseball games: "Half the pleasure of the baseball fan in this country is to make all the noise he can."[40]

While progressivism fell out of vogue during World War I, boxer James Sakomoto founded the Progressive Citizen's League in 1921 to push back against Alien Land Laws that prevented Japanese Americans from owning property. Sakomoto denounced the Seattle-spawn Immigration Act of 1924 that reduced Japanese immigration, then founded the Japanese American Courier League in 1928 to funnel community factionalism in Seattle's Nihonmachi into sports. That JACL baseball teams often beat white Seattle squads did little to ingratiate them to the surrounding community.

When Japanese warplanes attacked a US military base at Pearl Harbor,

Hawaii, on December 7, 1941, slurs became ubiquitous in Seattle newspapers and appeared in area graffiti, signaling an escalation toward incarceration.[41] Although Seattle mayor John Dore had been seen giving the Heil Hitler salute at a Seattle rally funded by the Nazi Party in 1939, panic over German Americans in the city was at this time virtually nonexistent. In February 1943, President Roosevelt authorized the forced removal of all Japanese Americans to concentration camps.[42] Incarcerated in the Minidoka Relocation Center near the town of Hunt, Idaho, Seattle's seven thousand Japanese Americans worked under the auspices of the War Relocation Authority to publish the *Minidoka Irrigator* after arriving in the desert.[43] When the long first winter at the American concentration camp finally thawed, it was reported that a golf course, basketball courts, and baseball diamonds were under construction by volunteering prisoners. In July 1943 the Minidoka baseball team played the camp's military police, sinking the cops by thirteen runs.[44]

The anti-Asian sentiment of the original age of reform had set the stage for the Japanese American incarceration a generation later. Consequently, it would be a mistake to say that the inclusivity of the Progressive Era had been restored during the New Deal. In the embers of Seattle prejudice, what was never possessed could never be recovered.

Concession Stand

After Firebug torched Dugdale Park, Seattle labor leader Dave Beck urged his friend—beer magnate Emil Sick—to get involved in the baseball business.[1] Sick agreed. He purchased the Seattle Indians, renamed them the Rainiers after the ale company he owned, then financed a new fifteen-thousand-seat arena on the grounds of the torched ballpark. At Sick's Stadium the Rainiers went to the Pacific Coast League championship every year from 1940 through 1943. They won three titles. Thirsty Seattle fans poured into their new ballpark and bought suds by the gallon at stadium concession stands. The Rainiers fulfilled Beck's prediction that Sick would "be a big man in this city and sell lots of beer" by building a good baseball team and a ballpark to watch them in.[2] But by the end of World War II, it was Beck who was the bigger man in Seattle, on the path to becoming one of the most powerful men in the country.

Born June 16, 1894, David Daniel Beck spent his formative years in Seattle after his family moved there in 1898, taking a job as a laundry truck driver while a teen and working his way up the ranks of management in the Teamsters Union.[3] As the Progressive Era turned into the Roaring 1920s, Beck loathed leftists who agitated for the Seattle General Strike in 1919. "You lose more in pay than you get from the raise," he once said of striking.[4] His business-friendly brand paid off: in 1947 Beck was named executive vice president of the Teamsters, the largest and richest union in the country. "Our aim," Beck said, "has been to develop better understanding between industry and labor. This is our contribution toward a better relationship between all classes."[5]

The years 1945 through 1973 are referred to by some economists as the "golden age of capitalism" because of the enormous boom created for the white American middle class after World War II.[6] Conciliatory unionists like Beck, big businesses like Boeing, and American politicians arrived at a macroeconomic consensus. In exchange for industry subsidies and a population socially engineered to support private enterprise, corporations would pay the government's high tax rates. In exchange for livable wages from their employers, laborers would largely agree to minimize strike activity. With the public sector promising social entitlements, cheap housing, and a comfortable retirement, workers punched the clock day in and day out, asking not what their country could do for them, but what capitalism could do for the country. Key concessions between big socioeconomic stakeholders created record productivity, record prosperity, and record profits.

A reflection of this new status quo, American sports after World War II were defined by the partnership of elite athletic labor with disciplinarian team management, replicating the economic consensus between bosses and organized labor embodied by Dave Beck. In Green Bay, Wisconsin, coach Vince Lombardi commanded the Packers to five NFL titles and two Super Bowl wins in the 1960s. In Boston, Celtics center Bill Russell and coach Red Auerbach created basketball royalty, winning eight straight NBA championships from 1959 to 1966. In New York, manager Casey Stengel guided the star-studded Yankees to seven World Series wins between 1949 and 1960. Even in boxing, once the domain of rugged individualists, the manager and cornermen became equal partners, with coach Cus D'Amato coaxing Floyd Patterson to the world heavyweight championship in 1956. A fledgling industry with the advent of *Sports Illustrated* in 1954, sports media focused increasingly on team management alongside athletic labor. "Like other great industries, baseball is in the age of the organization man," the magazine's editorial board wrote in 1958. "A baseball manager must have the financial acumen of a corporation president."[7]

Lucrative games gave racial minorities opportunities to climb America's class hierarchy. But the ladder wasn't sturdy: when Black athletes had bad games or voiced radical political opinions, white spectators castigated them. Sportswriters tarred Black athletes as unable to handle big-game pressure after Brooklyn Dodger ace pitcher Don Newcombe's shutout was broken up by a home run in the ninth inning of the first game of the 1949 World Series.[8] Already controversial because of his association with Malcolm X and the militant Black Muslims, Muhammad Ali became an iconoclast when he denounced the Vietnam War.

The "golden age of capitalism" was defined as much by who it included as by who it left out. In the celebration of industrious athletes with "blue collar" work habits in the heyday of American manufacturing, disabled athletes were seldom represented. Regressive views of women's participation in sports were reflected by the wageless labors of women in the home. New suburbs created by a partnership between government and the private sector barred nonwhite residents. Consequently, big slums and blighted areas sprang up in US inner cities. These unequally distributed benefits of the American social order sullied the economic consensus built by the liberal heirs of the original progressive movement—and ultimately doomed it.

After World War II minority residents of northern liberal cities suffered unemployment and segregated schools. Civil rights injustices sparked riots. By the late 1960s, US policymakers spoke of an "urban crisis," its roots irrigated by decades of exclusion. Though it flowered for a generation, postwar American progressivism already contained the seeds of its own demise.

4th Inning

PEAK PERFORMANCE, 1945–1949

Five feet three inches and 115 pounds was all that stood between mighty Jim Beaty and a place on Tacoma's Lincoln High School men's tennis squad. To keep his spot on the team in the spring of 1947, all he had to do was win a singles match against a classmate who challenged him for the last spot on the team. Shockingly, Beaty had nothing for his opponent, who rolled him in straight sets: 6–2, 6–1. "She beat me," he said, when asked for an explanation from the team's coach. "What can I do?"[1]

As it turned out, nothing much. Beaty tried three more times that spring to win back his place on the team. The girl beat him thrice. In advance of 1947 Cross-State League matches against Puget Sound–region competition, all-male Lincoln High welcomed their new teammate: Marilyn Kropf.

Born June 29, 1930, in Tacoma, Kropf was a promising talent in girls' tennis when she won Beaty's spot, going undefeated in match play and winning the singles championship in her class. When Everett High refused to play Lincoln because they had a girl on the team in April 1947, the story drew syndicated newspaper coverage from the Associated Press, entreating a national readership to witness the moral injury of Everett's cowardice in real time. An Everett official explained that "the rules are all worded in the masculine, and custom has frowned on mixed competition."[2] Administrators found no such statute against intergender competition on the state books. Lincoln offered a compromise: four-on-four play with no Kropf. Everett shirked again, saying they would only play if Kropf were swapped for a male. Lincoln moved on, only to have Bremerton High also refuse to play them.

Where Everett had no response for the media blitz initiated when they refused to play Kropf, Bremerton went on the offensive. In June 1947 school leaders told the Associated Press about their school's progressive sports culture, showcasing a young woman who excelled at women's tennis and women's football.[3] That the controversy surrounding Kropf was about girls competing with boys—not one another—escaped Bremerton's public relations game plan.

"I can't help it if I'm a girl," said the sixteen-year-old Marilyn Kropf during the controversy her mere presence caused. "I hope I'm not causing any trouble." Her story was given clumsy, frequently creepy treatment by sportswriters; a national news write-up referred to her as "pretty and shapely."[4] Rather than use Kropf's achievements to reflect on stereotypical gender roles, a Tacoma sportswriter used the refusal of rival schools to play Kropf as an excuse for rank homophobia: "What happens in Everett, do the boys dance with the boys up there?"[5]

Some Seattle writers looked down on Tacoma as their little sibling city, a smugness heightened by Kropf's age and gender. *Seattle Times* sportswriter Emmett Watson devoted a paragraph to parsing the deficiencies in Kropf's game, noting her shaky backhand and struggles with play at the net.[6] "The little German-Irish miss isn't a great player," he concluded. Observations made by Watson's expert eye about the shortcomings of mighty Jim Beaty's game never saw the light of print; as Kropf was good enough to defeat Beaty four consecutive times, no further appraisal of his talent was ever necessary.

* * *

Historically, Seattleites had a habit of referring to their city and its institutions with she/her pronouns that made women seem like passive beneficiaries of male heroism instead of active agents in the city they lived, worked, and recreated in. The rhetorical tactic fashioned Seattle into a submissive female saved from depravity by hearty men. In a 1908 call for a new UW football coach, *Washington Alumnus* argued the college "needs a personality at the head of her athletics."[7] Welford Beaton's 1914 history *The City That Made Itself* called Seattle's male settlers the catalysts of "her" rapid development: "The reason for her growth lay in the stout hearts of her warriors."[8] Later, historian Roger Sale wrote: "Seattle's great attributes seemed to be her harbor and her forests," feminizing women and nature all at once, while giving subtle linguistic license to the exploitation of both.[9] Far from passive, settler women shaped and formed Seattle.

In the Progressive Era, white Seattle women established an opera house and lobbied for a new public hospital. Historian John C. Putnam relays that at the turn of the century, "women participated in nearly a dozen unions, including locals for beer-bottlers, telephone operators, cigarmakers."[10] In 1914 the Seattle Police Department "hired" unpaid Black Seattle woman Corinne Carter. On the force she rescued Black domestic servant girls living in slavery-like conditions in Seattle and later established a YWCA chapter that offered Central Area physical fitness facilities for "Negro Health Week" in 1947.[11] For Seattle women seeking full entry into American life, sports were an important proving ground.

Black women in Seattle were the future, their position within the city's social hierarchy forecasting labor conditions and strategies of resilience replicated by others many years later. For the broader society, the flight of men from households, workplaces, and positions of power in service of World War II created new opportunities; as the rate of employment for Seattle women increased 57 percent between 1941 and 1946, the national divorce rate doubled.[12] Women worked as mechanics and machinists, embodying the Rosie the Riveter iconography that illustrated their worth to the wartime economy. Chewing gum tycoon Philip K. Wrigley capitalized on ascendant American women when he created the All-American Girls Professional Baseball League (AAGPBL) in 1943. Later immortalized in the film *A League of Their Own*, this all-white story of economic empowerment leading to sports triumph traced a template trod earlier by Black Seattle women.

With a roster composed entirely of Black women, the Seattle Owls baseball team played its home games at Sick's Stadium in the 1930s, won the Washington State Softball Championship in 1938, and captured the 1939 city championship. In the process they reproduced the grit of Seattle Black women who served as the backbone of their beleaguered community. As America recovered from the Great Depression in the late 1930s, the Black unemployment rate in Seattle (24.3 percent) was second only to Milwaukee; because the downturn hit Black men in Seattle particularly hard, Black women entered the labor force to support themselves and

Four members of the Seattle Owls, 1938. The Seattle Owls were a team of Black women who captured local trophies in the late 1930s. They sported Depression-era fashion that would resonate in later years. Museum of History and Industry, Seattle, Al Smith Collection, 2014.49.19.01.01.

their social networks, finding employment as domestic servants and service workers.[13] Working for a living produced a hard-won confidence. Photographs of the self-assured Seattle Owls squad depict a team of tight-knit competitors, bandaged by the baseball hustle but still debonair enough to don hoop earrings with caps and jerseys—an ahead-of-its-time sartorial play later copied by postindustrial women of all races. In the Seattle Owls baseball team, the triple pressures of race, class, and gender adversity had created diamonds.

After the Owls dismantled a white women's Bremerton team 21–1 to clinch the 1938 title, the *Seattle Post-Intelligencer* dubbed them the "Brown Bombers," spotlighting their "powerful batting attack and smooth-working defense." Before long, Black women's labor bolstered the American defense establishment.[14] Of the 329 Black workers employed by Boeing at its plants in Seattle and Wichita during World War II, 280 of them were women.[15] These "Black Rosies" integrated Boeing in Seattle, simultaneously advancing race and gender progress domestically while aiding the fight against authoritarianism abroad.[16] In factories and on the field of play, the presence of fewer white men facilitated the creation of a more fair city.

When servicemen returned to the United States after the war, they brought with them a predilection for partying that had fermented in American military bases. Seattle was already a hotbed of debauchery. When a US military doctor declared in 1943 that "Seattle's V.D. situation is appalling," he wasn't referring to Victory Day; the *Washington Post* devoted a two-part series that year to Seattle's efforts to contain gonorrhea and syphilis.[17] Jazz halls and cabarets in Pioneer Square and the Central Area were frequented by soldiers, sex workers, and society types, lubricating the sporting life as pimps and gamblers placed huge wagers on pool and horse racing. Seattle cops were a corrupt protection racket at this time, soliciting bribes from establishments in exchange for police protection. Down in Pioneer Square, the Garden of Allah was a cabaret that opened in 1946 as one of the first gay-owned bars in the country.

Garden crowds took in uproarious gender-bending performances and minstrel shows.[18] A boxer with an imposing physique, Black exhibitionist Michael Phelan performed in drag at the Garden; Vaudevillian dancers executed elaborate synchronized displays in shoes decidedly not meant for athletic activity. Tipsy audiences egged the ersatz athletes on like fans at the ballpark.[19] An organ blared. If gender was a performance, the show didn't stop at sporting events with straight male athletes.

Shirley Maser was a regular at the Garden of Allah, calling it "a home away from home" in the book *An Evening at the Garden of Allah.* "The first time I went to the Garden, I was just coming out."[20] During the day Maser played playground softball in a league sponsored by the Seattle Park Department; at night she recalled taking in the physical feats of "super butches at the Garden, the gals dressed up like guys."[21] Women drove an uptick in Seattle playground activity that doubled from 1948 to 1949.[22] Maser played in the Park Department's Northwest Women's Basketball League—one of the teams was named the Pabst Blue Ribbons: "I remember going to the Hub, Seattle's first lesbian bar, and seeing some of the girls on the team."[23]

Seattle women athletes who didn't conform to traditional gender roles after World War II stepped into civic spaces created during the Progressive Era. The parks where Shirley Maser played sports were established during the "City Beautiful" movement; the Garden of Allah was located in the basement of the Arlington Hotel, opened in 1894 as a salon.[24] In the 1940s Jane Addams's "age of association" was evident in the joyous camaraderie of trans, gay, and lesbian Seattleites. Unfortunately, some progressives believed the place for queer Seattleites was in prisons and mental institutions.

Pioneer Square had been the center of LGBTQ+ life in Seattle since the frontier period. If the area south of Lake Union was Seattle's "heart," then this neighborhood near Puget Harbor was its gut—a microbiome of mill workers, manual laborers, and racial and sexual minorities who made the metropolis's rise possible. North Seattle was the land of strivers, real estate prospectors, and refined neighborhoods. Pioneer Square was the district of sex workers, wage laborers, and seasonal employees living in single-room-occupancy hotels. City officials in the Progressive Era frequently tried cleansing this area with policing. They criminalized the perceived rots of drinking and prostitution in Seattle's gut. Whatever flourished there might spread to the rest of the city. Consequently, reformers also cracked down on gay life.

Beginning with a Washington State law that banned sodomy in 1893, most aspects of gay and trans existence in Seattle were suppressed. As a state legislator, "progressive" George Cotterill spurred a 1909 law that criminalized fellatio—an act he believed gay men were predisposed to perform.[25] Cops harassed trans Seattleite Harry Allen at the turn of the century, citing them for bogus biking infractions when their real crime was cross-dressing.[26] During the New Deal women suspected of being lesbians were subject to involuntary commitment in hospitals built with New Deal funds; family members of Seattle actress Frances Farmer had her evaluated

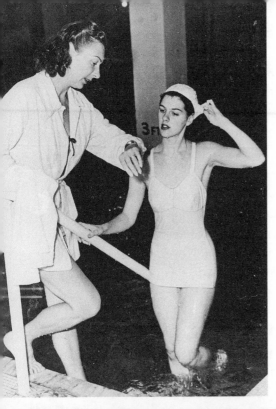

left Helene Madison (left) and Marilyn Luper (right) at Seattle's Moore Pool, 1949. Once the titleholder of every women's swimming record in existence, Madison fed the tributary of the sport by training Oregon upstart Luper. Courtesy of the Seattle Municipal Archives, item 31086.

below A ball handler in a Seattle Parks women's basketball league deftly executes a screen-and-roll play in a packed gymnasium, circa 1949. King County Archives, Series 467, Park System 1949–1998, box 12, folder 6.

at Harborview Medical Center in 1944 and then admitted to Western State Hospital, where she remained until 1950, her incarceration a symbol of LGBTQ+ persecution in Seattle.[27]

Because cities are defined by the absence of space between individuals, all movement on urban terrain is political. To move freely in the method of one's choosing is an expression of power; to be restricted, evidence of repression. Rights granted or fought for are animated by the urban athlete, their mobility an embodiment of political liberties.[28] In October 1947 a Seattle woman who loved motorbiking was given an ultimatum by her boyfriend: keep the bike, or keep the beau. "He knew she'd have her heart set on a new cycle model instead of a new dining room set," said the *Seattle Post-Intelligencer*. "So, he told her to choose. The woman returned her bike in tears."[29]

Seattle athletes who broke societal gender molds found a vehicle for liberation in motorbiking. Shirley Maser joined the all-woman Motor Maids of America, founded in 1940. The club had a small but dedicated Seattle ridership of about two dozen who competed in grueling races on muddy trails and rode casually to pick up coffee. The riders caused rubbernecking on city streets with their sartorial choices: newsboy caps, baggy jodhpur pants, long-sleeve button-ups, and white gloves. "We prided ourselves on being clean cut," a cyclist remembered.[30] Seattle women riders like Peggy Joslin—who trained for a three-hundred-mile endurance ride in the autumn of 1947—were socialized to accept second-class citizenship. Nevertheless, they rode. When asked to choose between the sport she loved and a boy she liked, Joslin got on her bike and sped away.[31]

* * *

When Gil Dobie died in 1948, sentimental musings about the old prick poured into the Seattle sports world. The Associated Press praised his "tackle-smashing" teams and called him a "stern and exacting taskmaster." Washington quarterback Willie Coyle fondly recalled what a jerk he was: "No smile, no handshake, no 'Glad to see you at Washington'— nothing but a pair of black eyes peering coldly."[32] It was as if the trauma of world war and the social destabilization of shifting gender roles inspired nostalgia for the seemingly less-complicated masculinity of a bygone era—a masculinity that Dobie once epitomized.

With due respect to General Patton's command of the Seventh United States Army during World War II, America would never again see a leader of men like Gil Dobie, who captained Washington to nine straight undefeated seasons from 1908 to 1916.[33] Washington football fans old enough to remember the legend's winning ways missed him maybe more than ever. After the war the Huskies posted a shabby record of 19–27–1 in the years spanning 1945 through 1949. Ugly losses piled up. A 28–0 drubbing by USC in October 1946. A 6–0 stinker against Oregon in October 1947. A 46–0 spanking at the hands of Notre Dame in November 1948. A September 1949 game in Minnesota promised to be a massacre—and it was. But the game was nonetheless noteworthy: Washington arrived as two-touchdown underdogs, left as 48–20 losers, and made the trip on the chartered maiden flight of a B-29 bomber plane repurposed for domestic air travel.

In 1949 round-trip tickets from Seattle to Minnesota cost $1,500 (in 2023 dollars); because the rituals of commercial passenger flight were still a novelty, it's plausible that the Huskies lost their defense in baggage claim, or forgot to pack it altogether.[34] In any case, aerospace was the next frontier—a new place for men to be pioneers, and for everyone else to exit the cockpit. In the 1940s, Douglas Aircraft drew tens of thousands of workers to its wild-west manufacturing centers in Oklahoma City and Los Angeles; Boeing planes manufactured in Wichita and Seattle dropped atomic bombs on Japan, ending World War II. Afterward, Boeing aspired to become America's main purveyor of passenger aircraft. In the August 1947 edition of its glossy periodical *Boeing Magazine*, the company recruited a US Air Force general to elaborate on the breakthrough of passenger air travel: "Seattle will have a special role in making people conscious of the potential in the Air Age. As a civilizer, the airplane succeeds the covered wagon and the railroad."[35] Boeing was thus a settler of the skies, destined to manifest corporate dominance on Seattle's aluminum-colored horizon.

An heir to Gilded Age industrial giants, Boeing rebranded "progress" as private enterprise. The July 1946 *Boeing Magazine* write-up, "Progress Is a Two-Letter Word," predicted breakthroughs for commercial aircraft travel: hovercraft, space travel, and supersonic jets.[36] Boeing benefited greatly from Seattle's cheap public power utility, from the subsidies steered its way by US congressmen Henry Jackson and Warren Magnuson, from the security of publicly funded research and taxpayer-subsidized defense contracts.[37] Flying in the face of facts, the company claimed in the March 1947 edition of *Boeing Magazine* that "there was no financial support from the government for the Flying Fortress. It was strictly a pioneering venture." The corporation's "progress" didn't consist of public policies and social reforms that made its rise possible but of the privatized wizardry of warfare and consumer air travel.

Boeing Magazine bragged about the aircraft that flew the Washington football team to Minnesota, christening their plane "Husky Special." "Since the forward pass was introduced to American football in 1906, teams have become more aerial minded," the magazine said before the game. "The Huskies were the first team to charter a Stratocruiser. They were in Minneapolis a few hours, a steak dinner, and 127-half-pints of milk later."[38] Aside the article, editors included a picture of the team ogling flight attendants, atop the caption "the Huskies make like wolves as two stewardesses stroll past."

If *Boeing Magazine* was the staged photo of a big, happy corporate family, then *Aero Mechanic* was the messy Thanksgiving dinner fight. The print newspaper was the press organ of Aeronautical Mechanics Union Lodge 751, the Seattle division of the International Association of Machinists union. When unionized machinists went on a five-month strike in 1948 from April until September, *Boeing Magazine* omitted all mention of it. *Aero Mechanic* agitated. "WE HAD TO STRIKE," proclaimed the paper on April 22, 1948. "We're not interested in Boeing company propaganda. DID YOU KNOW that the cost of living in Seattle increased 27.8 percent since we received our last wage increase?"[39]

In *Capitalist Family Values,* historian Polly Reed Myers describes how *Aero Mechanic* "pushed for fraternal solidarity among union members to create a separate blue-collar shopfloor identity."[40] The newspaper used sports to further class consciousness. In January 1946, *Aero Mechanic* praised wrestlers in San Francisco for joining the American Federation of Labor. A March 1946 cartoon depicted unions as a mountain climber guiding "HUMAN PROGRESS" up the peak of "HIGHER STANDARDS OF LIVING," and an autumn 1948 comic spoofed the coming federal election as a car race between worker-friendly candidates and their anti-worker opponents.[41] Throughout the latter 1940s, *Aero Mechanic* detailed baseball games, ski parties, and hunting excursions participated in by union members. A union bowling league strengthened ties between members.

Seattle City Light bowling team, 1946. During the Progressive Era, Seattle voters elected to create the first public power utility in the country in 1910. In later years, the decline of bowling's popularity exemplified the tattering of America's social fabric. Courtesy of the Seattle Municipal Archives, item 19660.

Solidarity spawned teamwork: a week into the 1948 strike, with workers supporting one another by delivering meals to the picket line, *Aero Mechanic* happily reported that "our motorcycle squad is doing a fine job relaying messages and running important errands."[42]

Although the solidarity of Seattle's machinist union was extended to white women, it was denied African Americans altogether. *Aero Mechanic* was generally supportive of white women in the Boeing workforce, praising their participation in the machinists' strike in 1948, but the newspaper exhibited casual sexism and homophobia. Beneath a September 1948 photo of a woman crossing the picket line, a caption mocked the strikebreaker's "beaten dog looks."[43] A 1946 editorial skewered the "queer" idea of free health care during a smallpox outbreak, indicating an underlying conservatism beneath the union's surface-level egalitarian goals.[44] Though Local 751 disallowed African Americans from joining, *Aero Mechanic* demanded that Black laborers refrain from taking jobs vacated by striking white workers.

* * *

Seattle Rainiers infielder Alfred Niemiec was nervous. On a train trip between games in April 1946, he confessed to a friend that he thought the Rainiers would try to move on from him. Thanks to Niemiec's hitting and defensive versatility, the Rainiers won three Pacific Coast League championships in the early 1940s. Niemiec was the highest-paid player on the team. But he had gone away to war and come back, and three years was a long time to be away from the game. Riding down the scenic Pacific coast, Niemiec's friend told him if the Rainiers let him go, he could seek redress through the Veterans' Protection Act of 1944, which guaranteed that returning soldiers could come back to jobs they left in service of the war effort. In Seattle the infielder's worst fears were confirmed: on April 21, 1946, the Rainiers informed Niemiec of his unconditional release.[45]

Niemiec's friend was Tony Lupien, a first baseman who was demoted to the Pacific Coast League by the Philadelphia Phillies earlier in 1946; he would later coauthor *The Imperfect Diamond*, a history of labor activism in professional baseball. In his book, Lupien described how the Fraternity of Professional Baseball Players fought the majors in the Progressive Era to install a "batter's eye" in centerfield so hitters could see incoming pitches; thirty-eight batters died of head injuries in 1915.[46] *The Imperfect Diamond* detailed Lupien's own struggle with the gutless Phillies, who dumped him for a younger player after Lupien returned from his tour of duty. While he didn't have the funds to fight Philadelphia in court, Lupien urged Niemiec to take on the Seattle Rainiers, believing Niemiec's firing to be an egregious violation of the GI Bill of Rights.

Niemiec listened. The team of lawyers afforded him by the draft board argued that in the five games Niemiec played for the Seattle Rainiers before they released him, his production hadn't fallen off. Seattle responded by forming an all-star team of lawyers, farmed from the front offices of Major

League Baseball; as the Cold War prompted paranoia about communist influence in American life, the league wanted to stamp out radicalism in all ranks of the sport. A *New York Times* headline about the Niemiec trial announced on June 15, 1946: "RIGHTS OF BALL PLAYERS UNDER SERVICE ACT TO BE TESTED."[47] A week later, Judge Lloyd Black ruled in Niemiec's favor, condemning the hypocrisy of owners who capitalized on American enthusiasm for the national pastime while giving the boot to returning soldiers. "In the matter of Alfred J. Niemiec against the Seattle Rainiers, I am going to take the prerogative of the baseball umpire," the judge wrote, ordering the minor league Seattle team to reinstate Niemiec. "Allowing the employer to discharge Niemiec is a far cry from the sportsmanship Americans expect from baseball."[48]

Niemiec's court victory against Seattle Rainiers management indicated that public sentiment had shifted at least partially in favor of the country's workaday laborers. The war bolstered America's manufacturing core, making it big and strong enough to ask more of big business, more of American politicians, more of the managerial state that was created by the New Deal and fortified after World War II. If corporate behemoths like Boeing and shady baseball clubs were Gilded Age holdovers, they now had to contend with an age of guilds.

At the same time, the GI Bill of Rights upheld in *Niemiec v. Seattle Rainier Baseball Club* didn't extend to women and Black veterans. Post–World War II social entitlements like the GI Bill flowed to the family through men, who married women (often subject to wageless domestic labor). During World War II social expectations of women had shifted somewhat when they demonstrated the full extent of their worth to the capitalist economy; the return of US servicemen promptly reinstituted retrograde gender roles. The Chicago Co-Eds stopped play in 1950; the All-American Girls Professional Baseball League immortalized in the film *A League of Their Own* folded four years later. In *When Affirmative Action Was White: An Untold History of Racial Inequality in Twentieth-Century America*, historian Ira Katznelson details how the GI Bill was a whites-only entitlement, quoting a 1946 article in the *Pittsburgh Courier* that bemoaned "the sorry plight of Negro veterans."[49]

The racial exclusivity of Seattle's Local 751 union mirrored the general racial exclusivity of mid-twentieth-century capitalism. Because social entitlements and higher wages secured by organized labor created postwar prosperity in the United States, racial exclusion created racial disparities. After its defense industries helped America win a war against Nazis, Seattle remained a segregated city.

Briefly in the summer of 1946 the Seattle Steelheads played games as members of the West Coast Negro Baseball League. The small operation had a team in Portland owned by Jesse Owens, the sprinter who had humbled Germany's track-and-field team at the 1936 Olympics. The Seattle squad was owned by Abe Saperstein, founder of the Harlem Globetrotters.[50] Despite the star power and big names behind the team, major newspapers in Seattle devoted no reporting to the Steelheads. Play ceased after about a month. A year later, the *Seattle Post-Intelligencer* heaped praise on Jackie Robinson for integrating Major League Baseball in April 1947: "Sports is one field of human endeavor in which tolerance can pay off in cash. Baseball executives are hunting Negro players whose stardom can be cashed in on."[51] Robinson's assimilationist achievement depleted the Negro Leagues, subjecting Black players to even worse labor conditions than their white counterparts in the 1940s and 1950s. In politics, African Americans were excluded, denied access to capital; in sports, they were included to create capital for others.

America's exclusionary guilds, discriminatory entitlement programs, and segregated sports were not "broken" systems. They were working as intended. American progressives had created their ideal body politic; for American progressives, this is what peak performance looked like.

"REVENGE SPORT," 1950–1959

5th Inning

The year Elgin Baylor committed to play basketball at Seattle University in 1955, Seattle cops were sent there for racial sensitivity training.[1] The Seattle Police Department had just one Black officer in the 1950s—a decade, wrote Quintard Taylor in *The Forging of a Black Community*, when they "held racist attitudes about Black citizens, frequently stereotyping them as criminals."[2] Back in the 1930s, the Roosevelt administration's New Deal had redlined Black Seattle with maps generated by government surveyors for America's housing industry; predominantly minority neighborhoods were designated as ineligible for private investment and federal funding, and were more prone to overpolicing. Baylor's new school was in one of these districts: located due east of the "heart of the city" beneath Lake Union, the Central Area was 90 percent Black in the 1950s. It housed 75 percent of Black Seattle's population in only nine census tracts.[3]

Seattle photographer Al Smith's black-and-white pictures of African American life in the 1950s document a joyful Central Area community etching out an oasis of happiness in segregated Seattle, with Black city dwellers riding Ferris wheels, fooling around, imbibing jazz and cocktails at Seattle clubs where Ray Charles and Quincy Jones played.[4] The community's biggest press outlet was the weekly *Northwest Enterprise*, founded in 1920 to highlight stories of Black civil rights progress and business affairs. The *Enterprise* also had dedicated sports coverage. Ever since slavery, Black Americans celebrated athletes as symbols of dignity under racial oppression. In *Forty Million Dollar Slaves*, author William C. Rhoden wrote: "For those in bondage, the image of the strong black body was positive. The black athlete's grace presented a counterimage to prevailing stereotypes of blacks as slump-shouldered, shuffling bondsmen with heads bowed and knees bent."[5] White plantation owners lived in fear of Black physical supremacy, often devising cruel ways to assert dominance. The practice of "buck breaking" involved publicly flogging and sexually assaulting renegade enslaved peoples to crush insurrectionist morale. Later, lynching became mass entertainment.[6] With the spectacle of white cruelty over Black bodies etched into the cultural DNA of the United States, sports competition—particularly interracial games pitting Blacks against whites—came with raised stakes.

An integrated Jesuit school in the Central Area, Seattle University had a reputation as a liberal haven; the college's integrated basketball squad was known in basketball circles as "the United Nations team."[7] Baylor spent two seasons as a Seattle University Chieftain (1956–57 and 1957–58), averaging 31.2 points and 19.8 rebounds, becoming a prized NBA prospect, and embodying Black Seattle's resilience in the face of racial prejudice. Born Elgin Gay Baylor on September 16, 1934, Baylor attended Spingarn High School in Washington, DC, before coming west. When his Idaho college ended its basketball program, a local sponsor of amateur athletics convinced him to give Seattle a chance. Baylor bit. His one condition for playing at Seattle University in 1956 was that he could bring a couple of his DC buddies with him: "I went to college, and that never would have happened without Elgin," said teammate Francis Saunders.[8]

Seattle's new star was basketball's first aerial artist, a six-foot-five forward with springs for legs. Baylor shot finger rolls and fadeaways before Air Jordan got off the runaway; he dominated on the boards before Dennis Rodman was born. In *The Book of Basketball*, Bill Simmons called Baylor the "godfather of hangtime."[9] After garnering national attention in the hometown of Boeing, Baylor introduced altitude to a still-segregated NBA.[10] At a time when racial discrimination was the law of the land, racism would deny him and his adopted city a championship triumph.

* * *

Floyd Patterson was heavyweight champion of the world when Elgin Baylor began playing for Seattle University in 1956. He didn't get there by pulling punches. "Boxing is a revenge sport," Patterson once said. "Revenge then and there, not tomorrow. It may take a round or two, but I'm going to get you back."[11] After Rocky Marciano retired in 1956, Black boxers like Patterson reigned, holding the title of heavyweight champ for 6,936 of the 7,512 days between the real Rocky's retirement on April 27, 1956, and the debut of the film *Rocky* on November 21, 1976.[12] The movie was a racial revenge fantasy, positing a fictional world where a white nobody could go toe-to-toe with a Black champion. A 1957 match in Seattle between Floyd Patterson and a local white challenger is the closest thing to *Rocky* that ever happened in real life: an amateur getting a shot at the championship belt in his professional debut.

Boxing was the sport of unbridled male aggression, a universally relatable contest of physical supremacy with fewer rules than football and more unmasked violence than hockey. Working classes of color had historically found leisure in other sports: In his 1946 memoir *America Is in the Heart*, Seattle Filipino migrant worker Carlos Bulosan describes playing baseball with Alaska Indigenous women while stationed there for cannery work. But as male breadwinners achieved socioeconomic supremacy after World War II, *mano a mano* fisticuffs grew in popularity, mirroring the reinstatement of traditional gender roles that had waned briefly in the latter 1940s. Black men in particular—subject to emasculating police abuses and unpredictable swings in employment status—bought into boxing as a symbol of self-determination. When African American Chicago White Sox outfielder Larry Doby cold-cocked white New York Yankee pitcher Art Ditmar on the field in 1957, *Ebony* magazine celebrated: "After a decade of observing the no-fight-back edict prescribed for Jackie Robinson, Negro players have reached the position where they can assert themselves on a man-to-man basis."[13]

Floyd Patterson became the champ after knocking out Archie Moore in the fifth round of their November 30, 1956, match. The shadow of doubt dulled the gold sheen of his title belt. At age twenty-two, Patterson was the youngest fighter to ever become champ; white fans believed the retired Rocky would have made mincemeat of him. The ruling caste of boxing at this time was a clique of mafia members, oddsmakers, and sportswriters, most of whom detested Patterson and his iconoclast white manager, Cus

D'Amato, for not greasing the right palms on their rise to the top. Because D'Amato didn't kiss the establishment's ring, Patterson was viewed as a people's champ, beholden to no corrupt interest, answerable to nobody.[14] Consequently, D'Amato incurred resentment from the pugilist literati who framed Patterson as an unproven Negro, holder of a title that belonged to a white man.

Boxing brass sought revenge. They found it in the Pacific Northwest: in June 1957 a white challenger from the suburbs of Seattle flew to New York and kindly invited Floyd Patterson to fight.

* * *

Director Stanley Kubrick's 1955 film *Killer's Kiss* is an early masterpiece from a cinema giant, a film noir shot with chiaroscuro cine-matography that illuminates the inner turmoil of cursed characters with sharply contrasted shadow and light, black and white. The film follows a boxer who aspires to start a new life with his blonde bombshell, if only they could escape New York City for his spacious ranch in Seattle. In fiction and in fact, nice and quiet Seattle was an antidote to what ailed the rest of urban America.[15]

In postwar America, noir films like *The Naked City* (1948) and *The Asphalt Jungle* (1950) projected bleak pictures of city life in the United States. Crooks and gangs loomed in unlit alleyways; booze and jazz corrupted children. Elsewhere in mass media, the 1957 *Redbook* magazine documentary *In the Suburbs* juxtaposed noisy cities with peaceful suburbs. Pundits and policymakers were similarly pessimistic about the fate of major metropolitan areas.[16] As the speed of suburbanization quickened with cars and freeways, *Business Week* conceded in 1954 that "the big city is still the magnet that pulls people into its orbit, but the pull is stronger in outlying areas than in the heart of the city."[17]

Seattle's advantage over the rest of urban America was always its proximity to wide-open spaces, its rare synthesis of urban amenities and ruralesque sprawl. In *Seattle and the Roots of Urban Sustainability*, historian Jeffrey Craig Sanders describes how after World War II, "Seattle swelled with returning veterans [and] former farmlands on the edges of the city took on a new identity as suburbs."[18] In 1954 the city annexed neighborhoods north of its 85th Street border, extending its limits to 145th Street. Between 1940 and 1970, Bellevue grew from 1,177 residents to 61,196; Renton from 4,488 to 25,878; Seattle from 368,300 to 530,800.[19] Away from the heart of the city, the growth of Seattle's suburban extremities took place on a canvas of color.

Land confiscated from Bellevue's Japanese American community during wartime incarceration became a lucrative real estate holding in the hands of white developers. After President Dwight Eisenhower signed the National Interstate and Defense Highways Act in 1956, construction on Interstate 5 slashed through Seattle's Chinatown and destroyed six thousand homes. Boeing wrote and enforced racially restrictive housing covenants in its immense Seattle-area real estate holdings. North Seattle neighborhoods Wallingford, Green Lake, Queen Anne, and Ballard forbade nonwhite homeownership. Selectively enforced vagrancy laws turned the city into a "Sundown Town" where racial minorities were arrested for appearing in public spaces after dark.[20]

In exclusive enclaves, white Seattleites lived lives of suburbanite charm, going to golf courses, taking in Seattle Indians baseball games, and attending Seafair—an annual summer celebration started by civic boosters in 1950 to commemorate the centennial of contact between white settlers and the Indigenous people in Seattle. The cornerstone of the civic extravaganza was the hydroplane competition, in which a nonwhite driver didn't appear until 2004.[21] "This was the beginning of Seattle feeling like a grown-up city," remembers Leonard Garfield, executive director of Seattle's Museum of History and Industry.[22] "Every kid in Lake Hills, Bellevue, where I grew up, had a mini-hydroplane behind their bikes." Lake Hills was built on farmland taken from incarcerated Japanese Americans.[23]

* * *

Some basketball fans at Seattle University decided it was hang time. When the Chieftains struggled early in the 1958 season, dropping to 3–4 after an 81–75 loss, unknown perpetrators lynched an effigy of the team's white coach twice, on nooses dangling from the college science building and on a campus utility pole.[24] Following a promising 1957, a subpar start to the 1958 campaign wasn't what fans had in mind. After the hanging, coach John Castellani instituted a more free-flowing style of play centered around Elgin Baylor. Seattle ripped off twelve wins in a row to close the 1958 season, then won four games in the NCAA Men's Basketball tournament to advance to the national championship game. Awaiting them was a team that personified the color line that cut the United States in half.

In four decades as head coach of the Kentucky Wildcats (1930–72), Adolph Rupp didn't recruit a Black player until 1969.[25] In public he remained silent on attempts to integrate the college; in private he excoriated the university for attempting to integrate his team.[26] Rupp was known to use the n-word prolifically, deploying the slur when describing the Black neighborhood demolished to make way for Kentucky's basketball arena. To capture the NCAA Men's Basketball title, Seattle University would have to defeat a villain who represented the racial divide their integrated team defied.

A game belonging equally to the peach baskets of rural areas as to the asphalt courts of urban America, basketball animated the country's regional and racial identity crises. Cops on the court, most college referees were white; many harbored attitudes that placed integrated teams at a disadvantage. Elgin Baylor watched Kentucky's semifinal match against Temple, appalled at the clear favoritism being paid to Rupp's players over Temple's integrated squad. Kentucky prevailed. "I sure hope we don't get these refs," Baylor said, a day before Seattle got those refs.[27]

* * *

Was this a joke? Cus D'Amato thought Pete Rademacher was full of it. One million dollars for a shot at the champ wasn't a serious offer. After Floyd Patterson defended his title in July 1957, Rademacher raised the ante, forming an LLC that solicited investments from white Seattleites and businessmen who wanted to see somebody pulverize the uppity Patterson. Rademacher's new offer was $2.6 million.[28] D'Amato accepted—on two conditions. If Rademacher somehow won, Patterson got a rematch; in addition, Team Patterson would select the referees, ensuring a fair fight. The two sides agreed to an August 22, 1957, date at Sick's Stadium in Seattle. For the first time ever, an amateur would have a shot at the title in his first professional fight.[29]

To prepare, Rademacher set up camp in Issaquah, a segregated Seattle suburb whose population doubled between 1950 and 1960. In white Seattle's orbit the fight became a racial spectacle. The August 19, 1957, issue of *Sports Illustrated* ran an open letter from white Yale-bred boxer Eddie Eagan, preemptively placing him in the lineage of other white heavyweight champions.[30] In the same issue a feature titled "The Champ Meets a Veep" compared Rademacher to Christopher Columbus.[31] In his biography of Floyd Patterson, writer Alan Levy cracked the fight's racial code: "Rademacher proved to be a winner with the All-American hero-hungry press. He was a farm boy who had grown up in rural America. He had served as a lieutenant in the U.S. Army. Rocky Marciano conspicuously helped Rademacher train, adding to the racial dimensions."[32]

Born Thomas Peter Rademacher on November 20, 1928, in a town two hours east of Seattle, Rademacher was a "Great White Hope" straight out of central casting.[33] While nursing a bicep injury in a military hospital, Rademacher had an epiphany. "I dreamed that if I can win the gold medal, I can challenge the winner of the Patterson-Moore title match."[34] Days later, he ravished Russian fighter Lev Mukhim to take gold. Defeating a Soviet man during the Cold War gave Rademacher the aura of success needed to challenge Patterson.

Serious observers knew that this fight was a serious mismatch. Floyd Patterson was heavyweight champion of the world, having just defeated slugger Tommy Jackson in the tenth round of a fight scheduled for fifteen. Pete Rademacher was some guy who had never been in a professional fight, let alone one that went past three rounds, let alone one with the best fighter alive. Some Black boxing fans felt D'Amato dented Patterson's dignity by making him stoop to tussle with a white amateur.[35] Pennsylvania congressman Hugh Scott wrote to Washington governor Albert Rossellini, urging him not to televise Rademacher's slaughter, but banning the fight from television only ensured that more spectators landed in Seattle seats.[36] All-white crowds visited Issaquah to watch Rademacher train.[37] The hype machine kept rolling.

At his training camp outside Seattle, a Georgia journalist called Patterson "boy" during an interview.[38] When Emmett Watson asked Patterson about his reaction to the hype surrounding Rademacher, the champ did not mince words: "I think this is a White Hope fight. If I had been white, they never would have put up $2.6 million for this. I've never wanted to win one more."[39] Later published in Watson's book *Digressions of a Native Son*, Patterson's remarks weren't printed before the fight because *Post-Intelligencer* editors feared they'd provoke a race riot in Seattle. In the press Rademacher had it both ways, becoming both celebrated hero and sympathetic favorite.

But it was Floyd Patterson, born January 4, 1935, who bounced around in a Brooklyn reformatory school as a youth. "I come from a ghetto, and boxing is a way out," he remembered.[40] At a time when performers like Al Jolson, Judy Garland, and Shirley Temple mocked African Americans with shameful blackface performances in the 1930s and 1940s, Patterson suffered self-esteem issues as a kid. He penciled an "X" over a class picture of himself, telling his mom, "I don't like that boy."[41] Outside the ring Patterson was soft-spoken; in it, strangely vulnerable. On March 13, 1961, he beat the hell out of Ingemar Johansson, then cradled him like a baby and dragged him to his corner. A boxing journalist for more than sixty years, Burt Sugar was amazed: "I've never seen anything like that in the world of sports."[42]

Patterson was a thinking man's fighter who understood the political dynamics that made him one. In an *Esquire* magazine essay he diagnosed a sick society's obsession with his sport:

> The prizefighter in America isn't supposed to shoot off his mouth about politics, particularly when his views might influence the working classes. The prizefighter is considered a dumb, half-naked entertainer. He's supposed to stick to his trade—keeping his mouth shut and pretending he hates his opponent. There's so much hate among people that they hire prizefighters to do their hating for them. We get into a ring and act out other people's hates. I think boxing is a good thing. I don't think it should be abolished, because the elimination of boxing will not eliminate the hate people have, and the wars. If people didn't have boxing they'd invent something else, maybe something that wouldn't give poor people a chance at the big money.[43]

While the press framed Pete Rademacher as the all-American icon, Patterson was the wholesome sports hero most of the country didn't want to recognize. "If there's a key to the Patterson personality," a 1956 feature in the Black-targeted publication *Jet* observed, "it's that he's the sole support of his mother and father, eight brothers and two sisters, and his own wife and child."[44] Asked to describe his "greatest ambition" by *Ebony* magazine, Patterson talked about escaping New York for the "fresh air of the country."[45]

In the fresh Pacific Northwest air of his training camp near Seattle, a Universal Studios newsreel captured Patterson training, battering the speed bag, jumping rope, assaulting thin air while picturing Rademacher's face on the other end of swift jabs and stiff hooks.[46] Through 1957, the sports noirs *Fear Strikes Out* (1957) and *Monkey on My Back* (1957) played in local movie theaters, priming Seattle audiences for a black-and-white fight.

On August 22, 1957, seventeen thousand ticketholders shove into Seattle's Sick's Stadium to see the unprecedented scenario of a Black titleholder fighting an unqualified white amateur. Hundreds more gather by the fencing around Sick's Stadium, hoping to catch a glimpse. To blind them, the fight's promoter shines a white spotlight into the dark Seattle night.[47] Rademacher enters the ring wearing white robes; sheriffs escort him.[48] The mostly white audience roars with approval, then denies Patterson the same praise, getting testy with the champ for taking his time into the ring, milking the moment, embracing the hate. At six feet two, Rademacher weighs 202 pounds and has a reach of seventy-seven inches. The muscular Patterson is six feet even and 187 pounds, with a shorter reach of seventy-one inches.

When the first round begins, Rademacher uses his height and length effectively, keeping Patterson at bay. The champ times Rademacher's delivery, swaying like a metronome, getting a sense for the rhythm of his opponent's attack. In the second round, Patterson begins to box, fighting not with his arms but with his feet, in a game of positioning that boxes Rademacher into uncomfortable angles. Patterson gets close to Rademacher to mitigate his superior reach. The amateur handles the pressure well; he cracks Patterson with a solid right, sending the champ to the canvas. Rademacher prances, celebrating apparent victory. The crowd's roar gives a spectator a heart attack, killing him.

* * *

Played in Louisville, Kentucky, on March 22, the 1958 NCAA Men's Basketball championship game pitted "Rupp's Runts" against the "United Nations Team"—an integrated squad from Seattle against a Jim Crow legion led by a man named Adolph. Before the game, a Black Seattle University player was denied service in a Louisville hotel.[49] After opening tip-off, Seattle pushed to a 21–16 lead. They went up eleven midway through the first half. Baylor was cooking Kentucky's white guards. Seattle was threatening to run away with it.[50]

The game slipping away, Adolph Rupp and structural racism took control: Rupp devised a strategy to take advantage of the racist referees officiating the game. On defense, he would run Baylor through a series of screens and switches, forcing him to shadow guards who had a clear path to the basket by the time he caught up to the ball.[51] Baylor would either have to concede points or risk fouling; his competitive fiber wouldn't allow him to do the former. The refs hit Baylor with two questionable fouls early in the game, then saddled him with a third as Seattle started to widen its lead. With three-quarters of the game left to play, Baylor was close to a fifth foul, which would result in his ejection from the game. He protested the officiating; a ref told him to "shut up and play, boy."[52]

To protect Baylor and stall Kentucky's momentum, Coach Castellani slowed the game to a glacial pace, resorting to the losing style of play that made Seattle fans lynch his likeness earlier in the year.[53] The adjustment played into Rupp's strategy of making Baylor expend energy and risk foul trouble while playing defense. Early in the second half, the refs bludgeoned Baylor with a quick fourth foul, one away from mandatory ejection. To protect Baylor, Seattle switched to a zone defense the team hadn't played all year. It was all too much to overcome. At the end of a game that was less championship coronation than racist charade, Kentucky prevailed 84–72. A *Sports Illustrated* recap praised Rupp as an "old master" who "outfoxed"

Seattle.[54] In the magazine's portrayal of the game as a meritocratic triumph, no mention was made of disparities in officiating that affected its outcome.

Before the tournament the Harlem Globetrotters offered Elgin Baylor $202,000 to leave Seattle and play for Harlem.[55] Baylor declined, setting his eyes on the postseason glory eventually denied him in the title game against Adolph Rupp. He would go on to enjoy an accomplished career in the pros as a Los Angeles Laker. A US Army reservist, Baylor was stationed in Fort Lewis in Tacoma during the 1961–62 NBA season, only playing on weekends when he could obtain a pass to get off the base and averaging an impossible 38 points and 19 rebounds in the games he played.[56] "Elgin was the greatest player I played with," remembered a Seattle University teammate.[57] "I don't put anybody above him."

Nobody could leap over him anyway.

* * *

Seeming mostly to have lost his balance from the force of Pete Rademacher's punch, Floyd Patterson fared better than the fan who died of a heart attack earlier in the fight. The champ rose to his feet to finish the second round. Cus D'Amato had always inspired his fighters to convert fear into positive action.[58] With the knockdown, Rademacher had earned Patterson's full attention.

Patterson came out in the third round and knocked Rademacher down twice with the "peekaboo" style of D'Amato, who taught fighters to keep their hands high near their heads in a self-protective stance before striking. Though Rademacher's punches came in crisp one-twos in earlier rounds, Team Patterson correctly predicted the amateur wouldn't have the conditioning for a professional fight. By the third round, Rademacher's jab was flaccid as cooked linguine, his punches coming in predictable lunges that left him exposed. Patterson, meanwhile, got stronger as the fight went on, his stamina relative to Rademacher's fatigue a result of the peculiar alchemy of pugilism and anatomy. The novelist Joyce Carol Oates once wrote in *Life* magazine that taller fighters like Rademacher must punch at "a downward angle, utilizing only their shoulder and arm muscles."[59]

Fighters like Patterson, who have more compact frames, are better able to use their legs to spring upward than taller fighters, generating more force with a bigger muscle group that fatigues less quickly than those in the upper body. Rademacher's size advantage was now a liability.

In the fifth round Patterson allows a flailing Rademacher the illusion that he can be hit—except when Rademacher swings like a mad dad trying to swat a housefly, the champ counters, unloading a volley of punches to his head. Rademacher crumbles. Patterson dismissively waves his hand, as if to tell his opponent to stay down. By now, the once-frenzied Seattle audience has been reduced to a nervous murmur, grumbling like a baseball crowd whose starting pitcher is suddenly getting shellacked in a game that was once a shutout. Patterson scores three more knockdowns. On the last of these he tries to help Seattle's Great White Hope off the ground.

In the sixth round the fight's pace slows to a crawl. Patterson goes for the figurative kill. Rademacher continues lunging, trying to land a Hail Mary. Patterson waits for an opening. He pounds Rademacher in the face. When woozy Rademacher staggers forward, Patterson hits him again with a hard right. Rademacher gets up, only to be erased by an uppercut. A three-punch barrage from the champ delivers the amateur to the canvas for the seventh and final time. As the referee raises Patterson's arms in triumph, Sick's Stadium is silent—the sound of not a single hand clapping.

The next day, journalist Royal Brougham wrote in the *Seattle Post-Intelligencer* that "the fast-punching Negro boy from New York showed why he is the best fighter in the world."[60] A week after Patterson's victory, Elvis Presley rocked Sick's Stadium, giving Seattle crowds the triumph of white showmanship in another Black-dominated field—rhythm and blues music—that Rademacher couldn't bring them in boxing.[61] "Whiteness retains its value as a 'consolation prize,'" writes critical race theorist Cheryl Harris. "It does not mean that all whites will win, but simply that they will not lose, if losing is defined as being on the bottom of the social and economic hierarchy, the position to which Blacks have been consigned."[62]

Seeing Black Seattle's growing numbers and visibility in the mid-twentieth century, white Seattle rallied.[63] The Washington State Legislature passed a 1957 law allowing primarily Black neighborhoods to be displaced if they were deemed blighted. In 1958, Seattle City Council updated the city's exclusionary zoning code to "protect" strongholds of neighborhood segregation with "safety and morals."[64] The 1961 Washington State Supreme Court decision *O'Meara v. Washington State Board* permitted mortgage companies to racially discriminate. The 1960 case *Price v. Evergreen Cemetery Co. of Seattle* allowed city cemeteries to deny burial based on race—a morbid ruling that became deathly relevant as police continued profiling and executing Black Seattleites, prompting the American Civil Liberties Union to call for a city hearing on discriminatory cop behavior in the city.[65] As the retrenched 1950s turned into the revolutionary 1960s, the persistence of police harassment drove Black Central Area resident Jesse Glover to begin taking self-defense courses. He became the first student of a Seattle martial arts instructor named Bruce Lee.[66]

Though it seemed to many that the nonviolent tactics of Dr. Martin Luther King Jr. were the only reasonable response to racial oppression, incrementalism wasn't the only way forward. On a midsummer Seattle night in 1957, darkness needed only six rounds to whip white.

The Montlake Landfill near Husky Stadium, 1954. Civic reformer James Ellis addressed the destruction of Seattle's natural environs in the late 1960s. As a result of his efforts, voters approved funding for a domed stadium but declined to build Ellis's proposed forty-seven miles of comprehensive rail transit in 1968. Courtesy of the Seattle Municipal Archives, item 44896.

6th Inning

FORWARD THRUST, 1960–1969

What kind of home-field advantage was this? Montlake Landfill near Husky Stadium was a seventy-four-acre cesspit that absorbed Seattle's trash. Eighty-five dump trucks a day deposited old furniture, clothes, outdated appliances, dirty diapers, and food waste in the swamp of rot. In spring 1965 city officials deployed falcons to scare away the twenty thousand seagulls who feasted on the junkyard every day. The area could be smelled before it was seen. King County's sewer system siphoned local feces into the once-brilliant waters of nearby Union Bay and Lake Washington, causing them to look like split pea soup. In 1920 this area had been the site of Seattle's first traffic jam; in 1969 the *New York Times* described Seattle as beset by "overflowing freeways and brown haze"—some of it produced by the new floating highway connecting Montlake to Seattle's eastside suburbs. Indicative of the pollution problem marring midcentury urban America, Husky Stadium had become a hellhole.[1]

Seattle was unprepared for the growth of the post–World War II period. The city's population had increased by half between 1940 (368,302) and 1960 (557,087). Its reputation grew as a frontier city with all the promise of older East Coast urban areas but fewer of their problems. Opened April 21, 1962, with a telegram sent by President John F. Kennedy, the Century 21 Exposition in Seattle was a six-month celebration of tech, capitalism, and aerospace that elevated the city's profile even further. Boosters at the Washington Athletic Club used Cold War subsidies to construct the Pacific Science Center and the Seattle Center Coliseum (later KeyArena and then Climate Pledge Arena). The 1962 World's Fair gifted Seattle its most identifiable landmark: the 605-foot-tall Space Needle, designed to resemble a flying saucer on a tripod.[2] Seattle was ready for its close-up.

The films *It Happened at the World's Fair* (1963) and *The Slender Thread* (1965) showcased Seattle on the silver screen. The ABC television show *Here Come the Brides* (1968–70) reanimated its white settler past on primetime. The attention allured new residents. The February 1967 *Los Angeles Times* feature "Puget Sound Emerging as Megalopolis" declared "prosperity and growth are evident everywhere."[3]

Problems were also everywhere—fixable ones, but problems all the same: problems measured in traffic, contests between ethnic groups, a lack of housing units for new residents, and truckloads of trash. And everywhere in Seattle were signs of a distracted populace, lured away from fixing big city problems by pop culture and consumerism. The first shopping mall in the country, Northgate, opened in 1950. Dick's Drive-In debuted four years later, adding several locales in the 1960s with no seats, just parking lots. On local television *The J. P. Patches Show* (1958–81) made light of the Montlake Landfill, centering its plot around a clown who lived in a shack by the dump. On First Avenue, peep shows and porn theaters catered to the refined tastes of Seattle spectators. If Seattle wasn't careful, it would find itself hollowed out and spent, its natural splendor depleted by nonchalant city dwellers who wouldn't know what they had until it was gone. Though President Lyndon B. Johnson made Seattle the pilot of his 1966 "Model Cities" program that combatted urban decay with recreational facilities and housing, much work remained to make Seattle an environmental haven.

Environmentalist activist Jim Ellis saw trouble on the Seattle horizon, befouled as it was by freeway smog. "There are warning signs that urban conditions are engulfing in their potential trouble," the reformer said in a 1966 speech at the Seattle Rotary Club. "The conflict between people and vehicles growing more deadly—the air we breathe changing its composition—involuntary segregation exploding its charge of injustice. Masses of self-centered people march sightless into a sea of blinking signs."[4] Born August 5, 1921, in Oakland, California, James Reed Ellis led the campaign that created Metro in 1958, a Seattle-area agency that built sewage treatment plants to clean up Lake Washington.[5]

The water became clear again. Jim Ellis wasn't done saving the world.

* * *

Kentucky Coach Adolph Rupp got his comeuppance. In 1966, Texas Western University toppled the segregated Kentucky Wildcats in the NCAA title game. Coach Don Haskin started five Black players in the game—a first in NCAA tournament history—on the way to his 72–65 win.[6] The victory was immortalized in the 2006 movie *Glory Road*. Written by and for winners, dominant portrayals of history shoved Seattle University out of the frame, indifferent to an almost-before-its-time civil rights victory that could have been achieved when Seattle played Rupp in 1958. After Elgin Baylor left Seattle University, the school's basketball program gradually faded away from prominence as local fan excitement shifted to baseball and football.

A few months after Texas Western beat Kentucky, news dropped that the National Basketball Association (NBA) would be placing a team in Seattle. The details were unceremoniously revealed in a brief *Seattle Post-Intelligencer* write-up, the story squished atop a blurb about Washington State officials who wanted to spend $10 billion on highways instead of mass transit.[7] Though they sprang into action two years earlier to try to lure the Cleveland Indians to Seattle in 1964, none of Seattle's white boosters stepped forward to run the team. It fell to two opportunistic Los Angeles businessmen to ensure Seattle didn't fumble its basketball team away. After buying the Seattle team's rights for $15.7 million, Eugene Klein and Sam Schulman held a naming contest for the new NBA squad before its inaugural 1967–68 season. Voters christened them the "SuperSonics," after a Boeing airplane project that provided tens of thousands of jobs in the city. Still, local embrace of the team was mostly mute.

Basketball had an image problem. With the retirement of white greats George Mikan and Bob Cousy and the rise of Black stars Bill Russell and Wilt Chamberlain, the NBA had become palpably Blacker in the 1960s. The players let people know it. Basketball's African American elite threatened to strike before the 1964 All-Star Game over a labor dispute with exploitative team owners. A Seattle SuperSonic and president of the NBA players' union, Paul Silas later remarked that "white people generally look disfavorably upon blacks who are making astronomical amounts of money if it appears they are not working hard for that money."[8]

What many Seattle sports fans really wanted was baseball and football. The former was the national pastime for a century and counting, and the latter rose in popularity alongside postwar suburbanization and increased television consumption. Super Bowl I between the Green Bay Packers and Kansas City Chiefs was simulcast on CBS and NBC; mega-stadiums with huge parking lots popped up on the outskirts of big cities. In December 1966, *Seattle Times* sportswriter Hy Zimmerman argued that "mere membership in the NBA does not make Seattle a big league city. It takes baseball."[9] Weeks earlier, Seattle's sports commentariat expressed envy when New Orleans voters approved the construction of a new football stadium.[10]

Seattle fans were so thirsty for pro baseball and football that in 1963 they backed the space-age idea of a floating stadium in the heart of the city—not near Lake Union but *in it*. The cockamamie plan for a floating stadium fascinated *Sports Illustrated*, which called attention to "the concrete pontoons that would hold the structure level in a windstorm." Fans dreamed of boating to games.[11]

Had Seattle voters approved the Bogue Plan in 1912, the resulting subway hub in the heart of the city may have made a floating stadium in Lake Union feasible. But strategists couldn't find enough area parking spaces for the automobiles the arena would attract. The city's Planning Commission advised against the idea, prompting voters to reject the facility in 1964. Its floating stadium dead in the water, Seattle had to find another way into the big leagues.

* * *

Jim Ellis had an idea: What if Seattle sports fandom were parlayed into environmental conservation? Ellis fused Seattle's egoistic enthusiasm to enter the big leagues with more basic concerns about the climate. He called the campaign "Forward Thrust": an electoral slate of thirteen ballot initiatives for Seattle-area capital improvements—including subway transit and a new sports stadium—put before King County voters in a February 13, 1968, special election.[12]

To appeal to all sides of the Seattle electorate, Ellis flanked his ambitious vision for forty-seven miles of subway with such popular programs as playgrounds, public housing, sewer improvements, and the sports stadium. The hope was that the slate of measures would create a positive aura for Forward Thrust as a whole, ensuring the passage of the subway system in particular.[13] To anchor the campaign, Ellis convened a campaign committee with two hundred members; 90 percent of them white, only one woman, and most of them Seattle business owners and engineers.[14] On the campaign trail Ellis pitched a stadium and mass transit as the amenities Seattle needed to become a world-class city.

America was preparing to put a man on the moon; why couldn't Seattle put a subway in the ground? The 1968 Forward Thrust election was a referendum on space-age optimism, the limits of postwar progressivism tested by a transit proposal that had polarized Seattle voters a half century earlier. "Seattle blew a chance to build itself into a Paris of the western hemisphere when it rejected the plans of Virgil Bogue," wrote *Seattle Post-Intelligencer* political columnist Shelby Scates of Seattle's 1912 urbanist heartbreak.[15] Forward Thrust reiterated Seattle's civic ambition: the city could enter the big leagues with mass transit, MLB baseball, and NFL football. In 1968, Seattleites of a certain age may have remembered the first-ever professional football game in Seattle, a 34–0 drubbing delivered by the Chicago Bears to a local team of "All-Stars" in 1926. Forward Thrust promised payback for years of East Coast condescension.[16]

Before the election a cartoon in the *Seattle Post-Intelligencer* showed New York Yankee superstar Mickey Mantle banging on a door with Forward Thrust's logo, begging "CAN SEATTLE COME OUT AND PLAY NOW?"[17] To make the big-league leap, Seattle had to overcome the loser mindset that kept it bottom-feeding with smaller towns of urban America, unable to challenge the Chicagos, the Los Angeleses, the New Yorks. When the Forward Thrust campaign turned out thirty-five hundred volunteers in one weekend to knock on doors and make phone calls, Seattle sportswriter Emmett Watson was stirred: "They're up against the negativism that afflicts all communities, of which Seattle has more than its fair share."[18]

Forward Thrust tried using sports and transit to unite Seattle behind an audacious vision. But it was stranded on a political isthmus—ravished from the right as a costly bureaucratic kraken and lampooned on the left as social engineering by the white-collar gentry. Walter Crowley, editor of a leftist University District newspaper, slammed Forward Thrust as "grossly inadequate," later skewering it as "changing the linen aboard the Titanic." Conversely, developer Vic Gould called Jim Ellis "a communist." The newspaper *King County Democrat* ran a cartoon of Ellis with money-bags atop a caption that read "Forward Lust"; critics accused the lawyer of corruption, since the bond firm where he worked would have handled some of Forward Thrust's debt.[19] Ellis hoped for the best on election day. But his hope was divisive.[20]

On February 13, 1968, the Forward Thrust measures for improved fire service, a bolstered sewer system, and parks succeeded by passing the 60 percent "yes" vote threshold required for county initiatives. Gloriously, with 62.3 percent, so did the measure for a multipurpose stadium that eventually resulted in the construction of the Kingdome. The ratification of the stadium signaled to the big leagues that Seattle meant business, leading to the arrival of the Seahawks in 1976 and the Mariners in 1977.

But sports weren't at the center of Ellis's vision. Mass transit was. A majority of King County voters approved the rail transit bond with a 50.8 percent vote share, but that was shy of the needed 60 percent threshold. Residents of inner-city Seattle largely supported the subway—so did affluent voters in the suburbs. It was white working-class voters who betrayed the subway, dismayed by the lack of blue-collar representation on the Forward Thrust committee, and swayed by the General Motors–funded opposition to mass transit. Ellis wanted a subway to make a modernizing urban community more cosmopolitan; the campaign moniker "Forward Thrust" suggested force, movement, progress. But his associates and the campaign they ran had too little in common with a complex King County electorate.

This was 1968. On the one hand, a national civil rights movement, a burgeoning sexual revolution, and antiwar protests roiled. *Seattle Magazine* covered it all, with risqué stories about Black Panthers, LGBTQ+ Seattleites, and hallucinogenic drugs.[21] On the other hand, reactionary voters recoiled from radical activity that pushed the postwar progressive consensus to what they thought were unreasonable extremes; no small part of Seattle-area opposition to mass transit was the tacit fear that more buses and trains would mean increased integration. Forward Thrust reproduced a historical trope in progressive failure: attempting to appeal to all sides, then alienating most.

Ellis's campaign patronizingly appealed to women by emphasizing the Kingdome's potential to host fashion shows; campaign surrogates said the covered stadium would help them protect their hair and makeup.[22] Contrary to popular belief, the highest aspiration of many Seattle women wasn't to become trophy wives in luxury stadium suites—they were out winning trophies of their own. Seattleite Anne Quast won the US Women's Amateur Golf Championship in 1958, 1961, and 1963 under *three different surnames* because she ended two marriages that clashed with her athletic ambitions.[23] She won Seattle sportswriter Royal Brougham's unfortunately titled "Man of the Year" award in 1961. So did Doris Brown Heritage, a Seattle runner who became the first woman to dash an indoor sub-five-minute-mile (4:52) in 1966.[24] Though the first Double Dutch Championship didn't take place until 1974, the fast-twitch game of rhythm and speed was a fixture for Black women and girls who were largely ignored in the conversation about sports in 1960s Seattle.[25]

Women athletes in Seattle made use of city space—golf courses, parks, streets—substantiating their political engagement in the city's affairs with athletics. In architect Fred Bassetti's 1968 documentary *What Is So Great about Seattle?*, a Seattle woman declares: "If you go downtown, it gives you a feeling of being part of a cosmopolitan area. Otherwise, you could just live in Puyallup."[26] That year, a civic group found Seattle women were twice as likely as men to ride the bus.[27] Black studies scholar Judson Jeffries illustrated how "Seattle women kept the Seattle Black Panther Party afloat in the 1960s, facilitating the distribution of free shoes, free lunch, and free healthcare in the 1960s."[28] Forward Thrust's lack of direct appeal to these blocs of voters likely cost Ellis's campaign valuable votes in a tight election.

Like women, Indigenous people didn't have much of a place in the Forward Thrust campaign. Historian Coll Thrush wrote in *Native Seattle* that "in the 1960s, political and cultural developments brought Indian people to the center of urban life."[29] Primary among these were the "Fish Wars," which pitted Indigenous people who depended on salmon fishing for subsistence and spiritual fulfillment against white fishermen who felt entitled to Seattle's colonized waterways. Native activists in 1964 defied colonial law by fishing without obeying game restrictions in the Puyallup River.[30] It was an effective political spectacle, igniting violent opposition from angry whites in the Washington State Sportsmen's Council, while becoming a cause célèbre for Marlon Brando and Dick Gregory. Direct action led to a 1975 Supreme Court decision (*United States v. Washington*) that affirmed the right of Indigenous Washingtonians to fish in their ancestral waters. That the environmental activism of Seattle-area Natives was potent enough to inspire federal legislation while being completely ignored by Forward Thrust reflected poorly on the campaign's inclusive environmental pretensions.

Indigenous Seattleites joined other ethnic groups in asserting their place in Seattle's social fabric in the 1960s. Following watershed federal immigration reform acts in 1952 and 1965, King County residents of Asian descent numbered 29,141 in the 1970 census, doubling their 1940 population of 13,972.[31] Asian Americans in Seattle were less likely than other voters to believe that government programs like Forward Thrust would meet community needs—a possible residue of the Japanese American experience of internment.[32] At the same time, enthusiasm for athletics built community for socially outcast Asian Americans. In his 1957 novel *No-No Boy*, author John Okada used baseball to signify the patriotism of Japanese Americans returning to Seattle after the World War II incarceration.[33] Forward Thrust and its baseball boosterism nonetheless underperformed among Asian American voters.

In 1962, Seattle City Councilman Wing Luke became the first municipal officeholder of Asian descent in the United States.[34] Luke stood in solidarity with Black Seattle, sticking his neck out to support a 1964 initiative that would have outlawed racial discrimination in Seattle's housing market if white Seattle voters didn't emphatically reject it.[35] Not coincidentally, Black voters were 16.2 percent more likely than other voters to support Forward Thrust's public housing measure. Had only Black Seattle voters cast ballots for Forward Thrust's rapid-rail transit initiative, it would have passed by a clean 60–40 margin. Despite this base of support, a Forward Thrust campaign staffer confessed to *Seattle Magazine* that his campaign "never once [asked] 'what are we going to do for the Negro?'"[36]

If Black Seattleites were underrepresented in the Forward Thrust campaign, the disabled were invisible. Though the 1960s were a high-water mark of liberalism in the United States, pervasive views about disability hadn't progressed much since the days of forced sterilization laws. When Babe Ruth visited Seattle for an exhibition game for a Seattle children's hospital in 1924, local papers referred to the kids as "cripples"; a generation later, while women, people of color, and sexual minorities petitioned for greater sociopolitical freedoms, the disabled seemed the last group in American politics it was still permissible to discriminate against. Though hundreds of disabled Seattleites participated in the first-ever Washington State Special Olympics in 1968—racing and leaping their way to greater visibility—they went ignored by Forward Thrust. What accommodations did sports arenas and rapid transit have for Seattleites who had difficulties ambulating on their own, or who had mental illnesses that were subject to stigmatization in public settings?

As Seattle craved big-league status in the 1960s, sports were a site of struggle to make it the truly progressive city it had never been. Jim Ellis's campaign did little to appeal to groups outside the political mainstream, which contributed to its failure. Insistent that Forward Thrust's subway could succeed with another shot, officials in Seattle urged Ellis to try, try again.

* * *

After the arrival of the SuperSonics flopped, Seattleites in search of a specific kind of big-league attention were finally satisfied. In 1967 the American League awarded Seattle a professional baseball franchise, on the condition that the city construct a new arena. When voters passed the Forward Thrust new ballpark measure in 1968, Seattle's new team was temporarily allowed to play at Sick's Stadium. After a naming contest, they were called the Seattle Pilots, their technicolor off-yellow home uniforms and sky-blue road outfits with red highlights jumping off the screens of Seattleites who could afford more than black-and-white televisions.[37]

Seattle fans weren't colorblind. Sportswriter John Owen speculated that expensive ticket prices at Sick's Stadium deliberately kept Black and low-income fans from attending the games.[38] Site of the racial proxy battle between Floyd Patterson and Pete Rademacher, Sick's Stadium was located in the Mount Baker neighborhood, a part of town changing from

Sick's Stadium, 1965. Seattle's first big-league ballpark, the stadium hosted the
Seattle Pilots for a single season in 1969 until they relocated to Milwaukee. Seattle
was awarded the Mariners in 1976 after King County sued the American League.
Sick's Stadium was demolished in 1979. Courtesy of the Seattle Municipal Archives,
item 77130.

predominantly Italian to predominantly Black. Many white Seattleites
were reluctant to visit the Pilots in their suddenly colorful neighborhood
surroundings.

Despite the demographic incentive to do so, the Pilots did nearly nothing
to market the team to Black Seattle.[39] The Pilots were less integrated than
the average 1969 Major League Baseball team. Seattle general manager
Marvin Milkes expressly forbid the hiring of "a Negro" for any of the team's
management positions. Jackie Robinson had integrated Major League Baseball in 1947.[40] Still, the sport's preservation of the "less complicated" times
before civil rights protest and neighborhood integration was central to its
commercial appeal. In his 1970 book *Ball Four*—a wildly popular noncon-
formist account of the 1969 Seattle Pilots season—Pilots pitcher Jim Bouton
detailed how baseball's establishment was out of touch with the times:

This afternoon, [Seattle Pilots pitcher] Gary Bell and I drove up to the Berkeley campus and listened to speeches—Arab kids arguing about the Arab-Israeli war, Black Panthers talking about Huey Newton. Gary and I are concerned about making money in real estate. These kids are concerned about Vietnam, poor people, black people. They're concerned about the way things are and they're trying to change them. I wanted to tell everybody, "Look, I'm with you. I understand you're doing the right thing."[41]

The Seattle Pilots found it difficult to do the right things on the field: they allowed the most runs in 1969 and had the third-worst batting average. On Saturday, May 31, 1969, Seattle's fragile ego suffered the fate it feared most—embarrassment on national television. The hapless Pilots committed five errors on NBC's *Game of the Week*, losing to Detroit, 3–2. Big-league ambition soon turned into bitter disappointment.

With dwindling fan attendance at Sick's Stadium and the new Kingdome taking longer to build than league officials hoped, the Seattle Pilots were forcibly moved to Milwaukee in 1970. In response, local officials sued. The debacle reminded Seattle historian Roger Sale of the city's railroad saga in the Gilded Age, prompting him to decry Seattle's tendency to debase itself for attention from capitalists. "In the big leagues," he wrote, "established money and power can seldom be trusted."[42] Until the Seattle Seahawks arrived in 1976 and the American League gifted the city the expansion Mariners as a lawsuit settlement with King County in 1977, all that big-league Seattle fans had were the SuperSonics—and the hope that they'd never suffer another humiliating franchise relocation again.

* * *

While the Pilots sputtered, Jim Ellis reloaded. Times had changed since the February 1968 Forward Thrust election. November 1968 saw Richard Nixon become president on a platform that addressed concerns about the environment; Nixon created the Environmental Protection Agency on January 1, 1970. Ellis turned down an invitation to become the agency's first-ever director, believing he could be more impactful in Seattle.

A second Forward Thrust election to build mass transit in Seattle was scheduled for spring 1970.[43] With the success of the Kingdome in the 1968 campaign, Ellis could no longer use a stadium to entice King County voters into supporting his primary goal of mass transit. Nixon's 1968 campaign suggested a new approach.

The centerpiece of Nixon's campaign was a calculated appeal to white voters who thought the civil rights gains of the decade had spilled into lawlessness.[44] Nixon narrowly lost the King County vote 46.00 percent to Hubert Humphrey's 47.05 percent, but segregationist George Wallace captured 6.62 percent of the King County electorate, meaning a majority of Seattle-area voters wanted a law-and-order-style conservative as president.[45] The Forward Thrust committee paired Ellis's coveted subway system with a $40.2 million proposal for new police stations and county jails.[46] In the second Forward Thrust election, mass transit met mass incarceration.

Seattle in the 1960s was preoccupied with policing. On the political right, a reported 47 percent increase in crime from 1968 to 1970 stirred political reaction to big diverse blocs of new city dwellers.[47] On the political left, repeated incidents of police brutality led to radical tactics from Black activists. The Seattle chapter of the Black Panther Party was founded in 1968, not to reform cops but to call into question the institution of policing altogether. In the political center, good government reformers criticized the corruption of Seattle police officers who solicited bribes in exchange for selective enforcement of the law.[48] In the debate about policing, Ellis picked a side, aligning the second Forward Thrust with law and order. A progressive Republican, he had revealed himself to be a Republican nonetheless.

Under different circumstances, Ellis's ploy might have worked. But when the market for commercial aircraft grew oversaturated in the late 1960s, Boeing laid off twenty thousand employees between 1968 and 1969. Seattle's economy crashed. Boeing canceled the supersonic plane in 1970 after the project was the subject of federal budgetary scrutiny, terminating even more jobs. Seattle underwent a devastating recession, prompting tens of thousands of people who had been drawn to the city by Boeing aerospace jobs to leave. Seattle's tailspin reached a tragicomic low in 1971, when two pranksters erected a billboard that read "WILL THE LAST PERSON LEAVING SEATTLE TURN OUT THE LIGHTS" on a highway just outside Seattle.

In this recession capital-intensive public projects like Forward Thrust were seen as dangerous to a suddenly vulnerable economy.[49] The powerful King County Labor Council sided with conservative anti-tax groups to oppose Ellis's subway plan. The kiss of death had been delivered.

On Tuesday, May 19, 1970, all four Forward Thrust ballot initiatives were defeated. Community centers and additional sewer improvements fell well short of the needed 60 percent "yes" vote threshold; only the carceral initiative for new jails and police stations won more than a 50 percent vote share but also failed to pass. For the third time in half a century, a subway measure in Seattle failed, falling well short of even a simple majority, with a 46 percent vote share.

Washington senator Warren Magnuson had secured $7.3 billion for Seattle's subway before the 1970 Forward Thrust election. All voters had to do was say "yes" and there would be shovels in the ground. After the loss the funds were awarded to Atlanta, Georgia, where construction started promptly on the Metropolitan Atlanta Rapid Transit Authority. In the competition between American cities, one town's trash was another's treasure.

* * *

After the failed 1968 campaign for inclusive public housing and mass transit, Forward Thrust did a conservative heel-turn in 1970, pairing subways with new jails. The maneuver's demise mirrored the broader disintegration of progressive movements in the United States. The initial Progressive Era of 1893–1919 faded when progressives like Ole Hanson exchanged an age of reform for the punitive pursuits of the Red Scare, Prohibition, and crackdowns on labor unions. The postwar consensus of 1945–68 fell apart in similar fashion. As groups excluded from America's "golden age of capitalism" grew increasingly outspoken, many progressives receded, became conservatives, and denounced America's emergent left wing.

When Forward Thrust recruited the first Black umpire in Major League Baseball to campaign for a new arena in 1968, white Seattle sportswriter Royal Brougham showed his reactionary streak. While in the city, umpire Emmett Ashford stumped not just for a new stadium but against the radicalism of the Black Panthers, saying "the youngsters of my race must realize they can't get respect without earning it." A progressive, Brougham joined the increasingly conservative chorus: "We'd buy a ringside seat to see Emmett Ashford in a match against [the Black Panthers]," he wrote. "Leaders like Ashford do more to solve serious racial problems than all of the radicals put together."[50]

In some moments, sports could symbolize the cross-racial harmony dreamed of by Dr. Martin Luther King Jr. Floyd Patterson and Cus D'Amato took on boxing's bigoted establishment; Texas Western's integrated triumph over Adolph Rupp was a triumph over segregation. But as the climate of the country changed, sports substantiated the political divisions that simmered beneath the surface. They'd soon bubble over. When the SuperSonics announced Black point guard Lenny Wilkens as the team's player-coach in 1969, some Seattle fans not used to seeing African Americans in positions of power sent hate mail. At the November 1972 groundbreaking ceremony for the Kingdome's construction, Asian American youths threw mud balls at elected officials, protesting a new stadium they feared would bring congestion and disrespectful drunks to Seattle's nearby Chinatown. In choosing a new stadium over a new subway system, Seattle voters selected a symbol of collective harmony over its substance. Subsequently President Lyndon B. Johnson's "Great Society" would be ground to dust.

Jim Ellis did everything he could to stave off the reactionary tide, including participate in it. After the failed 1970 attempt to use mass incarceration to entice voters to build mass transit, he ended up in the hospital with stress-induced stomach issues.[51] Back during the peak of postwar political optimism, the visionary unveiled his plan for pro sports and Seattle subways in a November 3, 1965, speech: Ellis argued that "with World's Fair Zip" Seattle could enter "a golden age and become one of the great cities of man." That same day, the *Seattle Times* declared "another city chooses progress" when San Diego voters approved a new stadium.[52]

With its World's Fair and big-league aspirations, bustling Seattle was obsessed with matching the progress of its peers. But because that progress was shallowly defined, it was therefore shallowly realized.

7th-Inning Stretch

Seattle cop Roy Burt chased people down at Green Lake when they smoked weed. Every day, he took off his uniform and ran the Green Lake loop three times. The 8.4-mile scamper didn't leave him too tired to punish parkgoers for their crimes: feeding ducks, letting their dogs off leashes, smoking marijuana while taking in brilliant Seattle sunsets. "I've run down a lot of suspects," Burt said in November 1976. "I tell them anytime they want to run, let me know."[1]

After the failed May 1970 Forward Thrust mass transit initiative, Burt was part of a growing movement of Seattleites who traversed the city on foot. The first annual Seattle Marathon took place on November 15, 1970, with thirty-eight runners turning out to the University of Washington student athletics facility at 11:00 a.m. in hopes of torturing themselves.[2] The college's running club plotted the course: a loop of thirteen miles to be run twice, taking runners from the University District to Seward Park and back. Rain and wind chased participants. Seventeen didn't finish. Four hours, five minutes, and twenty-six seconds after the opening gun, the last of the runners returned, narrowly beating out the early sunset of a cloudy late-autumn Seattle day.

Why would anybody do this to themselves? Novembers in Seattle are a wickedly dim time of year where light dwindles swiftly as the December solstice approaches. Hostile tacks of cold rain are common. Local legend had it that as the first colonists arrived in the area that became Seattle on November 13, 1851, white women wept when their boat approached the shore; their sunbonnets drooped in the coastal mist.[3] Because they didn't belong, settlers went to great lengths to bend Seattle's terrain to their whims—cutting holes in the land, draining rivers, and taming tall inclines. But even after dramatic regrades paved area humps, Seattle remained very curvy, running up the city's steep hills causes the h___t to work harder, often leading to tunnel vision.

And yet the number of participants in the Seattle Marathon grew: from 38 in 1970 to 137 in 1975. From 350 runners in 1976 to 980 in 1977, 2 of whom were paraplegics, riding custom hand-operated tricycles. In 1978 the run had 1,950 participants, corporate sponsorship from Safeco Insurance, and enough resources to spare a bowl of clam chowder to whoever crossed the finish line. Some of the runners were decked out in new gear attained from an apparel store offering a 26.2 percent discount before the race. The local ABC affiliate captured the preening marathoners on television; gaggles of Seattleites cheered in person. The tenth annual Seattle Marathon on November 22, 1979, had 2,791 registered runners, a third of whom were first timers.[4]

Seattleites had grown accustomed to seeing joggers in sweat suits on the city's greenways; many found them annoying. At Green Lake a rivalry broke out between runners, cyclists, and regular pedestrians. Police broke up altercations in the spring of 1977. The Seattle Parks Board intervened, adding new signs and a special trail for joggers.[5] The runners kept running.

A twenty-four-year-old student who won the Seattle Marathon in 1978 told the *Seattle Times* he "runs mainly for his 'mental health.'"[6] America was a stressful place to live. After Nixon's administration was caught burgling the offices of the Democratic National Committee in 1972, Americans reported feeling record levels of distrust in their own government.[7] After hitting an all-time peak in 1973, real wages in the United States fell as if descending a Seattle hill, bottoming out in the coming years as American corporations sought cheaper labor costs abroad.[8] Because oil-exporting Arab countries protested Israeli encroachment on Palestine, gas prices soared in 1973. The bloody Vietnam War unfolded on television, bracketed by unsettling nightly news segments that made America seem possessed by a belligerent zeitgeist. In November 1971, D. B. Cooper hijacked a passenger aircraft bound from Portland to Seattle, jumping out of it with a bagful of money, never to be seen again. Charles Manson led a deadly sex cult, resulting in the trial of the century in 1970, only to be outdone by Seattleite serial killer Ted Bundy a few years later.

There was a lot that Americans could not control, but one thing that many of them could: their own bodies, which they subjected to the cruel and unusual therapy of running long distances in short shorts. American urbanites did this en masse starting in the 1970s, with millions identifying as runners and annual marathon competitions sprouting up in New York (1970), Seattle (1970), Portland (1972), and Chicago (1977).[9] With many Americans suffering lower wages and rising stress levels, was it a coincidence that running became popular as the golden age of midcentury social entitlements unraveled?

Jogging satisfied the anti-conformist counterculture that led many Americans to turn to self-help books, psychedelics, and mindfulness exercises in the 1960s and 1970s. It was equally at home in a coming era of out-of-control consumerism, when shoe companies would swoosh in to monetize the personal pursuit of physical fitness. Darting between two major epochs was the solitary runner—stretching on park benches, feet pounding the pavement, eyes fixed on some distant point on the American horizon.

7th Inning

FADEAWAY, 1970–1979

In week nine of the 1978 NFL season, the Seattle Seahawks played a heart-stopping game against the visiting Denver Broncos. As the Seahawks prepared for their divisional showdown against Denver on October 29, 1978, journalist Royal Brougham wasn't objective. He never had been. Day after day, Brougham, who started writing for the *Seattle Post-Intelligencer* in 1910, hyped Seattle sports in his "Morning After" column, proselytizing the power of athletics to bring the city accolades and attention. After the Seahawks beat John Madden's Oakland Raiders on October 22, 1978, they pulled within a game of Denver and Oakland for the AFC division lead. Before the October 29 game against the Broncos, Brougham gassed Seattleites, telling readers the Seahawks had real potential as Super Bowl contenders.[1]

The delusion was titanic. In their two and a half years of existence, the Seahawks had yet to have a winning record at any point in any season. But sports were a performance of civic spirit; to have a chance, cities had to believe they had a chance. And nobody believed Seattle had a chance as much as Royal Brougham.

At the spry age of eighty-four, Brougham watched the Seahawks and Broncos while peering through binoculars from the Kingdome press box.[2] He saw Denver score a field goal on their opening drive and watched Seattle answer with a forty-four-yard touchdown strike from quarterback Jim Zorn. Fourth among twenty-eight NFL teams for most touchdowns scored, the high-flying Seahawks pushed their lead to 14–3 in the second quarter. Denver scored after they intercepted Zorn at the Seattle thirty-six—but it must have seemed to Brougham that Seattle was benefiting from most of the game's bizarre breaks. In the second quarter Seahawk defenders tackled

Bronco kicker Jim Turner on a fake field goal attempt after they noticed he entered the game with sneakers instead of kicking cleats. Turner proceeded to miss another field goal. The first half ended with Seattle up 14–10.

The Seahawks and Broncos played a comedy of errors in the second half. Seattle fumbled on its own nine-yard line, leading to a Denver score in the third quarter. Zorn removed himself from the game to deal with an injury, assured Seattle coaches he was good to go back in, and immediately threw an interception upon returning. Denver's offense gave the ball right back to Seattle. With the clock winding down, the Hawks turned the ball over yet again, then quickly recovered when a Broncos defender tried a silly lateral pass to a teammate during the return. With time running down, they kicked a field goal to tie it, 17–17.

Sixty-three thousand Kingdome attendees braced for overtime. The tragicomic suspense was more than Royal Brougham could take. As the score tightened, so did his chest. Late in the game, he collapsed. The Seattle Seahawks had given their number one fan a heart attack.

Born September 17, 1894, in Saint Louis, Missouri, Royal Brewster Brougham once told a friend "all I want to do is be a sportswriter."[3] He became an institution. Brougham came of age during the Progressive Era, and his civic gusto was a product of the age of reform. When the Seattle Metropolitans went on their Stanley Cup Championship run, Brougham told Seattle how much a trophy would mean to young Seattle in the pages of the *Post-Intelligencer*, then moonlit as the Mets' team statistician. When many Seattleites his age receded from civic engagement during the hedonistic 1920s, Brougham organized Babe Ruth's 1924 Seattle visit to lift the spirits of disabled children at the city's pediatric hospital. When Seattle swimmer Helene Madison represented America at the 1932 Olympics, Brougham questioned why youth athletes couldn't be compensated for their labor, then used his column to raise funds for Madison. When Madison's life unraveled in the 1940s after she fell ill with cancer and was arrested for shoplifting food, Brougham solicited donations to help her rebound.

When Japanese Americans returned from incarceration camps, Seattle's Nisei community thanked Brougham for pushing the American Bowling Congress to remove its "whites only" clause. Brougham lobbied to end racial exclusion in the city's golf courses. When white Seattleites clois-tered into ethnically exclusive enclaves in the postwar period, Brougham wrangled to bring the all-Black Harlem Globetrotters to town in 1952, a move that gave Seattle University the cachet to recruit a start like Elgin Baylor. And when Seattle had the chance to attract the NFL and MLB in the 1960s, Brougham campaigned for the Forward Thrust ballot measure that resulted in the Kingdome's construction. By the 1970s the sports prophet of Puget Sound had made it to the promised land: Seattle was a bona fide big-league city, with teams in America's three major leagues, plus a competitive football program at the University of Washington. For seventy years, Brougham made Seattle sports his life's work; the city repaid him by sending him to rest.

Taken out of the Kingdome media suite on a stretcher, Brougham had a life-or-death question for the stadium elevator usher on the way down to the ambulance: "What's the score?" With timing running out of the sudden-death overtime period, Denver marched to Seattle's one-yard line. The Seahawk defense stopped the Broncos on three successive goal-line plays. Denver kicker Jim Turner missed a close-range field goal attempt, ensuring the game would end in a tie—except Seattle was flagged for having twelve men on the field.[4] Turner nailed his next try, plunging the Seahawks to 4–5. Brougham expired the next morning. "It may have been reported that Royal Brougham died of a heart attack," wrote sports columnist Em-mett Watson after his idol's death. "But if the heart symbolizes spirit and tenacity, he didn't die of that. He just got a little tired at the end."[5]

* * *

Briefly, in 1975, sophomore football prospect Warren Moon was classmates with a man who helped integrate the National Basketball Association. Warren Moon was a Seattle pioneer in his own right, a young man venturing to play the quarterback position in an era when it was largely denied to Black athletes. Spencer Haywood, meanwhile, was a bona fide basketball star, taking college classes in his spare time and moonlighting as a campus jazz show radio host while playing for the Seattle SuperSonics. Life was good. At a time when the average player salary was almost $700,000, the six-foot-eight, 225-pound forward was on a six-year, $8 million (both figures in 2023 dollars) deal with Seattle.

Back in 1971, the US Supreme Court had ruled in Haywood's favor in the case *Haywood v. National Basketball Association*, when he sued the NBA over a rule that disallowed players from entering the league unless they were four years removed from high school. After the Sonics were blocked by the league when they tried to sign him, Haywood successfully argued in court that the rule was discriminatory: most players who were impacted by this rule were Black, poor, and playing basketball to get out of poverty. The NBA knew this. Slowing the flood of young, gifted, and Black players was a way for conservative white team owners to control how their league was perceived and to retain power in it. "I ain't Jackie Robinson," recalled Haywood. "But I was, in a way."[6]

Journalist David Halberstam's *The Breaks of the Game* relays that in the 1970s "the NBA's players came from the ghettos of cities in the postindustrial age; but its new markets were in Denver, Portland, Seattle, Phoenix, Salt Lake City and San Antonio."[7] With the civil rights movement still smoldering, professional basketball seemed caught in a bind: How would the NBA market a Black, urban sport to a growing white, suburban fan base? On *NBA on CBS* broadcasts in the 1970s, musical cutaways to commercials toggled between blonde crooner Olivia Newton-John and Black-led soul band MFSB—a telling act of musical vertigo that signaled basketball's attempted cross-racial appeal.

The 1977 NBA Finals between the Philadelphia 76ers and the Portland Trail Blazers modeled the demographic tensions that tugged at the league.[8] Led by Julius Erving and his Afro, the 76ers were the squad of high-flying hoopers with bombastic styles of play forged on the concrete courts of big cities like Philly. Portland was the establishment favorite, with white center Bill Walton, a white head coach, and a mostly white fan base. The contest of racialized contrast produced the largest television rating ever for an NBA Finals. After Philly blew a 2–0 series lead and lost the series, an article in the *Philadelphia Daily News* predicted the city's white fan base would turn on Black players: "In white Philadelphia, there will be conversations about the team's lack of heart. The talk will be about how the n——s choked."[9]

As Portland hoisted the championship trophy, Lenny Wilkens watched from Seattle with disgust.[10] Wilkens was the SuperSonics' director of player personnel in 1977; from 1974 to 1976 he was the head coach of the Portland Trail Blazers and one of only five Black NBA coaches since the league started in 1946. It was Wilkens who mentored Bill Walton during his rookie and sophomore seasons, helping to mold the young hippie into the NBA Finals MVP he became. It was Wilkens who coaxed the Trailblazer roster into winning form, crafting the nucleus that won the championship. And it was Wilkens who Portland management fired in 1976, replacing him with white coach Jack Ramsay. The very next year, the Trail Blazers were champs. That was Lenny's team. Only it wasn't anymore.

Beneath a calm demeanor, Wilkens simmered.

Born October 28, 1937, Leonard Randolph Wilkens was raised in the Bedford-Stuyvesant neighborhood of Brooklyn. After a stint with the St. Louis Hawks, he was traded to Seattle in 1969. When Wilkens took on the role of player-coach, Seattle fans sent the team hate mail.[11] But the team improved under him, posting its first winning record in franchise history in 1972. While the two were teammates in Seattle, Wilkens saw Spencer Haywood's struggle as intertwined with his own. African Americans in managerial positions were as rare as empowered Black players. Like Haywood, Wilkens was a pioneer of post–civil rights professional sports, navigating the world of white elites with few roadmaps for doing so.

Reinstated as Seattle's coach during the 1977 season when Bob Hopkins was fired after the team started 5–17, Wilkens noticed something about Seattle's roster: they were talented but top-heavy.[12] Most of the action centered around big-men Marvin Webster and Bruce Seals. Seattle had a brilliant trio of Black guards in Dennis Johnson, Fred Brown, and Gus Williams. But they weren't being trusted to guide the team. The NBA's racial hierarchy dictated its division of labor. In basketball, guards play much the same role as quarterbacks on the football field. Usually the smallest players on the court, good backcourt players show sound decision-making and a coolness under pressure that many white observers of the sport didn't believe African Americans possessed. A 1968 *Sports Illustrated* feature that exposed racism at UW football also showed that white sports management reserved "thinking" positions like quarterback and point guard for whites.[13] To bracket a mostly Black game with the reassuring balm of Caucasian expertise for white audiences, the TV program *NBA on CBS* hired two white floor generals—Rick Barry and John Havlicek—as analysts in the 1970s.

Lenny Wilkens would have none of these typecasts. A former point guard, he gave the car keys to Seattle's guards, allowing them to control more of the action. The downsized Sonics started winning.

Seattle finished the 1977–78 regular season by going 42–18 after Wilkens replaced Hopkins, ending the year with a 47–35 record. In the first round of the playoffs, they knocked off Kareem Abdul-Jabbar's Los Angeles Lakers, then took on heavily favored Portland—the team that had discarded Sonics coach Lenny Wilkens. To Wilkens, the series was so personal that his assistants had to beg him to stop seeing the games in terms of a personal pursuit of revenge.[14] The series may've mirrored America's tumultuous racial dynamics; but thinking about it that way didn't help Seattle defend Portland's intricate high-post offense. The Sonics took the first game in Portland, then caught a fortuitous break—specifically, in Bill Walton's foot, which fractured during Portland's Game Two win. The Sonics won three of the next four games to advance to the Western Conference Finals, where they dumped the Denver Nuggets. A league laughingstock at the start of the season, the Seattle SuperSonics were representing the NBA's Western Conference in the 1978 NBA Finals. By making serious noise, the Sonics added to the national clamor about Seattle.

As other cities suffered the loss of jobs, tax revenue, and stability during deindustrialization, Seattle was relatively steady. Boeing bounced back; the local economy rebounded. Seen from afar, the city's progressive-seeming way of smoothing over its conflicts—its image of unperturbed urban cool—stood out. City cops expected a June 1978 neighborhood meeting about pollution in West Seattle to become contentious; hardly anybody showed up. Everybody was watching the Sonics, who added to Seattle's utopian gloss.[15] In 1972 author Nard Jones scribed a trade hardcover for Doubleday Books called *Seattle*, its New York–based publisher billing it as "a fresh look at one of America's most exciting cities." Jones lauded the local sporting culture, the immaculate outdoor climes that inspired Seattleites to ski, play golf, frolic in parks. In 1975, *Harper's Magazine* ranked Seattle the "least-worst city" in the country. In May 1978, *Sports Illustrated* described "Sonicsteria" among Seattle residents: "If you've been near a floating bridge or an aircraft plant, [you've heard] the good people of Seattle blow their lungs out over the SuperSonics."[16]

If we're being honest, Seattle didn't deserve this team. Its sporting establishment couldn't be bothered to celebrate the arrival of the NBA in 1967. Most sports fans were enchanted with football and baseball, games that had a more hallowed American heritage—games that could be more easily coded as white. But a funny thing happened on the road to big-league recognition: the Sonics got there first.

As of 1978, the young Mariners and Seahawks were years away from being contenders. The Sonics were the only competitive professional ball game in town. On their backs were built the rest of pro sports spectatorship in Seattle: the big crowds that showed investors and the press that it could be a big-league city; the sales tax and parking fee revenue that fattened the city budget and showed politicians, bars, and restaurants how to capitalize on a team's deep playoff run. The rejected stone of Seattle sports had become its cornerstone. A Black newspaper circulated primarily in the Central Area, the *Seattle Medium*, knew what time it was: "Whether on the court or in the courtroom, Seattle is a colorful basketball team. They laid the groundwork for the other franchises that grace the city today."[17]

It wouldn't be an exaggeration to say that the Seattle SuperSonics helped lay the groundwork for modern men's professional basketball. Spencer Haywood readied the league for young Black talent with his pathbreaking lawsuit. Hired as head coach of the Sonics in 1973, Bill Russell had been the first Black coach in the league when Boston hired him in 1966; in Seattle in 1967, Lenny Wilkens became the second. Years before the exploits of Isiah Thomas, Michael Jordan, and Stephen Curry, Wilkens turned Seattle into the first guard-led team in NBA history to make a real run at the championship. Sonics public relations staffer Rick Welts sold this mostly Black team to a mostly white city, planting stories in area press about players' charitable exploits for human interest appeal to white readers, while offering discounted tickets to readers of the *Seattle Medium* for Black History Month. In the process Seattle became the first petri dish for the coming viral explosion of the NBA's commerciality.[18]

Though the Sonics fell short to the Washington Bullets after losing a Game Seven heartbreaker at home, Seattle embraced professional basketball to an extent that seemed extremely unlikely a decade earlier, when many didn't care about its arrival in Seattle. The city was on the doorstep of something special: its first major league championship since the Seattle Metropolitans in 1917. A Sonics title would mean big-league triumph the city coveted for decades.

Before moving there permanently in 1979, the Sonics played the last two home games of the 1978 playoffs at the Kingdome, a stadium located on a plot of land where Seattle engineers dredged mounds of soil to make way for the coming railroad in 1895. Seattleites congregated by the hundreds—the thousands—watching from docks and ships as a soil-pumping boat turned open sound into solid ground. Manufactured civic ambition was a spectator sport. Fifty sets of train tracks would crisscross this artificial tideland, fueling Seattle's twentieth-century rise. When elected officials broke ground during the Kingdome's opening construction ceremony in 1972, they pulled up spikes that tethered rail lines to this man-made terra firma, clearing space for the new stadium. One avenue of civic ambition made way for another: Seattle's sports were a new path to respect and recognition, literally built upon the railroad that put the city on the map.[19]

In the 1978 NBA season, 504,668 fans went to pro-basketball games at the Coliseum. The Sonics represented a city of audacious settlers. At a pep rally after their Finals loss in June 1978, team management promised Seattle fans they'd win the NBA Championship next season.

* * *

Earlier in 1978, quarterback Warren Moon led the University of Washington to the last big Seattle sports triumph witnessed by Royal Brougham. Played annually in Pasadena since 1902, Brougham called the Rose Bowl "one of the world's great spectacles."[20] Moon rose to the occasion, throwing for 234 yards, running for two touchdowns and passing for another, and earning Player of the Game honors. When he glided to the end zone to give the Huskies an early lead, NBC Sports television announcer Curt Gowdy said: "This fella was booed. But he's arrived this year." The

The construction of the Kingdome following the 1968 Forward Thrust election brought the Seahawks and Mariners to town. Courtesy of the Seattle Municipal Archives, item 195628.

pat remark concealed the complicated political dynamics that had orbited Moon since he landed in Seattle: he was a Black quarterback in a segregated city, exceling at a position many didn't believe African American athletes could play.

A transfer from a California community college, Warren Moon won his starting job by outcompeting Chris Rowland, a white Seattleite and local favorite. In Moon's memoir he recalled getting jeered by Washington's mostly white fans at Husky Stadium: "I tried not to let it bother me. It still hurt."[21] As Moon went 11–11 in his first two years at Washington, friends and family heard people in the stands using slurs. Moon confessed he played better on the road.[22]

Though big-name athletic recruits were often pampered, Washington was unfriendly to Black athletes. The 1968 *Sports Illustrated* exposé "The Black Athlete: A Shameful Story" revealed that UW football had restrictive quotas limiting the number of African Americans who could play for the school. Washington officials penalized Black players for dating white women.[23] The UW race problem became a political spectacle in 1970 when three football players quit the team, citing loyalty tests issued to players by head coach Jim Owens. In 1971 the Black Seattle newspaper *The Facts* decried the "sophisticated institutional racism" of UW coaches: "In this age of overt racism, racism can be perpetrated by a facial frown, by a change in voice when talking to Blacks, by the turning of backs when Blacks come upon the scene."[24]

Harold Warren Moon was born November 18, 1956, and grew up in the affluent Baldwin Hills section of Black Los Angeles. When he moved to Seattle in 1975, he had allies. Under a media microscope for his football program's discriminatory past, coach Don James chose Moon as a starter, then stuck with the quarterback as he found his footing.[25] Moon also had an advocate in Gertrude Peoples, a UW athletic recruiter who helped ease minority athletes into campus life.[26] Still, Moon's on-campus support system couldn't protect him from instances of bigotry in Seattle. In a 1976 issue of *The Daily*, a UW sportswriter entertained whether it was time to lynch the quarterback because the Husky offense was struggling.[27] Many white Seattleites refused to tolerate a Black quarterback.

Integration in Seattle was a bumpy, incomplete ride. The city's voters rejected a 1964 measure for housing desegregation. Seattle schools were still segregated. A majority of King County voters—56 percent—supported Richard Nixon's 1972 reelection, doubling down on the "law and order" rhetoric he aimed at civil rights protestors. After Martin Luther King Jr. was assassinated in 1968, American cities exploded in charged riots and demonstrations, further alienating moderates who believed the civil rights movement moved too quickly even when King was alive. Moon's tenure at UW was a political football, pitting reactionaries against reformers and radicals, the Black freedom struggle against racist backlash.

Deindustrialization further fueled racial unrest. Throughout the 1970s major corporations left heavily unionized northern cities. Seattle had technically retained its industrial base in the 1970s, with jobs along the waterfront remaining intact. But the 1969–71 Boeing recession simulated the economic insecurity seen in other cities during deindustrialization. When faced with civil rights statutes and empowered minority workers, segregated Seattle unions tried to close ranks: after the US Department of Justice determined that Seattle unions had declined to accept Black workers, Black labor organizer Tyree Scott protested in 1972 to ensure that minority contractors were employed in the construction of the Kingdome.[28] Throughout urban America the perception permeated that African Americans were being given an unfair advantage.

"The hard-fought victories of the Civil Rights movement caused a reaction," wrote historian Carol Anderson in *White Rage: The Unspoken Truth of Our Racial Divide.*[29] In 1976 a white student sued the University of Washington after it denied her admission, asserting that she had been a victim of "reverse racism."[30] In a 1977 edition of the UW student newspaper *The Daily*, a Seattle attorney argued that affirmative action programs "resulted in the displacement of whites by unqualified applicants."[31] In the socioeconomic context of deindustrialization—and the political context of civil rights backlash—Warren Moon appeared to angry white fans as a diversity hire, one more unqualified minority being given a handout.

Moon was quick to point out he had *earned his place* as a starter.[32] The job of quarterback had been a bastion of racial exclusivity, with many sportswriters long asserting that Black athletes didn't have the smarts to excel at the position. When Joe Gilliam beat out Terry Bradshaw in training camp to become the starting quarterback of the Pittsburgh Steelers in 1974, *Sports Illustrated* shined a spotlight on his skin color, announcing "PITTSBURGH'S BLACK QUARTERBACK" on the cover of its September 23, 1974, edition.[33] After Gilliam led the Steelers to a 4–1–1 record, Pittsburgh coaches received hate mail and replaced him with Bradshaw, who posted comparable numbers to Gilliam and had a number of games that were worse than any by the ousted Black quarterback.

Pittsburgh was a segregated northern city. Activists tried to integrate its schools; the city resisted. The saga was replayed in Seattle, where mad white parents mobbed an October 1970 meeting where the Seattle School Board mulled busing Black, brown, and poor students into white and affluent schools.[34] In a last-ditch effort to avoid being sued by the federal government for violating civil rights law, the city made busing mandatory in 1978. *Seattle Weekly* writer Fred Moody wrote that "white Seattle congratulated itself on voluntary integration and moved to private schools to avoid it."[35]

And yet there went Warren Moon, the most prominent Black student in the city, leading Washington to victory. He noticed a change in Husky fans as he grew into his starting job: "We were beating USC on November 12, 1977. I ran for a touchdown. Fans chanted my name."[36] He thought of giving fans the middle finger. Instead, he savored the moment. Warren Moon didn't bus for equal opportunity in Seattle—but he did have to make a run for it.

* * *

White Seattle wanted what Washington, DC, had. Not its public housing developments or its murder rate. Not its soul food restaurants. Not its tradition of Black resistance to white racism, typified by the home of abolitionist Frederick Douglass, which sat atop a hill in the city's Anacostia neighborhood. And certainly not the moniker "Chocolate City," given to DC in 1975 by the funk group Parliament in acknowledgment of the group's Black fan base there. No, white Seattle wanted an NBA Championship. And the rest of the city did too. The Sonics had managed to do what few politicians or elections could: unite Seattle in pursuit of the same goal.

After the 1978 NBA Finals, the *Seattle Post-Intelligencer* tried to pivot to politics: "The party's over. This community must turn its attention to schools and unemployment. Maybe those problems will be easier to face now that we've had time off, a time when throwing a ball through a hoop was of world-shaking importance."[37]

Whatever. Sports were exciting. Sports made people happy. Sports brought them together. A Central Area kid later known to the world as Sir Mix-A-Lot went to Sonics rallies in the late 1970s. A young fan in Bellevue named Jenny Anne Durkan followed the team. A Washington, DC, pundit said the Bullets' title "was a sociological happening that restored pride to this community."[38] Basketball gave white city dwellers another way to lay claim to the city, and gave Black and brown people pride and a sense of belonging. Sports gave people a good time by giving them back what their politics took from them.

Sports were civic dopamine, the pleasure hormone released when doing

After the SuperSonics came to town in 1966, Metro bus service began in 1973. Pro sports and mass transit crossed paths when Sonics ads featuring star guard Slick Watts appeared on bus façades, 1978. King County Archives, A07–056.

drugs, having sex, or watching a beautiful sunset. Politics were civic cortisol, the stress hormone released while arguing or sitting in traffic. Calls to get the city to "refocus" on civic affairs had it all wrong. Seattleites weren't watching the Sonics to forget about their politics; they were watching the Sonics to feel better about them.

The Seattle SuperSonics started the 1978–79 season winning seven straight games.[39] By season's end, they set a franchise record for wins at 52–30, captured the NBA's Pacific Division, and finished seven games ahead of rival Portland, which finished fourth. Seattle drowned the Lakers 4–1 in the first round of the playoffs, then eclipsed the Phoenix Suns in the Western Conference Finals. They were back in the NBA Finals, where a familiar foe awaited them: the Washington Bullets.

After the Bullets flew to an 18-point lead in Game One, the Sonics staged a furious comeback that fell just short. They took the next three games. The champs were on the ropes. With Game Five looming, Bullets

NBA Finals game, Sonics against the Washington Bullets, 1978. While many opposed mandatory busing to integrate the city's schools, the Sonics' NBA Finals runs in 1978 and 1979 invited diverse crowds to the Kingdome. King County Archives, A08-065.

coach Dick Motta resorted to psychological warfare, telling reporters that Sonics guard Dennis Johnson was susceptible to pressure because he shot 0–14 in a Finals game the year before.[40] Whether he knew it or not, Motta was trafficking in a racial stereotype, resurrecting the old notion that Black players lacked the "clutch gene" to succeed under pressure. The trope first started in the late 1940s, when white sportswriters misrepresented Black Brooklyn Dodgers pitcher Don Newcombe's playoff performance as a way of undercutting the integrationist movement spearheaded by his teammate, Jackie Robinson.[41] Lenny Wilkens stuck up for Johnson: "Dick has to use any psychology he can to motivate his team. Tell him don't hold his breath." Motta would eat his words.

Game Five of the 1979 NBA Finals was played on June 1, 1979, in Landover, Maryland. Seattle's guards were a revelation in the game. Though it later became commonplace, a guard-oriented team led by an all-Black backcourt had never won an NBA Championship. The Sonics were on the verge.

Up two with a minute to play, Seattle needed a basket to seal the title. *NBA on CBS* commentator Rick Barry predicted the Sonics would run the crucial possession through one of its guards. Bullets assistant coach Bernie Bickerstaff beckoned Washington to double-team Seattle point guard Gus Williams as he crossed center court; they were a step late. Williams drove, drew three Bullets defenders, then dished to Dennis Johnson. The target of Motta's trash talk, Johnson leaped into a balletic fadeaway shot.

* * *

In a sport where taller players have a decided advantage, it might be said that the fadeaway is a weapon the meek use against the mighty. It's a bad shot: to create space against larger or overaggressive defenders, the shooter projects the ball while drifting away from the opponent and the basket. Like the step-back three-pointer, critics decry the fadeaway as passive, a sign of a player shying away from physical contact. It screams desperation, often launched as a last-ditch effort under duress, with no better options as the shot clock runs out. But at its most effective, the fadeaway is deployed by skilled guards who go to work where taller defenders lurk. In a game dominated by Goliaths, the fadeaway is the gumption of David.

Shot over three Bullets, Dennis Johnson's fadeaway rolled around the rim and found the bottom of the net: 95–91, Seattle. "Just what I was talking about," said Rick Barry, delighting in being right about something. Seattle and Washington traded fouls in the final seconds. Gus Williams hit two free throws to put the game out of reach. With triple zeroes on the clock, the scoreboard read Seattle 97, Washington 93. Lenny Wilkens and his assistants raised their arms in jubilation. An *NBA on CBS* chyron spelled it out:

Seattle SuperSonics

1979

NBA World Champions

The Sonics had done it. The *city* had done it. In the 1978–79 championship season, Seattle's average attendance per game increased a whopping 48 percent from the year before when the team moved to the Kingdome, vaulting Seattle to first place in the league in that category.[42] In a city with 493,000 people, 300,000 Sonics fans crowded downtown Seattle for the Super-Sonics championship parade on June 4, 1979. This was civic connection. The kind that contrasted with the polarizing 1978 busing mandate, that contrasted with the collective trauma of deindustrialization and baseless claims of "reverse racism." In the afterglow of the city's championship, a Seattle psychologist opined: "We were brothers under the skin because our team won."[43] Bright goldenrod Sonics T-shirts sold in Seattle department stores. Sonics baseball caps, bumper stickers, water bottles, ashtrays, key chains, and hand puppets hit shelves. Luther Rabb's commemorative disco cut "SuperSonics Do It" played in area nightclubs. A $575 gold SuperSonics pendant went on sale; a grinning Lenny Wilkens appeared next to it in Seattle newspapers.[44]

On one level the August 1978 *Jet* magazine write-up announcing Wilkens's entry into the ranks of NBA upper management in 1977 was a sign of racial progress. After Bill Russell accomplished the feat as player-coach in 1966, Wilkens was the second Black coach to ever win an NBA title. But sports triumph was easily tokenized. Law professor Mehrsa Baradaran's *The Color of Money: Black Banks and the Racial Wealth Gap* details how the Nixon administration sabotaged civil rights pleas with market-based solutions.[45] In a 1968 television ad titled "Black Capitalism," Nixon promised

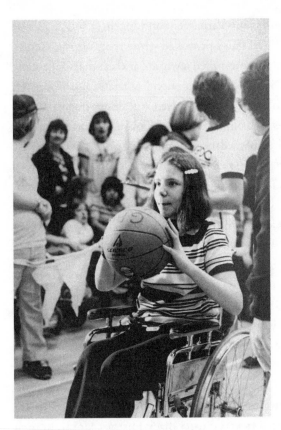

A Seattle youngster plays basketball at the Washington Games for the Physically Disabled, 1979. The Seattle SuperSonics won the NBA Championship that year, galvanizing Seattleites of all backgrounds. Courtesy of the Seattle Municipal Archives, item 196005.

that more Black business activity would end racial strife. Throughout the 1970s the pursuit of public aid, affirmative action, and political enfranchisement was funneled by federal policymakers into private enterprise. The celebration of personal minority achievement silenced dissent. Demands for desegregation were defanged. In the fetishization of African American athletes who made it out of destitute urban areas, materialism had become the de facto response to racial inequity.

All around America in the post–civil rights era, ethnic minorities saw long-delayed entry into the cultural mainstream. Until his untimely death in 1973, Bruce Lee was a bankable movie star on the rise whose water-like, formless approach to fighting was a by-product of his upbringing in Hong Kong. The summer of the Sonics' 1979 title run, Michael Jackson's *Off the Wall* climbed disco-pop charts, placing him alongside other popular Black acts like George Clinton's group Parliament and Earth, Wind & Fire. In the same way that civil rights gains provoked white reaction, the increasing acclaim for Black culture prompted a white backlash that spilled into sports: in a July 1979 "Disco Demolition Night" at a Chicago White Sox home game, white fans hurled racial invective while destroying records by Black artists of all genres.[46] A similar event took place in Seattle that year, when rock fans attacked a mobile dance floor blasting disco.[47] Nonetheless, Seattle newspaper *Seattle Medium* announced "the year of the great crossover for black music" in 1979, highlighting America's embrace of the same "funky black rhythms" displayed on the basketball court. Precious little of the co-optation trickled down to Black Americans at large, however, whose annual inflation-adjusted wages in 1979 ($34,476) were about half the national average ($67,784).[48]

To criticize Black capitalism is to walk a fine line. It's true that Black leaders in the mid-twentieth century believed economic empowerment was a prerequisite for equality; in 1964, Malcolm X described "Black Nationalism" as his "social, political *and economic* philosophy."[49] African Americans in redlined urban areas like the Central District owned fewer homes, fewer businesses, and had less capital than their white counterparts. The Sonics gave Seattleites in the margins representation. The team gave readers of the *Seattle Medium* discounted tickets during Black History Month in 1979. Coors beer company sponsored a weekly series of articles in the newspaper, with installments written by Sonics guard Fred Brown.[50] Black urbanites took pride in well-to-do Black athletes who blazed trails in sports.

Yet as a strategy for collective liberation, Black capitalism was filled with empty calories. Although they were enmeshed in the civic fabric of the city, only one player on the SuperSonics roster actually lived in Seattle; the rest commuted in from ritzy suburbs.[51] The economic impact of the Sonics' playoff run was $9.8 million in revenue for the City of Seattle; the revenue went almost everywhere—to bars, to parking stalls, to the same city government that allowed segregation to endure into the 1970s—except to the direct betterment of Black Seattle.[52] In his 1845 autobiography *Narrative of the Life of Frederick Douglass*, Douglass described the role of sports diversions in maintaining structural racism, with displays of Black-on-Black competition dissipating energy that might otherwise have gone to plantation revolt: "I believe sports are among the most effective means in the hands of slaveholders in keeping down the spirit of insurrection."[53]

Sports in Seattle were a largely hollow spectacle of social harmony. Not everyone was a fan. In 1979 the Sonics brought a Seattle-area couple to the brink of divorce. "Paul turns into a zombie if the Sonics lose and screams if they win," complained a Seattle woman named Cecile Andrews. "If there were women teams playing professional basketball, I might be able to get more interested."[54] Between 1970 and 1979 the US divorce rate increased by 50 percent; concurrently, women entered the workforce in rates not seen since the 1940s.[55] In *The Second Shift*, sociologist Arlie Hochschild detailed how women's economic empowerment in the postindustrial era didn't come with a shift in behavior from men who had grown accustomed to free domestic labor from the women in their lives.[56] Cecile was sick of Paul: "His expenditure of energy on the Sonics leaves him little time for household chores."

As the Sonics highlighted issues in the private lives of Seattleites, their impact on public life was also problematic.[57] Washington State governor Dixy Lee Ray expressed disappointment that the Sonics distracted from the 1979 state legislative session. County officials complained when community meetings for the county's Growth Management Plan were depopulated by Sonics games. Was the city valuing symbolism over substance? A June 10, 1979, letter to the *Seattle Times* begged the question: "Wouldn't it be incredible if energy expended for the Sonics (screaming, cheering, drinking, media coverage) was spent teaching our children, feeding the hungry, caring for the sick? The energy is there, but it needs to be channeled into other areas."[58]

After the "Great Society" failed to materialize in the 1960s, a rightward movement coalesced in the United States. Private gain diffused calls for greater public action. Commercialism became a facsimile for community. Sports stars like Warren Moon, Spencer Haywood, and Lenny Wilkens were tokens of integration, providing audiences a figment of progress on the field of play. Under pressure, progressivism faded away.

8th Inning

"I'M JUST HERE TO MAKE A FEW BUCKS," 1980–1989

Seriously, how did he not catch that? Seattle Seahawks tight end Mike Tice's replacement screwed up. In a game against the visiting Miami Dolphins, he bungled a play that should have been a routine reception. The crowd groaned. Tice turned to a reporter: "I could've caught that pass three times."[1] There was nothing he could do. Although Tice wasn't injured, he wasn't going back in the game. Like every member of Seattle's forty-five-man roster, Tice wasn't even in the Kingdome. Twelve days earlier, the National Football League Players Association had gone on strike.

It was Sunday, October 4, 1987. The Seahawks, the Dolphins, and every other NFL team was playing with replacement players. At the Pioneer Square sports bar Swannie's, Tice was one of two dozen official Seahawks who had gathered around bar televisions with beer, sandwiches, and fans to watch substitute Seattle players drop the ball. Droves of Seattle fans showed solidarity with the striking Seahawks. Union members derisively called the replacements "scabs," a term deployed a generation earlier by picketing machinists in the *Aero Mechanic* newspaper during the Boeing Strike of 1948.

Just as it took technical know-how to build a plane, it took real experience to convert on a crucial third and six—experience that couldn't be blessed onto hasty replacements.[2] Seattle fans noticed the subpar play of the scabs. They weren't alone. In every city with a striking NFL team, mocking monikers arose, maligning the impostor squads assembled by union-busting team bosses: the San Francisco Phoney-Niners, Pittsburgh Stealers, Los Angeles Shams, New Orleans St. Elsewheres, Los Angeles Masqueraders, Houston Spoilers, and the Seattle Sub-Hawks.[3]

The NFL strike kicked off after the September 21, 1987, game between the soon-to-be New England Fake-Riots and In-Lieu York Jets. At halftime, player union leader Gene Upshaw announced footballers would strike at 12:01 a.m.[4] Players followed through, holding out for higher wages, an end to random drug testing, larger pensions, and greater worker mobility in the form of free agency. The September 27 slate of NFL games was canceled. Teams scrambled to find replacements before play resumed on October 4.

Seattle defensive lineman Joe Nash was one of the Seahawks who gathered with fans and striking players at Swannie's. Though the cause was righteous, Nash was conflicted: "The game counts, so you hope they win. But you kind of hope they play terrible." The comrades got their wish. The slapdash Seahawks prevailed 24–20, but they didn't look so great.

Seahawks season ticketholder Marlene Colon was at Swannie's too, lunching with the Hawks wearing a T-shirt that read "NO ONE SHITS ON OUR HAWKS." She even kept her tickets, declining to profit from labor unrest by scalping them. She would never do that to her comrades: "They've been so sweet, visiting with us all day. No scabs can take their places."[5]

* * *

They came from out of the country, around the state, and across town. From tertiary football leagues, where they played; from junior college football programs, where they coached; and from hunting trips, where they were hunting. They were cops, high school guidance counselors, and floor workers at rubber processing plants. Some of them hadn't played football since college. At least one hadn't worked out in over a year. They were NFL tryouts who had been cut from team training camps earlier in the decade; injured former pros who had been discarded by a league with cruel labor practices. But now, they were being recycled.

They were the replacement Seahawks—the wannabes who suddenly were. Four dozen players in all, they were culled from the great scrap heap of athletic castoffs, survivors of a list of prospects that numbered three hundred. The search exhausted a Seahawks scout: "You wouldn't believe the places we've had to go to get these guys."[6] Some called in, sensing opportunity. Others were found in the wild. To get a running back, Seattle signed the owner of a Denver art gallery.[7] To track down a lineman in the Yukon, they got word to him through a park ranger.[8] Three other recruits traveled to Seattle, observed the disastrous state of Seahawks practice, and decided it wasn't worth it. "Nothing against the guys," a wide receiver remarked after absconding back to Bellingham. "You get a feeling if there are quality players, and it just wasn't there."[9]

Since its establishment during the Gilded Age, the game of football had been a sport of attrition; games were less won than they were survived. For a few weeks in 1987, the frontier ethic found its ultimate expression: In a league of self-interested prospectors, could Seattle's self-interested prospectors outlast the ones in other cities? A parade of opportunists appeared. Concert promoter Suge Knight played two games with the Los Angeles Rams; an assistant coach in Minnesota named Pete Carroll was ready to step in as starting quarterback. A newly minted Seahawks running back saw dollar signs: "The money I make in one game will be more than I'd make in two years at my job." Replacement fullback Rick Parros had no illusions: "I'm just here to make a few bucks."[10]

When the NFL players struck, the Seahawks asked for their property back: unionized workers traded in their blue uniforms and silver helmets for picket signs. Conflict ensued. Twenty striking Seahawks and their supporters assaulted a bus carrying replacement players to the team facility. A Seahawks linebacker swung a golf club at the scab convoy, causing it to hit a car.[11] Elsewhere in the wild wild West, striking Kansas City Chiefs patrolled Arrowhead Stadium with shotguns, looking for scabs.[12] When a crowd of four thousand went to watch the Philadelphia Eagles play the visiting Chicago Bears in the first game with replacement players, Philly fans pelted scabs with profanity and projectiles.[13] Picket signs outside Veterans Stadium read "FANS AGAINST SCABS" and "SCABS SUCK." They were signs of the times.

After first rising to national prominence as a second-rate actor who portrayed a Notre Dame football player named George Gipp in the 1940 film *Knute Rockne, All American*, President Ronald Reagan crushed a strike launched by the Professional Air Traffic Controllers Organization (PATCO) in August 1981, terminating the entire workforce and substituting them with replacements. Corporate America copied the game plan.

Labor historian Joseph A. McCartin describes Reagan's decimation of PATCO as the opening salvo in an assault on organized labor in the 1980s.[14] Mining corporation Phelps Dodge hired replacements workers in 1983 when its workers wouldn't agree to a wage freeze. In 1985, Hormel demanded a 23 percent wage cut from meat-packers in Minnesota, then reopened their plant with scabs when the meat-packers refused. As if manufactured on an assembly line, identical labor crackdowns occurred at Continental Airlines in 1984, Georgia-Pacific in 1985, Trans World Airlines in 1986, and the National Football League in 1987. In each case, McCartin writes, the stories were the same: "Employer demands triggered strikes, replacements were recruited, unions were routed." In 1986 the AFL-CIO was forced to concede that strikes were too risky. In a pamphlet titled *The Inside Game,* the labor federation advised: "When an employer tries to force a strike, staying on the job and working from the inside may be more appropriate."[15]

After he returned his uniform to Seahawks management to kick off the strike, star defensive back Ken Easley got the support of the King County Labor Council. The endorsement aligned the local AFL-CIO affiliate— representing seventy-five thousand Seattle-area workers—with Seattle's Pro Bowl safety, the most famous union shop steward in the city.[16] In 1987, 24 percent of Washington State workers were unionized—fifth among fifty states, but a far cry from the figure of 54 percent seen a generation earlier in 1954.[17] America was shifting from a manufacturing economy with unionized breadwinners to one predominated by contingent service labor. As labor became casualized, unions struggled. Organized labor in Seattle saw the football fight as a microcosm of their own.

The King County Labor Council excoriated NFL management in the October 1987 edition of its union newspaper, calling out league bosses for worker mistreatment. "A player has to have four years in the NFL to get his pension, and be age 55 before he can collect it," wrote the executive secretary of the Labor Council. "The average player's life expectancy after playing four years in the NFL is 52."[18] Football players went to work in hard hats to protect against brain injury. Seahawks were further endangered by playing on a thin layer of artificial turf spread over concrete at the Kingdome. Seattle workers who endured occupational hazards of their own supported the team.

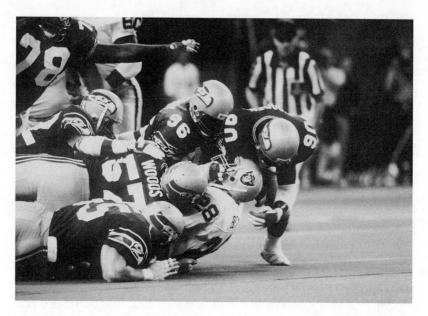

The Seattle Seahawks played on a thin layer of carpet laid over hard concrete at the Kingdome. Football was a brutal game played by glorified manual laborers with short careers. It embodied the increasing precariousness of work after Reagan-era America's backlash to organized labor in the 1980s. King County Archives, A08-065.

With its organized dockworkers, teachers, and nurses, Seattle had long been a union town. Strikes punctuated all the great revolutions—and counterrevolutions—in the city's history. A Ballard lumberman's strike in 1893 scared timber corporations who feared employees were on the road to radicalism when agitator Eugene Debs led a nationwide rail-worker strike a year later. Local production of guillotines ceased when Seattle sheet metal workers struck in 1902. In 1907 one thousand Seattle waiters shut down every unionized restaurant in the city; over the next decade, streetcar operators, taxicab drivers, ironworkers, coal packers, candymakers, telephone operators, and Industrial Workers of the World (IWW) militants also picketed, prompting Washington State to implement some of the first workman's compensation laws in the United States and setting the stage for the General Strike of 1919. After the Red Scare stifled proletariat uprisings that resurfaced during the Great Depression, Seattle cops turned machine guns on demonstrating maritime workers in the Battle of Smith Cove in 1934.

Later, the 1948 Boeing machinists strike signaled that the grand postwar consensus between labor, government, and big business had fatal fissures.

During the Energy Crisis of 1975, overworked Seattle City Light electricians staged the longest public employees' strike in Washington history; scabs were welcomed on the job when radical leftist group the George Jackson Brigade bombed a city substation in the rich neighborhood Laurelhurst, causing a thirty-six-hour power outage. Then in 1976—in the largest and most intense health-care labor stoppage in the country—fifteen hundred Seattle nurses fed up with harassment and low wages struck for two months. Seen in the grand scope of Seattle labor history, the 1987 Seahawks strike was less oddity than inevitability—a predictable consequence of class conflict between hard labor and heartless bosses in a frontier city. Running through the long saga of Seattle's incessant corporate shilling for railroads, lumber, airplanes, tech, and sports is a deep-red streak: the robust legacy of trade unionism that challenged capitalist hegemony wherever it tried to take root in the city.[19]

On September 26, 1987, one thousand fans and union members held a labor rally at the Kingdome for the striking Seahawks. Represented were unionized grocery store workers, concession stand attendants, food service employees, and electricians.[20] In the Kingdome parking lot, Seahawks players signed autographs for union members. "You have corporations all over America who try to sign the best executives," Ken Easley told fans in an autograph line. "Players want those same freedoms."[21] There was a clear class divide between football players and everyday workers. Unable to read the room, rookie linebacker Brian Bosworth showed up to the rally in a convertible. Union members looked past the inequity. "You think about how much money they make, and you think they're greedy," said a unionized electrician. "But our careers last 30 or 40 years. Theirs aren't."[22]

* * *

America was in the throes of a new Gilded Age. A time when Bill Gates was profiled as "one of the 25 most intriguing people" alive in *People* magazine in 1983, and his Seattle software company Microsoft grew to $846 million revenues in 1987.[23] A time when Central District entrepreneur Anthony L. Ray sold copies of his 1988 album *Swass* from the trunk of his car, made it onto MTV with the Seattle anthem "My Posse's on Broadway," and made it big with gold chains and brick-sized cell phones with the stage name Sir Mix-A-Lot. A time when, wrote economist Costas Lapavitsas in *Profiting without Producing*, "the income of the top 1% rose dramatically, approximating the levels of the 1920s. From the early 1980s onward, capital had the advantage against labor."[24]

Ever since it chased railroads and served as a jumping-off point for the Alaska gold rush, Seattle had been a booster city. Now, in the 1980s, it entered an era as materialistic as any other. A fish in water, the city thrived. In addition to computer software and rap records, Seattle sold itself. In 1981 the Seattle–King County tourism board nicknamed Seattle the "Emerald City" and netted a record $2.5 billion in tourist revenues.[25] In 1987 the Nordstrom family owned a majority share of the Seattle Seahawks. There was no way they could lose. If the strike ended, it was back to plush ticket revenues. If the strike continued, shoppers would keep mobbing the corporation's Seattle retail outlets on Sundays when they would typically be watching football. Thirty thousand people returned tickets before Seattle's scab game against Miami. "People are shopping more, it's incredible," said a clerk at a Nordstrom department store during the strike.[26]

Seattle grew glitzier in the 1980s, its fresh skyline visible from the deindustrialized coal plant Gas Works Park.[27] One million square feet of new office space came online downtown in 1984—much of it in the seventy-six-story Columbia Tower that opened that year. Nine other skyscrapers were under construction. After a generation of divestment from city centers in favor of suburbs, downtowns became fashionable again. And the fashion was for blandly appealing spaces for people to blow money in and leave. For example, in Houston's in the 1980s the Uptown District sprouted upscale commercial towers. In Seattle's Reagan years, activist Jim Ellis championed a glossy convention center that opened in 1982. Pioneer Square underwent a quarter-billion-dollar renovation. The shiny mall Westlake Center opened in 1988. Suburbs were once satellites of big cities; in the postindustrial period the relationship reversed.[28] Urban America became a commercial colony of outlying areas, the hearts of major cities controlled by the pacemaker of capitalist pursuit.

Everywhere in Seattle were road closures, construction cranes, craters. The 1980s development boom created new cityscapes to police, new yuppie labyrinths to seal off from city riffraff. Despite years of demonstrations from Capitol Hill residents who objected to it, the Seattle Police Department opened its East Precinct near Cal Anderson Park in 1986.[29] Later that year, King County officials opened a downtown jail that put a $179 million hole in the county budget, forcing officials to take funds from the tourism board to cover cost overruns; members of the Public Safety Employees Union threatened to walk off the job because the building's shoddy fire alarm system was unsafe.[30] In August 1987, Seattle Police launched a first-of-its-kind program in the country, putting officers on bikes so they could navigate the narrow capillaries of under-construction areas to capture shoplifters, issue parking tickets, bust drug dealers. Once a vehicle for the age of reform, bikes in Seattle had become a conduit for Reagan era repression of the urban poor.

Though targeted by the police, street dealers represented the commercialism of the 1980s better than anybody. High-end pushers sold powder cocaine to elites in the financial districts of urban America; pitchers of smokable "crack" cocaine moved mounds in the inner-city. "Selling crack made sense," writes journalist David Farber in *Crack: Rock Cocaine, Street Capitalism, and the Decade of Greed*. "With old-school industrial jobs disappearing, with unions in free fall, young men made choices."[31] The death of Maryland forward Len Bias—who overdosed on cocaine a day and a half after he was drafted by the Boston Celtics with a pick traded to them by the Sonics—instigated the federal War on Drugs. President Reagan gifted local law enforcement military equipment to combat the use and sale of narcotics.

University of Oklahoma linebacker Brian Bosworth became an icon of America's drug panic and its materialism. After Bosworth was found to have used steroids, the NCAA suspended him, relegating him to the sidelines of the 1987 Orange Bowl. NBC cameras caught Bosworth wearing a T-shirt that lampooned the NCAA as "National Communists Against Athletes." Going by the alias "the Boz," the linebacker built a brand on a bad-boy image, styling his hair in a blond mullet resembling the character Ivan Drago in the 1985 film *Rocky IV*. The Seahawks drafted Bosworth in

1987 and offered him the biggest NFL contract ever extended to a rookie: ten years, $11 million.[32] The Boz had parlayed his drug use into riches and fame; he was now at home in a city built by boosters.

Big as they were, Seahawks veterans noticed Bosworth's paychecks. Ken Easley designated Bosworth alternate union rep, putting him in charge of loaning money to poorer players on the team during the strike. Although Boz attended the September 26 labor rally, he was ambivalent about solidarity. "I just want to talk to Kenny," he said after signing autographs, tired of politicking.[33] Bored during practices the team held to stay sharp while striking, Boz let his dog Raider run onto the field.

The NFL players' union put up a good fight, but the comrades made a mistake. Because the union made free agency a sticking point in its negotiations with management, the majority of players—who would play a few years with one team before exiting the league—had little incentive to keep striking. Workers held out as long as they could, particularly in cities with long histories of labor activism.[34] But the strike eroded when superstars like Joe Montana and Eric Dickerson crossed the picket line. Seahawks star receiver Steve Largent also betrayed the union. On October 18, 1987, a 10 percent capacity crowd in Detroit—a city hit hard by the decline of unionized manufacturing jobs—watched him shred the replacement Lions for 261 yards on fifteen catches. When Seahawks regulars returned to the team, union loyalists gave Largent the cold shoulder.[35]

Capital won. Labor took the loss. Soon, so would the Seattle Seahawks.

* * *

Seattle's once-promising season careened into mediocrity. Expectations were raised for the Seahawks after they made a run to the AFC Championship game in 1983. When they selected Bosworth in the 1987 draft, *Sports Illustrated* predicted they would face the New York Giants in the Super Bowl.[36] But *Sports Illustrated* failed to consider that Seattle would have the season from hell.

As the strike endured, fan loyalty wavered. Accusations of greed landed not at the wingtips of the Seahawks' Nordstrom ownership group but at the cleats of their employees. The *Seattle Times* accused NFL players of elitism, asking, "When was the last time you saw a union man carry a golf club to a picket?"[37] Letters to the editor of the *Seattle Post-Intelligencer* beckoned the newspaper to stop using the insult "scab," skewered columnist Art Thiel for his pro-worker coverage of the strike, and said scab Seahawks were "a joy to watch."[38]

Fans trickled back to the Kingdome after the strike, spurring the Seahawks to three straight home wins. But enthusiasm was curbed when Los Angeles Raider running back Bo Jackson eviscerated Seattle on *Monday Night Football.* Jackson trucked Bosworth on a romp into the end zone, then jetted past him for a ninety-one-yard score on the way to a 37–14 plundering of the Seahawks on November 30, 1987. Seattle lost 13–9 to Pittsburgh on December 6. Kansas City owned them, 41–20, to finish the season. Humbled by a subpar end to the strike-shortened season, the 9–6 Seahawks traveled to Houston to play the Oilers in the AFC Wild Card round of the playoffs. Seattle met its match in Texas.

In the 1980s Houston seemed like the Seattle of the South: an enterprising town always on the lookout for ways to inflate its standing in the eyes of chattering pundits who dissected and ranked American cities. Plastic and petrochemical firms had been established there after World War II; the federal government followed, subsidizing housing subdivisions, paving miles of freeways, and directing federal subsidies to Houston when it launched a NASA center there in 1962. Opened in 1965, the Astrodome was the NFL's original concrete behemoth, forebearer of the template followed by the Kingdome when it opened in 1976. That year, Houston's mayor proclaimed: "We're the new New York."[39]

Few cities exemplified a decade of ribald materialism more than Houston. A whopping 80 percent of the city's jobs were tied to the gainful oil and gas industry in 1980; the Link Valley district was nicknamed "Death Valley" thanks to entrepreneurs in the fledgling cocaine trade. Observers fixated on Houston's spanking-new downtown and philanthropy-backed arts institutions, its sports teams, and college basketball stars Hakeem Olajuwon and Clyde Drexler. "Houston evolved into America's quintessential anti-government, anti-tax businessman's haven," writes Stephen L. Klineberg in *Prophetic City: Houston on the Cusp of a Changing America.*[40] The Bayou City wanted the same things Seattle wanted, and wanted them just as much. It had everything Seattle wanted, and maybe a little more. Seattle had a Space Needle; Houston, a Space Center. The AFC Wild Card game was a contest not simply between two football teams but between two frontier cities vying for supremacy.

Many sports fans believe their teams are subject to invisible forces stacked against their success. Followers of accomplished franchises know good luck will run out; lovers of losers fear failure is ordained. Material causes are more to blame than curses. The last team in baseball to integrate, the Boston Red Sox, self-sabotaged for decades by declining to sign many Black players and getting stomped by teams that did. When the Red Sox lost to the New York Mets in devastating fashion in the 1986 World Series, it was easier to blame the jinx of a 1920 trade that sent Babe Ruth to the Yankees than it was to state the obvious: Boston lost because it had a talent deficit created by segregationist team owner Tom Yawkey and later by anti-Black hostility among the city's fans. During the Celtics-Lakers NBA Finals showdowns of the 1980s, many Black Bostonians cheered for Los Angeles.[41]

In Seattle's case the "invisible forces" had always been socioeconomic. All things being equal, its teams would do well against smaller towns, typically lose to more storied East Coast cities, and struggle against other West Coast upstarts. Houston's hyperactive Chamber of Commerce had a talent for wooing big corporations and bold individuals; quarterback Warren Moon signed with the Oilers over his hometown Seahawks in 1984. The deciding factor in his decision not to play in Seattle was monetary: the Seahawks' Nordstrom ownership group didn't want to guarantee Moon's contract, compelling him to join the Oilers.[42]

Moon was the rock of the Oilers in 1987, serving as team union rep and making sure nobody crossed the picket line. Earlier in the year, Houston struggled; a recession caused a slowdown in the city's petroleum sector, and the Oilers had trouble moving the ball. Fans blamed their Black quarterback. Once a target of racial resentment in Seattle, Moon told reporters he was used to it: "The economy has a lot to do with it. It's made for a negative attitude."[43]

The 1978 Rose Bowl MVP remained resolute, guiding Houston to the playoffs. A good sport while enduring racism from University of Washington fans, Moon was now positioned to get revenge on the city that had jeered

Green Lake hoopers in north Seattle in 1980, two years before *Sports Illustrated* praised Seattle sports for "fostering civic pride and an uncommon urban vigor." Glowing profiles in national publications initiated a growth spurt for boomtown Seattle in the 1990s. Courtesy of the Seattle Municipal Archives, item 76211.

him in college. "I didn't show a lot of emotion, but I was concentrating to a greater degree than [for] any other game in my career," Moon said after throwing for 273 yards and completing twenty-one of thirty-two passes. "We knew we'd be able to run against Seattle. Everybody else has."[44] On January 3, 1988, Moon and the Houston Oilers defeated the Seattle Seahawks in an overtime heartbreaker in the Astrodome, because of course they did.

* * *

Seattle got whipped by Houston, a city called "the Buckle of the Sunbelt."[45] The North already had its Progressive Era, a period of rapid urbanization and political reform. In the 1970s and 1980s the Sunbelt had theirs.[46] A glut of corporations, industry, and employees fled there after the 1947 Taft-Hartley Act permitted Sunbelt states to pass "right-to-work" laws that weakened organized labor.[47] From 1940 to 1980 states below the thirty-seventh parallel increased their population by 112 percent, outpacing the Northeast and Midwest threefold.[48] In the postwar period activists won fights over busing and integration in Houston, Charlotte, and Atlanta, indicating changing attitudes about racial discrimination. Sports presented a safe avenue to negotiate the politics of the post–Jim Crow period, giving previously ignored southern cities capitalist clout and cultural legitimacy.[49] In addition to the exploding popularity of college football and NASCAR in the region, sundry professional sports teams were placed in the Sunbelt between 1970 and 1989: in Miami, Orlando, New Orleans, Phoenix, San Antonio, San Diego. Seattle had serious competition.

Just as colonial Seattle duked it out with Portland and San Francisco for Pacific coast supremacy in the late nineteenth century, the city had to grapple with rivals equally bent on becoming the marquee postindustrial metropolis of the United States. Seattle rapper Sir Mix-A-Lot pandered to the growing popularity of all things Sunbelt with his 1988 single "Square Dance Rap."

Though the Houston Oilers vanquished the 1987 Seahawks, Seattle fans still had a lot to look forward to. Standout prospect center fielder Ken Griffey Jr. entered the Mariners' minor league system in 1987. In the 1989 draft the SuperSonics selected Shawn Kemp, a supremely athletic power forward, then took promising point guard Gary Payton a year later. Suddenly stacked, Seattle's sports teams added to the city's swelling national stature. A 1982 *Sports Illustrated* feature about Seattle gushed over the parks it had created in the Progressive Era, the Forward Thrust initiatives that led to the Kingdome, its endless opportunities for outdoor recreation: "Through two decades of significant change and against a backdrop of the deterioration of American cities generally, Seattle has emerged as an inspiration, testimony to what urban living could be if cities were moderately populated, surrounded by water, and watched over by a citizenry that knows how lucky it is."[50]

While many US cities fought drug wars, deindustrialization, and declining public esteem, a new wave of national attention crested around Seattle. Tourists and transplants came and stayed awhile, some for the towering evergreens and waterfront views, others to make a few bucks. A rare jewel of urban America, capital couldn't wait to buy and sell the Emerald City.

9th Inning

FAKE LEFT, 1990–1999

No matter who prevailed in the 1996 NBA Finals between the Chicago Bulls and the Seattle SuperSonics, capitalism had already won. Chicago was where an influential group of economists stressed lowered taxes, removing regulatory restrictions on American corporations, and shrinking public expenditure on welfare. Described as "tough and smart" on the February 1982 cover of *Esquire* magazine, the ideas came to be known as "neoliberalism."[1] A plethora of lucrative companies called the Seattle area home in the 1990s, lured by Washington State's lack of a wealth or income tax: Microsoft, Nintendo, Costco, REI, Eddie Bauer, KeyBank, Washington Mutual, Boeing, and Starbucks. The two cities made one another. Chicago supplied the philosophical framework for a rise of corporate power; Seattle was proof of concept for free-market ideas. The 1996 NBA Finals pitted the city that created neoliberalism against the city that exemplified it.

In the endurance sport of American politics, neoliberals outlasted their competition. When *Time* magazine showcased neoliberal über-economist Milton Friedman in 1969, his views were far from the postwar orthodoxy of teamwork between labor and capital, government and big corporations. Shocks to the "golden age of capitalism" created a window of opportunity in the 1970s. Inflation soared because of the cost of the Vietnam War, while corporations grew impatient with the high tax rates that subsidized US entitlement programs. As America spiraled through a business recession, the laissez-faire ideas of Friedman's "Chicago School" of neoliberal economists gained traction.

After he was elected president in 1980, Ronald Reagan tapped Friedman as one of his chief economic advisers. Lowered taxes, decreased spending on social services, and deregulation of America's banking and financial sectors became the status quo. Corporate Seattle benefited from the success of the Chicago School. After acquiring Starbucks in 1987, Seattle businessman Howard Schultz targeted the Windy City as a new market.[2] Deindustrialized Chicago had shed tens of thousands of industrial jobs by the mid-1980s, many of them replaced by workers in the white collar and service sectors—the perfect clientele for coffee, the official performance enhancement beverage of postindustrial America. Schultz descended upon Chicago, opening dozens of stores while working overtime to combat unions formed by organizing baristas. By the 1990s, Starbucks operated thousands of stores worldwide, adding to Seattle's glowing national profile as a pro-business paradise.[3]

While Chicago supported corporate Seattle's success, two Seattleites assisted one of the Chicago School's great success stories.[4] In the birthplace of neoliberalism, Bulls guard Michael Jordan constructed a behemoth personal brand on being the consummate winner, flaunting sponsorships from Gatorade, Chevrolet, and McDonald's. Former Seattle SuperSonics publicist Rick Welts fertilized Jordan's rise. When Welts began work in the NBA front office in 1982, he wielded his experience of selling the Black Sonics to white Seattle. Under his tenure in the 1970s, the Sonics had been perennially among the league's leaders in fan support in the NBA. While professional basketball struggled with stereotypes of selfish African American athletes, Welts informed local press that Sonics players would be donating their playoff bonuses to poor Seattle youth.[5] At work for NBA commissioner David Stern, Welts courted corporate clients who formerly shunned the league; he lured AT&T and Denny's to sponsor new All-Star Weekend festivities in 1984. A by-product of marketing techniques first test-driven in Seattle, Jordan's legend grew when he won the slam-dunk contest at this exhibition in 1987 and 1988.

Thanks in part to Seattle filmmaker Jim Riswold, Michael Jordan couldn't be easily racially pigeonholed.[6] In 1986, Nike contracted the Sonics marketing staffer to direct a series of ads showcasing Jordan's personal charisma.[7] The commercials cast Jordan opposite Spike Lee, whose indie movie *She's Gotta Have It* inspired Riswold's edgy black-and-white cinematography. A University of Washington grad, Riswold directed commercials that catapulted Jordan's appeal as a pitchman for Coca-Cola, Hanes, and Wheaties. A famously vindictive brand ambassador with something to prove after an eighteen-month baseball sabbatical, Jordan and the Chicago Bulls set an NBA record regular season wins in the 1995–96 season, romping through the Eastern Conference to land back in the NBA Finals. The Sonics were only eight games behind Chicago's record pace that year; they grounded the defending champion Houston Rockets in the Western Conference Semifinals, on the way to their first NBA Finals appearance since 1979.

Two cities that wouldn't exist if it weren't for Gilded Age railroads, neoliberal Chicago and corporate Seattle were on a collision course.

* * *

Seattle had a Jordan of its own in Ken Griffey Jr.—a hypercompetitive superstar with prodigious athletic gifts that transcended baseball. Air Jordan's rising star was the outgrowth of a quarter century of policies and cultural trends that stimulated "Black Capitalism."[8] Griffey was this template's 2.0 version. Equally at home in the worlds of Sir Mix-A-Lot and the television sitcom *Frasier*, Griffey got shouted out in rap records while being a role model who chewed bubble gum instead of tobacco.[9] A Gatorade jingle urged kids to "be like Mike" in 1993, but it was Griffey whose autograph Jordan sought at Camden Yards during the All-Star Game that year.

Before Griffey, professional baseball in Seattle seemed cursed. And maybe it was: an ancient seafaring superstition held that an upside-down trident was bad luck for sailors. From the team's inception in 1977 until 1986, the Mariners made a topsy-turvy pitchfork an "M" on their hats and jerseys.[10] They missed the playoffs every year while doing so, failed to post a winning record, and came within ten wins of doing so only once. The Mariners removed the trident when Griffey landed in the team's farm system in 1987; they immediately set a franchise record for wins, posted a winning record for the first time ever in 1991, then did it again in 1993. Seattle was a franchise on the rise.

New talent was as big a factor as no tridents. In 1987, Mariner management promoted Edgar Martinez, from the minor leagues.[11] Seattle fleeced the Yankees for slugger Jay Buhner in 1988, a trade later immortalized in a 1995 episode of *Seinfeld*, when the irascible Frank Costanza berates Yankee owner George Steinbrenner for letting Buhner escape.[12] The Mariners acquired fireballer Randy Johnson in 1989, then sought a new skipper; Lou Piniella joined in 1993, bringing the winning ways he learned as an important part of the great New York Yankee teams of the 1970s and as manager of the 1990 World Series champion Cincinnati Reds. Seattle's assortment of talent coalesced under Piniella's leadership.

Managers manage and owners spend money, but professional sports are an entertainment industry driven by stars. In Ken Griffey Jr., Seattle had the brightest of them all. Born George Kenneth Griffey Jr. on November 21, 1969, Junior's dad had been a speedy base runner who won two World Series championships in Cincinnati in the mid-1970s. Though the Griffeys benefited from Jackie Robinson's integration of the sport in 1947, Black ballplayers still faced barriers. A year after Senior was traded to the Yankees in 1981, Junior joined him in the dugout. A Yankee Stadium field hand scolded them, saying team management didn't allow children so close to the field. Senior instructed his son to leave—but not before directing his attention to third base, where white Yankee third baseman Graig Nettles was fielding ground balls with his son. Junior noted the disrespect and harbored a lifelong hatred of New York.[13]

"When you're a center fielder, you're a different animal," Junior once said. "Everything hit to you is fair."[14] In a 1990 game against the Yankees in Yankee Stadium, Jesse Barfield hit what seemed a certain home run. As the ball drifted to the fence in left center field, Griffey darted, scaled the wall, and robbed a stunned Barfield. Junior laughed a hearty laugh of revenge. His dad greeted him in the dugout; the Mariners had signed him earlier in the year, making Senior and Junior the first father-son duo to play on the same team.

For years the trope of the absentee Black father was used to explain why a disproportionate number of African Americans lived in poverty. Senator Daniel Patrick Moynihan advanced the idea in his influential 1965 report "The Negro Family: The Case for National Action": "As a result of divorce, separation, and desertion, a very large percent of Negro families are headed by females. This family disorganization is found to be diminishing among whites."[15] Moynihan's baseless notion of Black "family disorganization" was used in the Reagan and Clinton years to curtail welfare subsidies that all Americans—including single Black mothers—benefited from. The wholesome father-son Griffey spectacle dignified the stereotype of the deadbeat Black dad by defying it. In a September 1990 game Senior and Junior hit back-to-back home runs.

The 1994 baseball season figured to be a great one for Junior, already a four-time All-Star. He won the July 11 Home Run Derby, baseball's equivalent of the NBA slam-dunk contest. When regular season play resumed after the All-Star Game, Junior had a shot at beating Roger Maris's 1961 all-time single season home-run total. But Griffey, in his own words, "picked a bad year to have a good year."[16] On July 19, four fifteen-pound ceiling tiles dropped from the Kingdome roof, crushing some empty seats.[17] County officials canceled all remaining home games, condemning the Mariners to play the rest of their schedule on the road. After the sky fell, the entire season came crashing down. In August 1994 the Major League Baseball Players Association went on strike to resist a cap on salaries that team owners wanted to impose. The season was canceled. Super Nintendo released a signature video game for Griffey in 1994 but had to give all players but Junior fake names because the players' union didn't license the game.

Stars like Griffey had the most to lose from the institution of a salary cap. Consequently, baseball's elite went to bat to end the labor unrest. On February 20, 1995, Ken Griffey Jr. and Jay Buhner traveled to the Washington State capitol to support a bill that would disallow replacement players from playing in the Kingdome.[18] "We're the ones sitting at home watching golf," pleaded Griffey during his testimony. "It's time people speak up."[19] The strike ended in spring of 1995. Junior's career in politics had only just begun.

* * *

With its ample opportunities for outdoor recreation and comparatively cheap housing costs, 1990s Seattle was a Peter Pan city that never grew up, thriving in an era where that was suddenly a good thing. The twentieth century saw world wars, ethnic conflicts, nasty proxy battles between capitalism and communism. Demonstrations for civil rights, antiwar protests, and labor disputes rocked American cities; but as the year 2000 approached, political scientist Francis Fukuyama's influential 1991 book

Ken Griffey Jr. wearing a Nike leisure suit at a 1993 press conference announcing his new Nintendo baseball game. Griffey saved baseball in the city of Seattle. Museum of History and Industry, Seattle, *Seattle Post-Intelligencer* (2000.107.19930511.1.08).

The End of History predicted a world united by consumerism. When the Soviet Union dissolved that year, capitalism stood as the global economic orthodoxy. A haven for big business, Seattle became America's "it" city—the frontier metropolis that would bridge the country's contentious twentieth century with its self-congratulatory twenty-first.

Just as the mythology of manifest destiny once held that the United States had a divine mandate to spread its wings from sea to shining sea, the new mythos of neoliberalism made Seattle the "shining city on a hill" described by Ronald Reagan. In *The End of the Myth*, historian Greg Grandin describes how the West was a blank canvas for President Reagan, who liked to deploy frontier imagery to project an image of a boundless American horizon: "Americans believed about the West not so much what was true," said Reagan, "but what they thought ought to be true."[20] The American West promised a fresh start. In the future it symbolized, there would be no racial conflicts in a country that had transcended them; no poverty for anyone who didn't deserve it; fewer regulations for corporations that created the country's prosperity. As the Sonics went on their playoff run in May 1996, a cover story about Seattle in *Newsweek* praised "the drive of CEO Howard Schultz" and noted the potential "civic-minded applications of Microsoft's untapped billions."[21]

When the USSR collapsed in 1991, not everybody celebrated. The Seattle newspaper *Freedom Socialist* mourned Soviet socialism, writing: "The ruling class gloats that the world's worker state collapsed."[22] The publication backed the city council campaign of democratic socialist Yolanda Alaniz, a union member and self-proclaimed "Chicana champion of the poor and underpaid."[23] She captured 17 percent of the citywide electorate in Seattle's November 1991 election; voters weren't in any mood for doctrinaire socialism.

On a well-attended campaign stop through Seattle's Pike Place Market on October 22, 1992, presidential hopeful Bill Clinton reiterated his promise to end welfare entitlements started by Franklin Roosevelt during the Great Depression. Twenty thousand onlookers cheered. Past Democrat presidents took on civil rights and built "Model Cities." Lyndon B. Johnson envisioned a "Great Society" in 1964; Carter decried the influence of consumerism on US life in 1979. Once elected, Clinton was content to be corporate America's pimp. "I'm not ashamed that I've asked countries to buy from Boeing, and I'll do it again if given half the chance," he said when he visited Seattle as president in 1993.[24]

Neoliberals like Clinton believed the free market's invisible hand could smooth over yesteryear's conflicts; many spectators wanted sports to do the same thing. In 1990, Atlanta mogul Ted Turner made Seattle the site of his Goodwill Games, an international sports competition that promised an end to the geopolitical squabbles of the Olympics during the Cold War. TBS and TNT cameras captured Seattle's scenic surroundings; CNN journalist Larry King opined: "Seattle has the friendliest people I've ever met."[25] Beneath the amiable surface, however, were long-standing divides. On a press tour through Seattle's Central Area, Soviet journalists couldn't understand why so many Black Seattleites still lived in poverty.[26]

Despite the happy face it presented to the world during the Goodwill Games, Seattle had a serious race problem. Aggressive police with a mandate to fight the drug war surveilled Black neighborhoods and killed innocent people. In 1995, Seattle cops testified that they "accidentally" shot unarmed Black Seattleite Antonio Dunsmore in the back of the head at the Garfield Community Center. They repeated the excuse when they shot a Black resident of the Central Area at point-blank range a year later.[27] Between 1992 and 1996 four Black Seattle churches fell to targeted arson—a time, wrote historian John M. Findlay, when "American white supremacist groups in the late twentieth century were attracted to the region as one place where their goal of an exclusively white population seems attainable."[28] Seattle was enlightened enough to elect Norm Rice as the city's first Black mayor in 1990, but in office he was subject to unconscionable racist smears. These were the kinds of conflicts that were supposed to belong to the gnarly twentieth century, not the coming twenty-first; to older history-bound cities, not "exceptional" ones like Seattle.

Seattle's political conflicts were sanitized with the whitewash of popular culture. When the city was more commercialized than ever, Nirvana and Soundgarden popularized the anti-capitalist angst of grunge originated by Black Seattleite Tina Bell. While wealth inequalities in the city widened, the sitcom *Frasier* (1993–2004) made viewers laugh at privileged three-piecers in affluent Queen Anne. While congestion made commutes a nightmare, a main character in the 1992 film *Singles* dreamed of a Seattle with adequate

Washington State teachers' union leader Constance Rice and her husband, Norm Rice, take in a Mariners game at the Kingdome, 1990. Norm was elected the first Black mayor of Seattle that year. Courtesy of the Seattle Municipal Archives, item 174211.

mass transit. While racial divides remained, Seattle rappers Sir Mix-A-Lot and Ishmael Butler (of Digable Planets) made the city seem a bastion of inclusive cool. The SuperSonics were the cherry on this sundae; a team that congealed all the things many hated about cities—noise, animus, the concentration of ethnic populations—into a fan-friendly physical performance. "People in Seattle are civilized, and what I love about the Sonics is that they're not like this at all," wrote white Seattle author David Shields in 1995.[29]

Led by mouthy point guard Gary Payton and the animated Shawn Kemp, the SuperSonics were a far cry from the corporate-friendly professionalism of the Chicago Bulls. *Sports Illustrated* labeled them "the most impudent team in the league."[30] A 1994 *Esquire* feature revealed a brash squad of Generation Xers who had group sex and talked mountains of shit.[31] Gary Payton cut a rap record; on KJR 950, play-by-play man Kevin Calabro called games with a speed and intensity that matched the Sonics themselves. Even head coach George Karl got in on the hip-hop bravado, dissing the rival Houston Rockets in the press. In the Sonics, nice and quiet Seattle had found a very loud civic avatar.

Seattle's raging civic ego was its basketball team; but when the squad offended white spectators, the results could be incendiary. After struggling Sonic guard Kendall Gill was diagnosed with clinical depression in 1995, a Seattle sports radio host mocked him: "If Gill were averaging twenty points a game, would we be talking about depression?" The old trope of Black athletes lacking the "clutch gene" to perform under pressure resurfaced after the number-one-seeded Sonics lost to the lowly Denver Nuggets early in the 1994 playoffs. When Denver's Dikembe Mutombo—a seven-foot-one center from Zaire—returned to play the Sonics the next year, Seattle sports radio anchors instructed fans to "white him out" with colorless clothing.[32] If Seattle had transcended the contentious politics of the past, it sure had a funny way of showing it.

In *Selling Seattle: Representing Contemporary Urban America*, media studies scholar James Lyons describes how America's urbanist illuminati anointed Seattle the city of the future in glowing magazine profiles and mass media in the 1990s. The city's sheening new downtown reflected that status, with FAO Schwarz, GameWorks, and Barnes & Noble all opening doors there in the decade. NikeTown was the grand temple of the capitalist archdiocese that downtown had become, its glass windows and tabernacle doors opening to worshippers of the altar mammon in July 1996. "They have a lot of stuff in here, I can spend so much money," said one of the faithful the day the sports apparel store opened, fulfilling historian Roger Sale's 1976 prophecy that "Seattle has become a great place in which to buy things."[33] The waning years of the twentieth century saw many Seattleites adopt the turn-of-the-millennium creed of materialism, replacing yesteryear's dead sea scrolls with lengthy receipts gleaned from a long day of shopping. Unfortunately the godlike invisible hand that economist Adam Smith said guided the free market reproduced Seattle's foundational disparities: "Half an hour from Planet Hollywood and NikeTown," bemoaned a July 1996 edition of the *Seattle Post-Intelligencer,* "there are Indians living in shacks as decrepit as any in Depression-era Appalachia."[34]

* * *

Back in the 1940s, *Boeing Magazine* rebranded "progress" as the pursuit of profit, separating the concept from social movements. Fifty years later, with the exploding commercialization of American sports and the concurrent valorization of the rich and famous, athletes became proxy politicians with huge platforms, expected to serve as role models for children while fielding questions more befitting of elected officials. As the 1996 NBA Finals between Seattle and Chicago began, reporters asked Michael Jordan if he had plans to inspect Nike's use of sweatshop labor in the company's industrial plants overseas.[35] Was the meddlesome media unaware that the prime minister of US capitalism was busy with the insurrectionist Sonics?

The Chicago Bulls trampled the Sonics in Game One of the Finals by a score of 107–90 on June 4, 1996, then won again two days later, 92–88. Back in Seattle for Game Three, the Bulls shut up Seattle and its noisy fans with brilliant ball movement and individual scoring from Jordan, who had 28 points at halftime. Chicago rolled, 108–86. "The first three games, Jordan ripped a hole in our ass," remembered Gary Payton.[36]

In the latter stages of his career, Jordan added a lethal fadeaway jumper to his arsenal, a weapon that was as physical as it was psychological. Because nervous defenders overplayed him, lunging while reacting to the icon's every move, Jordan learned to use their aggressiveness against them, faking left, then jumping right, falling away from the pressure instead of meeting it. Harvard professor Henry Louis Gates Jr. saw the shot as a metaphor for Jordan's cross-racial appeal, simulating his ability to misdirect racial type-casts into a celebration of American commercialism.[37] Whatever Jordan's offensive attack symbolized, Seattle had to find a way to stop it.

At the beginning of the series, George Karl had avoided having Gary Payton guard Jordan. Although Payton was the 1996 Defensive Player of the Year, Karl felt the team would benefit if the star guard conserved his energy for offense. When the Sonics went down 0–3, there was nothing left to lose. Payton frustrated Jordan in Game Four, holding him to a miserable 6-for-19 shooting night.[38] The Sonics prevailed, then followed up with an 89–78 victory in Game Five to make the series 3–2. Chicago's championship coronation had suddenly become competitive.

By design, the Seattle SuperSonics were a frenetic team with few set offensive plays. When they were playing well, as they did in Games Four and Five against Chicago, they engaged in risky traps to rattle their opponents and generate easy transition baskets on steals and turnovers. But Seattle's gift was also its curse. The Sonics could rack up home wins in the regular season when its crowd could rev their hyperactive defense; but when games slowed in tempo, they were less able to generate the same dynamism. With the series back in the Windy City, Phil Jackson focused on postindustrial Seattle's existential flaw: its inability to manufacture quality shots.[39] On June 15, 1996, the Chicago Bulls won Game Six of the NBA Finals, 87–75, to capture the title. League marketers were perhaps not displeased. Although the Sonics were a young team with a bright future, Michael Jordan was worth billions in merchandising and ad revenue to the NBA, making him the face not just of basketball but global capitalism at large.[40] Jordan had a lot more to lose than Seattle, and so he didn't.

Although the Sonics didn't take the title, Seattle was nonetheless triumphant in its perennial quest to become a premier American city. As Seattle music and Seattle-set movies and television shows framed it as the hippest city in the country, the 1996 NBA Finals were one more platform from which to announce how cool it was. After Seattle's final home win of the season in Game Five against Chicago, *NBA on NBC* announcer Marv Albert was stunned to see Sonics fans stay at KeyArena to give the team an ovation. A fan waved a sign that read "LEGALIZE KEMP," a pun on contemporary debates about legalized marijuana. Seattle's rep as a forward-thinking city was reinforced.

The image of Seattle as a city floating above history was a fiction, but its social impact was real. The blockbuster 1993 film *Sleepless in Seattle* capitalized on the city's rep for scenic natural settings and high standards of living; a character played by Tom Hanks escapes neoliberal Chicago for the laid-back environs of the Emerald City, eventually falling in love with Meg Ryan, who flees Baltimore for Chicago, in search of what she calls "a real change." In real life many migrated to Seattle in search of a fresh start: Seattle's 9.1 percent population growth spurt between 1990 and 2000 was the largest in any decade since droves of midcentury workers had moved to the city to work at Boeing. The westward march was large enough to annoy Kurt Cobain, who in 1992 complained of bands pretending they were from Seattle in order to sign record deals. The invitation of Nirvana's hit single "Come as You Are" apparently didn't extend to grifters searching for their cut of Seattle's cultural cachet.[41]

There was no turning back now: the town that chased the railroad had arrived. But a recent sports triumph on par with the celebrated Chicago

Bulls and the dynastic Dallas Cowboys still eluded the city—as did a truly great ballpark. The Kingdome was falling apart. It was up to the Mariners to make Seattle an even bigger big-league city.

* * *

The Seattle Mariners saw firsthand how a new ballpark could excite a community. They were Cleveland's opponent for the April 4, 1994, debut of Jacobs Field, where President Clinton threw out the ceremonial first pitch. Throughout urban America team owners leveraged the sentimental ties that fan bases had to their franchises, pressuring political leadership into building new stadiums under the threat of relocation. Underneath the façade of "fan support" and "civic pride," sports franchises were behaving like any other corporation that packed up and left for greener outfields. Civic leaders craved the promised economic benefits of new ballparks that many credible economists maintained were dubious at best. Between 1990 and 2000 publicly funded baseball stadiums opened in Arlington, Atlanta, Chicago, Cleveland, Denver, Detroit, and Phoenix.

This was how cities worked now. During the "golden age of capitalism" from 1945 through 1973, US municipalities subsisted on steady tax revenue and federal funds. But the one-two punch of deindustrialization and neoliberalism created a new status quo where corporations fled the country for cheaper labor and lower taxes, and thus manufacturing jobs disappeared. Cities were subsequently forced to scramble for patchwork schemes to replace the steady revenue once provided by their plush tax bases. For struggling cities, sports became a new hustle.[42] The benefits were unevenly distributed.

In April 1995, Seattle hosted the NCAA Men's Basketball Final Four at the Kingdome. City officials placed a giant basketball atop the Space Needle and welcomed tourists to the shiny Washington State Convention Center; Microsoft held a virtual rally with ESPN to hype the games. With news cameras swarming, a group advocating for the city's homeless population staged a bold demonstration, setting up tents for a homeless encampment in a vacant lot near the Kingdome where the games were played. Seattle police swept the encampment and arrested all seventeen protestors.[43] With sports tourism part of the winner-take-all neoliberal social order, American cities had no time for losers.

A few weeks after the NCAA Final Four in Seattle, the 1995 MLB campaign started promisingly for the Seattle Mariners, who began the year 6–1. The M's then went on one of their vintage losing skids, falling to the California Angels by ten runs on May 5 and dropping eleven of its next seventeen games. On May 26, disaster struck. While chasing down a ball hit to right-center at the Kingdome, Ken Griffey Jr. sprinted face-first into the Kingdome's outfield wall, making an impossible behind-the-back catch but fracturing his wrist badly in the process. Pouncing to reinforce a neoliberal narrative that castigated baseball players for going on strike, the *Chicago Tribune* celebrated Griffey's catch as an example of "hustle" that would reattract fans who had been turned off by the labor stoppage.[44] The pro-capitalist moralizing was of little comfort to the Mariners, who would have to play the next three months without their star.

It was all the Kingdome's fault. Athletes played there on a thin layer of synthetic turf stretched over concrete, making injuries more likely than on real grass. Griffey had lobbied the stadium's keepers to tweak the outfield walls to make it easier for him to field.[45] When the Forward Thrust proposal for the Kingdome went before voters in 1968, one of its major selling points was its affordability. Seattleites got what they paid for—large and cheap, their ballpark looked like a brutalist Big Mac.

Sports fans everywhere took notice when the sublime Camden Yards opened in Baltimore in 1992. For years, modernist colossuses like the Astrodome and Kingdome were the national standard. Coincident with the waves of gentrifiers repopulating America's inner cities in the 1980s and 1990s, Camden started a new trend toward old-time ballparks in the city centers of urban America. Tim Kurkijan of *Sports Illustrated* called it "a real ballpark built into a real downtown of a real city," then lamented "the concrete flying saucers that landed in too many cities 25 years ago."[46] Emerald City officials turned green with envy.

While Ken Griffey Jr. was sidelined with injury, King County executive Gary Locke corralled the King County Council to place a countywide sales tax increase on the September ballot to pay for a new, natural grass, retractable-roof ballpark.[47] The park would be state-of-the-art, and the Mariners—

owned by the chairman of the Nintendo corporation—wanted the welfare state to pay for it. Otherwise, the Mariners would be relocated. With a vote on the new baseball stadium looming on September 19, the Mariners' 1995 season became a direct referendum on the future of professional baseball in the city. Had Seattle folded, voters may have been less likely to fund a new ballpark, and the M's would have been moved. But under Lou Piniella's leadership, the Mariners managed to tread water, going 37–38 in Griffey's absence. With Junior back in the lineup, Seattle faced a pressure cooker where their on-field performance would play a decisive role in determining the stadium vote. Their backs to the wall, they started winning.

After the Mariners were 54–55 on August 23, 1995, they won three of four games at home against the Yankees. Series wins against Boston, Baltimore, Minnesota, and Chicago followed. The Mariners swept the Kansas City Royals in early September while donning throwback uniforms celebrating the Seattle Steelheads Negro League team.[48] Seattle was suddenly within striking distance of the imploding California Angels, who at one point led the division by eleven games. In the thirty-four games between Griffey's return on August 15 and the September 19 stadium election, the falling Angels went 8–23, while the Mariners were 19–13. Seattle was making its case for a new stadium the best way it could. Teal "REFUSE TO LOSE" placards became ubiquitous, referring both to the Mariners' flood of wins and to the town's desire to keep the franchise. "We can't do this without the fans," Griffey said the day before the stadium election. "We need them at the games, and we need them at the voting booth."[49]

On the night of the September 19 election, the "yes" vote on the stadium held a narrow lead of four thousand votes. The odd-year primary had an unprecedented turnout of 52 percent. A deluge of absentee votes still remained to be counted. It had been a one-sided campaign, with the Mariners spending more than $586,000 in support of the effort. Corporate contributions came from Boeing and AT&T. Campaign operatives reported that on the day of the election, nearly a thousand volunteers called thirty thousand voters, begging them to go to the polls. By contrast, a group calling itself "Citizens for More Important Things" spent $48,800 total.[50]

In a city where homeless Seattleites slept beneath towering new highrises, anti-stadium activists hoped the absurdity of blowing taxpayer money on circuses instead of bread would speak for itself. They were right. A week after the election, King County officials called it: by the tight margin of 246,500 to 245,518—a difference of 0.19 percent—the stadium was defeated. Mariner management gave area officials until October 30, 1995, to find a way to fund a new stadium. Barring something strange, the team would most certainly be sold and relocated.

To save their season and remain in Seattle, the Mariners needed two miracles: one beneath the Kingdome's rotunda roof, and another beneath the Olympia statehouse's. After the September 19 stadium vote failed, the Mariners went on a brief slide but rebounded to win a one-game playoff against California to capture the 1995 American League West division on October 2. The win punched their ticket to the American League Divisional Series (ALDS) against the New York Yankees. Ken Griffey Jr. was a machine in the first two games of the series against his nemesis New York at Yankee Stadium, but Seattle lost both games on October 3 and 4. With the best-of-five series heading back to the Kingdome, the Mariners had to win three straight games to advance.

Meanwhile, a stadium deal seemed unlikelier than ever: There was speculation in Olympia that Democratic governor Mike Lowry would call a special session of the state legislature to authorize a ballpark funding package. Republicans controlled the House of Representatives and were reluctant to play ball. However rooted baseball may have been in American traditionalism, nostalgia wouldn't entice the Grand Old Party of budget hawks and austerity devotees to raise taxes. While Washington Democrats pushed for a stadium deal, the GOP masqueraded as populists by opposing this particular corporate giveaway. *Seattle Times* columnist Michelle Malkin—later a regular on Fox News—sounded rather like a socialist when she decried: "The civic charade whose primary objective is to distort market forces and government policy so that the many pay for the preferences of the few."[51]

Whatever Washington State politicians decided to do, the Mariners had to hold up their end of the bargain. In the ALDS against Gotham, Seattle had a chance to slay Goliath. It had a superstar who made it his personal mission to destroy the baseball team from New York, the city that Seattle settlers believed their colonial outpost would one day succeed. The Mariners could directly influence the political process by winning games to rally elected officials for a new stadium. Sport and politics collided, with hundreds of millions of dollars of public money hanging in the balance of balls and strikes, wins and losses.

In the two games in the Bronx, some degenerate Yankee fans threw debris at the Mariners. Jay Buhner vowed revenge, touting the consumer trinkets of his ascendant city: "We'll get back at them when they come to the Kingdome. We'll throw Starbucks coffee. Or some Windows '95 software. Or a Pearl Jam CD." At home in the Kingdome, Seattle won all three remaining games against New York, culminating in a Game Five epic that ended on an Edgar Martinez double that scored a speeding Junior from first in the bottom of the eleventh inning.

After advancing, Seattle took two of the first three games from Cleveland in the American League Championship Series (ALCS) on October 10 and 13. Seattle's playoff dramatics swayed enough statewide constituents to tell their state representatives to take action to save the team. In between Games One and Three of the ALCS against Cleveland, Governor Lowry convened an emergency session of the Washington State Legislature. The question at hand was simple: now that the Mariners were on the brink of their first World Series appearance in franchise history, which state reps would like to take credit for allowing the team to move to Tampa?[52]

On October 14, 1995, the state legislature approved a stadium funding package worth $625 million. With the Mariners two wins away from the World Series, politicians had overruled the will of Seattle voters to build a new ballpark. Two wins away from the World Series, the Seattle Mariners had saved themselves.

★ ★ ★

After public funding for the new stadium was secured, the Mariners took the most Mariners course of action possible: promptly losing three straight games to swiftly exit the playoffs. The weight of the season had finally caught up, the lactic acid of civic engagement sapping their tired legs. "I felt like I had all of Washington State on me as I pitched," said Randy Johnson of the postseason run.[53] Though the Mariners were

bounced from the playoffs and failed to make them the next year, Ken
Griffey Junior's celebrity grew anyway.

Like Jordan, Junior was a Nike-endorsed athlete with a signature shoe
after his bubbly Air Max 1s went live at NikeTown following the Mariners'
exit from the 1995 postseason. In their respective sports, the two players
were titans; they made consumers feel they could support the free market
and empower minorities—that is, be both traditionalist and progressive—
by buying their shoes. Nike marketers seized on Junior's popularity with
the ultimate publicity stunt. They would build him the biggest platform
possible. In 1996, they would run Ken Griffey Jr. for president of the United
States of America.[54]

During the 1996 MLB regular season, Nike's "Griffey in '96" advertising
campaign blurred fact and fiction. Although he received write-in votes
around the country, Griffey's name wasn't printed on any ballots. The fictional presidential run took place as a series of television commercials that
posited Griffey as the progressive pick for commander in chief. Seattle's
mascot—Mariner Moose—was staged as his running mate. Washington,
DC, funk genius George Clinton served as campaign manager. One of
the "Griffey for President" ads began with a grinning Junior superimposed
over a waving American flag; Clinton narrates that Junior has "the power
of a young Teddy Roosevelt."[55] In another ad Junior promises to legalize a
dangerous fielding game called "pepper" in all playgrounds. Clinton says
that Junior's friendship with the Mariner Moose demonstrates his commitment to animal rights. Though fake, the campaign stirred excitement.
"Griffey for President" bumper stickers appeared on cars in place of real
candidates. Phoenix voters hit the streets to campaign for Junior before
Arizona's February 1996 presidential primary.[56] Griffey tolerated the presidential hype initially but became annoyed when reporters peppered him
with questions about gay rights and reproductive freedom. "I got asked
'what is your stand on abortion?,'" Griffey said at the time. "The campaign
is not about that." Sick of it all, he pulled the plug on the presidential run
in September 1996.

America's political process had become the big butt of an elaborate
joke, such as the kind immortalized by Seattle rapper Sir Mix-A-Lot's 1992
celebration of fulsome derrieres, "Baby Got Back." Earnest political engagement seemed an absurd proposition when the resistance movements of the

1960s and 1970s were squashed, and when "Atari Democrats" looked more and more like Republicans, steering taxpayer money to boost tech tycoons like Bill Gates and Paul Allen.[57] A titular progressive, Bill Clinton signed the North American Free Trade Agreement in 1994, harming American unions and echoing Reagan's strikebreaking ways. If there was no real left, what was left to fight with?

The Republican Party didn't have to take control of the US Congress and House of Representatives to kick millions of vulnerable Americans off the country's welfare rolls in 1994 (they did, and they did). Clinton had eagerly campaigned on "ending welfare as we know it," then made good on his progress by replacing Aid to Families with Dependent Children with the work-for-welfare program TANF (Temporary Assistance for Needy Families).[58] Consequently, people who couldn't work for a living were punished for being disabled. Juxtaposed with this termination of financial assistance to America's most vulnerable, sports spectacles that celebrated the big and strong seemed like cultural legitimization of an unconscionably cruel social order. Millions watched as Seattleite offensive lineman Mike Utley was paralyzed during a game between the Detroit Lions and LA Rams in November 1991.[59]

In Seattle, widespread closures of public bowling alleys in the 1990s pointed to declining feelings of shared political destiny.[60] In his influential 1995 essay "Bowling Alone," author Robert Putnam had argued that the disappearance of organized bowling—together with reduced activity in American unions and shrinking membership in social clubs that were founded during the Progressive Era—pointed to the "notable decline of American civil society."[61] Though Putnam had a point, simple obits of progressivism don't tell the entire story. In spite of—or rather *because of*—its status as a capitalist hub, Seattle was a site of resistance.

As the city's voters mulled new taxes for the Mariners' stadium in 1995, a Seattle woman penned an anti-ballpark letter to the editor of the *Seattle Times*: "When I read of cuts in state social services, I must object to this frivolous amusement. Let's have money going towards our schools, community centers, and our public transportation system."[62] The Mariners' stadium vote appeared on the same ballot as the "Seattle Commons," a sixty-one-acre park in South Lake Union. To be located in the heart of the city where Virgil Bogue had proposed a grand subway station and public playfield in 1912,

FAKE LEFT

the plan was the brainchild of billionaire Paul Allen. Seattle voters rejected it, wondering why he couldn't pay for his own park.[63]

The same Seattle electorate that opposed stadium welfare and a corporate playground in September 1995 turned around and approved the construction of a new subway system in November 1996. After centrist Clinton was reelected and Republicans retained control of Congress, pundits that year pronounced the death of progressivism. Jeffrey C. Isaac wrote in *Dissent* magazine that "the 'social contract' governing American politics since 1945 has broken down, [repudiating] the spirit of progressive reform." Contradicting the doomsday analysis, 60 percent of Seattleites elected to tax themselves to build mass transit—an achievement that Seattle couldn't accomplish in the actual Progressive Era or during midcentury liberalism's peak in the 1960s.[64] If progressivism had expired, its specter was a force to be reckoned with.

For at least some of the hundreds of thousands of Seattleites who supported public funding for a new baseball stadium, something other than the corporate hegemony of billionaire team owners may have been a deciding factor. Quaint Camden Yards was a Progressive Era throwback to the halcyon days of April 1912, when the titanic ballparks Tiger Stadium, Fenway Park, and Crosley Field all opened within days of each other. Baltimore's beautiful ballpark resurrected a period when budding polities showed themselves off with great public works. Seattleites wanted in.

When it debuted in July 1999 in Pioneer Square, Safeco Field was quickly considered one of America's great baseball venues. Its airy steel webbing and retractable roof captured the rich interplay between raw nature and urban grandeur that defined Seattle. Safeco Field was a great place to watch a ball game with friends, with coworkers, with visiting family who wanted to understand the charm of this city, which had lured their relatives to pack up and move there. The source of Seattle's pull was in what *Sports Illustrated* called the city's "civic pride and uncommon urban vigor"—qualities especially on display in this big, beautiful ballpark.[65] It was love at first sight. The fact that the stadium which housed this affair was also a massive corporate swindle might have seemed, to some Seattleites, collateral damage on the way to a good time with great views.

The indoor Kingdome's days were numbered. Instead of cloistering into online chat rooms—arguing about the O. J. verdict or Clinton's cigars on nameless listservs—the ideal city for droves of Seattleites was one where mass transit took them out to a ball game.

While the Washington Huskies put together a national championship season in 1991, campus activists successfully lobbied that fall for a U-Pass program that was one of the first college transit subsidies in the country.[66] The reform recalled the 1918 expansion of the city's streetcar system, which permitted Seattleites to bypass angry motorists and Model-T traffic jams when Husky Stadium opened two years later. Through the 1920s, before the streetcar system was dismantled during the Great Depression, Seattle trollies bore placards advertising game times for UW football. Winning at sports and winning at city planning reinforced one another. Why did it have to stop with the Huskies?

When the Seahawks threatened to relocate in 1996, Seattle voters in 1997 narrowly approved a football stadium proposal to keep them in town with a new facility to replace the Kingdome. The Paul Allen–backed measure barely passed: voters saw Allen was rich enough to buy the Seahawks, which made him rich enough to buy his own stadium. But because the arena plan paid for itself with sales fees assessed at the stadium, already existing lodging taxes, and new state lottery games that people were free to play or not, it was more palatable to Seattle voters than the straightforward corporate giveaway of the baseball stadium that voters had declined in 1995. The details were perhaps a little convoluted for the layperson, but the big picture was clear: With the new subway approved in 1996 and the new stadium approved in 1997, Seattleites could soon ride trains to watch the Seahawks within city limits, bringing the college-town vibes of University of Washington football to the big leagues. For decades, Seattleites had found the game-day experience of marauding through the University District on the way to watch football infectious; with the Seahawks, they doubled down on sports urbanism. The triumphant football stadium proposal wasn't hurt by the fact that it would also be a professional soccer facility, activating a fervent fan base for the sport played on public pitches throughout the city.[67]

A century after the Progressive Era, Seattle was still a city whose central political preoccupations were playground and transit proposals, rivalries with other cities, and the role of corporate giants in determining the city's collective fate. The 1990s elections over stadiums and subways reveal a left-of-center city with serious concerns about wealth inequality and the influence of big businesses on civic life. Seattle voters narrowly rejected a public stadium subsidy for a team owned by Nintendo in 1995, narrowly approved one that carried more of its own fiscal water in 1997, and—in between, in 1996—approved the subway system that Virgil Bogue and James Ellis couldn't win approval for. Seattle fans cheered the Mariners' 1995 playoff run in the public arena they approved in 1968 but drew a line at building an aristocrat amusement park in the heart of the city in 1995. Though Seattleites lived in a city that mega-corporations called home, many of them balked when those corporations tried to run roughshod over them. In the final days of the twentieth century, their resistance took center stage.

Held from November 30 through December 3, 1999, the World Trade Organization conference was intended as a neoliberal jamboree, promoting free trade and corporate supremacy in the downtown Seattle confines that housed NikeTown, FAO Schwarz, and too many Starbuckses to count. President Clinton was supposed to make an appearance—instead, the conference animated Seattle activists who opposed the fake progressivism he had perfected.[68]

Seattle environmentalists protested globalization's ruination of the environment through war, corporate pollution, and factory-farm food. Consumer protection advocates decried goods made with sweatshop labor. Organized workers hit hard by deindustrialization called out Clinton's disastrous NAFTA deal. The anti-capitalist demonstrations were a mass media spectacle; when the din of Seattle police flash-bangs and billy-club cracks subsided, echoes of the 1919 General Strike could be heard in the Seattle night.

After city cops deployed chemical weapons banned in war on protestors, Starbucks CEO Howard Schultz refocused Seattle's attention on the issue that mattered most (at least to him): holiday shopping. "For us to have to close our stores during the peak Christmas season really is an injustice," said Schultz at a Sonics home game.[69]

A century after the age of reform, some progressives still faked left and went right.

Not everyone was fooled.

Pitching Change

Soundgarden was suspicious of the commercialization of everything around them. At the height of their popularity as the local NBA team did battle with Chicago in the NBA Finals, the alt-rockers were a musical guest on *Saturday Night Live* in May 1996. With "GO SONICS" plastered across Matt Cameron's kickdrum, they performed the hit "Pretty Noose," its lyrics decrying the "diamond rope, silver chain" keeping its narrator tethered to a life of "pretty pain." In the song's final measurers, singer Chris Cornell's voice drops a pitch to a sonic snarl, telling the materialist demon of his worldly affection: "I don't like what you got me hanging from." Record execs obliged by cutting the cord, ditching Seattle grunge in favor of faddish boy bands from LA and Orlando in the later 1990s. All that glittered wasn't gold, and Seattle wouldn't be glittering so much anymore at the turn of the century.

Sure as nimbostratus clouds cover the sun, the media spotlight on Seattle dimmed. After the World Trade Organization protests in late 1999, popular magazines reevaluated Seattle's status as urban America's trendiest city. The *New York Times* bristled at flash-bangs and pepper spray on the streets of "the happiest, mellowest city on the planet."[1] The British periodical *Independent* said: "Seattle may never be the same again."[2] Frontier Seattle's innocent façade had been punctured. Shortly thereafter, the tech sector of the US stock market peaked in March 2000, then collapsed, erasing the fortunes of some of Seattle's richest individuals. The city's bustling coffee shops and bookstores emptied; recession resulted in area population decline.[3] Seattle's sports simulated the city's rise and fall.

After losing to Chicago in the 1996 NBA Finals, the SuperSonics signed so-so white center Jim McIlvane to a massive contract, making him one

When he began playing for the Seattle Mariners in 2001, Ichiro Suzuki renewed a long tradition of Japanese American baseball in the city. Though segregated, Issei and Nisei ballplayers established thriving leagues in the Progressive Era. Courtesy of the Seattle Municipal Archives, item 177018.

of the highest-paid players on the team. That McIlvaine made as much money as Seattle's star player, Shawn Kemp, alienated Kemp terribly. Sonics management dealt away their disgruntled employee, and the team's subsequent slide into mediocrity had fatal consequences for the future of men's professional basketball in Seattle.

Briefly at the turn of the century, the Seattle Mariners were a bright spot. Ken Griffey Jr. felt slighted when Seattle management didn't incorporate his suggestions for the team's new ballpark. Junior wanted a stadium with short outfield fences, in hopes of one day catching Hank Aaron's career home-run record.[4] Instead, new Safeco Field was a pitcher-friendly stadium with faraway outfield fences and a canopy design that deadened deep balls in the thickly moist Seattle air. Fed up, Griffey departed for his home team Cincinnati Reds in early 2000. The Mariners prospered with a new core of Alex Rodriguez, Ichiro Suzuki, and pitchers Jamie Moyer and Freddie Garcia, making it to the 2000 American League Championship Series. Although they fell short to the eventual champion New York Yankees, fans were excited for the following year. After Rodriguez jumped ship in the offseason, the Mariners got even better.

When Seattle defeated the Anaheim Angels on Monday, September 10, 2001, their record improved to a dazzling 104–40. Seattle led their division by seventeen games, threatened to break the league record for regular season wins, and were clear favorites to win the World Series. The next morning, two passenger airplanes struck the World Trade Center in New York City. Eyewitnesses saw another plane hit the Pentagon. Still another, believed to have been bound for the US Capitol, crashed in rural Pennsylvania. After the terrorist attacks, professional baseball and football were delayed a week; when they returned, pregame rituals and halftime displays showcased a wave of performative patriotism. During baseball's seventh-inning stretch, the singing of "God Bless America" became customary.[5] A new nationalist tide took over American sports, its waves reaching from sea to shining Seattle.

Born October 22, 1973, Mariners outfielder Ichiro Suzuki became a case study on the state of American nationalism in the post-9/11 moment. Where in past seasons Seattle slugged home runs with Ken Griffey Jr. and Jay Buhner, this new iteration of the squad was tailored around the skills Suzuki picked up as a veteran in Japan's competitive baseball leagues: less power hitting, more base hits, better defense. Suzuki made highlight reels by sprinting to turn routine ground balls into singles. Pundits turned him into a parable about postindustrial America. In the same way that Japanese cars outlasted American autos with smaller frames and better gas mileage, Ichiro was framed as the cagey batter whose cunning efficiency conquered the national pastime. "Good riddance to stats-obsessed behemoths," said the *New York Times* on September 16, 2001. "Ichiro's Pacific Rim virtues of modesty and understatement mask a fierce devotion to success. [He's the] Honda that replaced the Oldsmobile."[6]

Just as many white Seattle audiences were wary of Japanese baseball excellence during the Progressive Era, fetishism of Ichiro often lapsed into bigotry. *Sports Illustrated* put him on the cover of its July 2002 edition, making his Asiatic physiognomy seem simultaneously intimate and foreign with an ogling close-up, while saying he had "no power, no peer, and no personality."[7] Behind the scenes Seattle sportswriters grumbled about Ichiro's standoffishness; fans wondered if he was pretending to not know how to speak English. Nobody could complain much: from 2001 to 2011, Ichiro won ten Gold Gloves, was one of baseball's best hitters, and missed only 34 of 1,782 regular season games. Still, there was a feeling among Seattle fans that though he was in the city, he wasn't of it. "I've struggled to understand what so much of Seattle had against Ichiro," wrote Mariners beat writer Geoff Baker. "After reading Lauren Hillenbrand's book about the Air Force experiences in a Japanese POW camp during World War II, it made sense. I believe people carry that sentiment over—even subconsciously—when looking at Ichiro."[8]

Although the Mariners won a record 116 games in the 2001 regular season, the vibes were all off after 9/11. Seattle made it back to the playoffs, advancing to face New York again in the American League Championship Series (ALCS)—but they had barely beaten Cleveland in a first-round series that highlighted the team's tendency to score fewer runs in their own new ballpark than they did on the road. The Yankees, meanwhile, looked like a team of destiny, riding high on sympathetic press attention that framed them as America's team after 9/11. An aura of guilt emanated from Seattle manager Lou Piniella as he sat in the dugout; once a beloved Yankee, he now had to deliver sports heartbreak to a New York fan base in search of something to feel good about after the bloodiest day on US soil since the Civil War battle of Antietam in 1862.

After dropping the first two games of the 2001 ALCS in Seattle, the Mariners stormed back to win 14–3 in New York. In a pivotal Game Four played on October 21 at Yankee Stadium, the Mariners took a 1–0 lead on a Bret Boone home run in the top of the eighth. On the mound, former Yankee Jeff Nelson had his old team completely smothered, wielding his knowledge of New York's hitters at the most opportune moment possible. Inexplicably, Lou Piniella made a pitching change. Seattle's bullpen surrendered three runs after Nelson left the game. The Mariners lost 3–1, then gave up twelve runs a day later to lose the series.

A symbol of their city's declining national esteem, the Seattle Mariners wouldn't return to the playoffs for another twenty-one years. When they made their next postseason run in 2022, American cities were two decades

Extra Innings

"LOSERVILLE, USA," 2000–2009

The Kingdome imploded and Seattleites couldn't look away. At twenty-five stories tall and two blocks wide, it was one of the biggest status symbols on the planet. For a quarter century since it opened on March 27, 1976, its 260 million pounds anchored the city in the big leagues. Mediocre for most of their history, the Seahawks compiled a respectable 100–77 record at the Kingdome; in their 1979 championship season the Sonics led the league in home attendance there. Come holy triumph or damned defeat, Seattle fanatics crammed into this citadel of civic connection: 434,100 attended the good reverend Billy Graham's eight-day evangelist extravaganza in May 1976. That set the world record for largest crowd ever for a single event. In the history books, the Kingdome had a place that could never be erased.[1]

But a single day shy of its twenty-fourth birthday, on Sunday, March 26, 2000, it would be reduced to rubble. Controlled Demolition, Inc. strapped 4,461 pounds of explosives to its roof. The Kingdome would implode at 8:30 a.m.

After a chorus of detonation devices, the concrete colossus took 16.8 seconds to crumble. Yellowish-brown soot billowed from the blast site in Pioneer Square, sullying a sunny Seattle morning. The pall reached as high as the Bank of America Tower's seventy-six stories. It left dust everywhere it drifted. It was Mount Saint Helens all over again. After the show Emerald City yokels marauded around Pioneer Square, cupping their hands to slide stadium detritus off car windshields into Ziploc bags; the rubbish could fetch a few bucks on the new website eBay.[2]

On the city's hilltop neighborhoods, some of Seattle's nouveau riche held swanky implosion-watch parties on the observation decks of high-rise condos. Some tech VPs and top-tier project managers congregated on rooftop bars, drinking mimosas and expensive microbrews while waiting for the final countdown. They rented the Smith Tower's thirty-fifth-floor panorama and charged $216 for champagne-brunch views of the stadium's demise.[3] Like their settler forebears who docked near the place that became Seattle in November 1851, they sailed their boats to Elliott Bay and set their sights on Pioneer Square. Unlike their settler forebears, these boats were motorized and had fully stocked liquor shelves.

Middle managers and IT grunts who couldn't afford front-row seats to the spectacle of destruction got together wherever they could. They went to visit that friend whose place had a semblance of a view. They shopped at Bon Marché. for something to wear to watch parties—Nordstrom if they could swing it. While awaiting their publicly funded stadium's demise, petite bourgeoisie partygoers cued REM's "It's the End of the World as We Know It" on a burned CD. As the debris settled, they played Queen's "Another One Bites the Dust" and the Verve's "Bitter Sweet Symphony," because that was the witty thing to do. The city's introverts—the silent, awkward, overwhelming majority of its population, to be sure—stayed at home and watched the KING 5 broadcast of the Kingdome's collapse. "I think a lot of people don't understand the destruction of a perfectly functional building," said anchor Jean Enersen.[4]

There's reason to believe faces of color were few and far between at Kingdome implosion festivities. In Chinatown the Asian Counseling and Referral Service (ACRS) held a gathering to dance on the stadium's grave. Some of the attendees were elders who had fought the stadium's placement in Chinatown; at the Kingdome groundbreaking ceremony in November 1972, they had thrown mud balls at elected officials. Organizers leveraged their civil unrest into public resources for Asian Seattleites in the inner-city. A nonprofit offering behavioral health programs and human services, ACRS grew out of this protest. "I don't have fond memories of the Kingdome," said Chinatown activist Bob Santos. "We got out of it what we wanted."[5]

Seattle spectators didn't come together to watch the Kingdome's implosion so much as the Kingdome's implosion revealed the city's divisions. The last time Seattleites gathered en masse was during the World Trade Organization protests in late 1999; three hundred police officers in riot gear

The Kingdome was imploded one day shy of its twenty-fourth birthday in March 2000, after Seattle voters narrowly approved tech mogul Paul Allen's stadium plan in 1997. Recycled concrete from the Kingdome was used to build Seahawks Stadium, later named CenturyLink Field and eventually Lumen Field. Courtesy of the Seattle Municipal Archives, item 100486.

patrolled the Kingdome demolition site perimeter, looking for civil unrest to stifle. With nothing to do, some cops in armor-covered vehicles let kids straddle their tanks for family photos. In the days leading up to the main event, the city eradicated a homeless encampment near the Kingdome; the *Seattle Times* said: "No wonder they feel at home here, near a building considered broken-down and washed-up."[6]

By imploding the Kingdome to build the football arena voters had elected to fund in 1997, Seattleites pissed away $668 million in civic debt for the new facility. At the time, five thousand Seattleites had no roof to sleep under. The *Seattle Post-Intelligencer* reported that those incarcerated at the King County Correctional Facility had the best vantage point of the waste of resources: "As the dome fell, prisoners cheered from their terrific view." The demolition registered a 2.3 on the Richter scale, gently shaking meal trays in the jail cafeteria.[7]

Seattle was supposed to be the city that transcended the old conflicts—a city above history. But at the turn of the century, it was sinking like everywhere else. Two weeks after the Kingdome implosion, the NASDAQ index collapsed, erasing the fortunes of Seattle's nouveau riche.

By cratering Seattle's economy, the "Dot-Com Recession" completed the damage to the city's reputation that the WTO protests had started: Seattle wasn't exceptional. If capitalism coughed, it would catch a cold. Seeing Seattle's declining cachet and the increasing outspokenness of unions at Boeing after WTO, Boeing announced in March 2001 that it would be relocating its corporate headquarters to Chicago. After Seattle and its economy crashed swiftly and in front of many spectators, rather like the Kingdome, reporter Kim Murphy penned a 2002 postmortem in the *Los Angeles Times*: "Seattle has fallen—from its place deep in America's restless heart, a city of snowy mountains and inland seas to which the disillusioned, ambitious, bored and broke from the rest of the country flocked in the 1990s—to where it is now, which is a city under siege."[8]

"Seattle hasn't had a lot to cheer about lately," said the *Seattle Times* on March 27, 2000, on what would have been the Kingdome's birthday.[9] A dream imploded with the stadium. The Kingdome was a public facility conceived as part of the Forward Thrust's civic improvements in the heady 1960s. It embodied the hope that American city dwellers could come together to solve their problems, and maybe have fun while doing so.[10] What the commentariat who ranked urban areas in major periodicals like *Time* and *Newsweek* wanted to see were cities with popular entertainments like pro sports. They wanted cities with lucrative industries and widespread prosperity, cities with the same arts and culture scenes that were being displaced in the stratified cities they praised, cities that pacified urban conflicts between groups that had all the power and those that had none.

One by one, the public literati that dissected and ranked urban areas realized that no city any longer satisfied the criteria for the "city of the future." Not Los Angeles or Cincinnati, with their turn-of-the-century civic flare-ups over police brutality. Not New York or Chicago, with their blighted neighborhoods and high crime rates. And certainly not Seattle, with its unsightly anti-capitalist protests, fleeing corporations, and growing population of people experiencing houselessness.[11] Consequently, public sentiment turned not just against individual cities but against urban America as a whole. The dream of the great US metropolis was dead. In the past, American cities were seen as *having* problems; in the year 2000, however, many believed they *were* the problem.

In 1997 conservative commentator David Brooks popularized the term "latte liberal" to describe what he called "upscale liberal communities, often in magnificent natural settings, often university-based, that have become the gestation centers for America's new upscale culture."[12] With its major research university, dot-com robber barons, and growing wealth inequalities, Seattle fit Brooks's description to a tee. Without intending to do so, he parodied the city precisely: "Latte towns were the birthplaces of coffee shops and microbreweries. The ideal Latte town has Native American crafts and software startups. You know you're in a Latte town when you can hop right off a bike path and drink coffee at a place with a pun-ish name."[13]

Conservatives wielded "latte liberal" as an epithet, characterizing liberal big cities as too socially permissive, too soft on crime, too emasculated.[14] What American conservatives objected to wasn't global capitalism (which they shilled for), but the complexities global capitalism introduced into American life. Those complexities were most evident in big cities. By attacking them, reactionaries had it both ways: celebrating the free market while wincing at the economic empowerment of women and minorities; deregulating capitalism while stigmatizing the immigrants whose cheap labor fueled it; stoking panic over terrorism in major cities while believing there wasn't much left in major cities worth defending.

In GOP-dominated federal elections in 2000, 2002, and 2004, Americans got accustomed to election-night maps dividing blue, urban America from its red, rural and suburban counterpart. The competition was on. Seattle was on the far left coast of the United States; as far as America's conservatives were concerned, that's where it was on the country's political spectrum as well. In the early twenty-first century, the city's sports animated the competition between urban America and everywhere else, and between urban America and itself.

***

Among the team names in the running were the "Emeralds," "Rainbows," and "Spin." Other Seattleites suggested the "Slammers," "Stealth," and "Speed." The Seattle "Hard Drives" ranked as one of the worst mascots ever suggested—in Seattle in 1999, and perhaps anywhere, ever, at any point in human history. Someone else offered the "Thunder," but what kind of name was that for a basketball team?

An eleven-year-old from Bellevue hit the game-winning name: "Seattle Storm, because they mean business." The WNBA had gifted Seattle a new franchise in 1999. After the city breezed past the mandatory threshold of fifty-five hundred season tickets sold, publicists in the league front office approved the name. The Seattle Storm were indeed in business.[15]

Women's sports in the United States are a barometer for alternating political climates of reform and regression. During the Progressive Era, women athletes provoked a backlash: a November 1915 article in the *Seattle Post-Intelligencer* cautioned that "girls cannot keep going day and night, playing tennis, golf, and hockey, and expect to keep a favorable balance in the bank of health."[16] City dwellers got used to biking women in "bloomer" dresses that gave them greater freedom of movement. As the Seattle Metropolitans went on their Stanley Cup Championship run, white women "Hockeyettes" played games at the segregated Seattle Ice Arena, with the *Seattle Times* noting their "disregard for tradition" in March 1917.[17]

After World War I the reinstitution of retrograde gender roles was bad news for women's sports. Not content to sit idly by as her husband instituted a Gilded Age redux in the 1920s, Lou Hoover—First Lady of the United States—shut down a thriving women's football league in Toledo in the 1930s. The cycle was repeated after World War II, as the return of men from the warfront curtailed the athletic activity of women and LGBTQ+ motorcyclists and dancers. As cooking, cleaning, rocking babies, folding clothes, and vacuuming took more physical grit than many men would ever know, many women awaited the opportunity to perform their physicality on a bigger stage.

The sexual revolutions of the 1960s and 1970s changed the game. After Congress ratified the Title IX constitutional amendment in 1972, American universities were legally obligated to afford women the same opportunities, in sports and academics, as men.[18] The legislation combined with the Civil Rights Act of 1964 to create a demographic revolution in sports. Just as the golden age of boxing expressed the primacy of male breadwinners in the mid-twentieth century, the growing popularity of women's basketball in the late twentieth century evidenced a deindustrialized, increasingly feminized labor force in which Black women accumulated professional degrees at a rate that exceeded their male counterparts.[19] By the end of the twentieth century, the best basketball players in the country were Black women: Cheryl Miller, Lisa Leslie, Sheryl Swoopes.

The increasing economic enfranchisement of Black women in the generation after the civil rights movement coincided with a decline in blue-collar jobs held by their male counterparts. Many decried this development, arguing that Black matriarchs were symptomatic of Black family dysfunction. Originator of the term "intersectionality," legal scholar Kimberlé Crenshaw pushed back in 1989, questioning why "the struggle against racism seemed to compel the subordination of the Black female experience in order to ensure the security of the larger Black community."[20] Echoing the Seattle Owls Club of the late 1930s, city dwellers in the late twentieth century got used to seeing financially self-sustaining Black women in team apparel and athletic shoes, hoop earrings and beanies—a much-copied postindustrial fashion statement born out of a new world of work. Founded as an NBA spin-off in 1996 the WNBA showcased the labors of post–civil rights era Black women athletes like no league before it.

In April 2000 seventy women attended tryouts for the Seattle Storm inaugural team at the Rainier Community Center. Robin Threatt stood out.[21] While in college, she had given Purdue coach Lin Dunn's teams nightmares in the early 1990s. Now, there stood Dunn on the Seattle sidelines, head coach of the Storm, watching the thirty-year-old Threatt make light work of grueling drills. She made the team. With a master's in marketing, she turned her back on her job as a peddler of heart medicine; Threatt would make $83,000 less as a professional basketball player than she did at the Du Pont corporation. She didn't care: "Anytime you have that fire in you to do something, you have to keep pushing on," she said in May 2000. "When I feel the option is no longer there, I'll go have more babies."[22]

Seattleites embraced the Storm with typical enthusiasm, the seeds planted by the US women's basketball team's November 1995 visit to the city. Six hundred girls from Seattle high schools turned out just to watch the team practice before its exhibition match against the University of Washington women's team; fifty-seven hundred rapt fans saw USA humble the Huskies, 92–47.[23] A study released by the American Basketball Council had shown that the number of women who played basketball spiked 23 percent between 1987 and 1995. A year later, the Seattle Reign of the American Basketball League displayed women's ball to modest but devoted crowds. The league folded in 1998, but not before setting a valuable precedent for the WNBA in Seattle and beyond.

Seattle joined the WNBA in 1999 alongside expansion franchises in Indiana, Miami, and Portland. Illustrating the distance between the league's elite and its new expansion teams, the mighty Houston Comets drained the Seattle Storm by 30 points in both of their matchups in Seattle's inaugural 2000 season.[24] In the June 2000 blowout, most of the 10,480 Seattle fans at KeyArena didn't leave early.[25] With "Gay Pride" nights and an ample marketing budget, the Storm activated passionate LGBTQ+ and women fans that other major leagues ignored.[26]

Robin Threatt played admirably in Seattle's inaugural season—her first and last in the WNBA—scoring 7.8 points per game while having thirteen steals in twenty games. As the Storm compiled an 8–26 record in 2000, fans hoped help was on the way.

* * *

Football was a man's game, a pure game, a game of integrity; a game of irreproachable moral fiber, incorruptible martial discipline, and crushing head injuries that were endured strictly for the honor of the game. It was a noble game—righteous in the same way that farming, fording a river, or fighting a war was. Much ink has been spilled about why the sport resonates as deeply as it does with American fans, rising in popularity parallel to modern suburbs and the mass spectacle of television; most of it falls short of author Frederick Exley's 1968 musing in *A Fan's Notes*: "Why did football bring me so to life? Part of it was my feeling that it was an island of directness in a world of circumspection. In football, a man was asked to do a difficult and brutal job. There was nothing rhetorical or vague about it. It smacked of something old, something traditional, something unclouded."[27]

In cloudy Seattle, voters approved Microsoft cofounder Paul Allen's plan for a new football stadium in 1997. The expectation was clear: in exchange for $300 million in public funds, the Seahawks would demolish football teams from rival cities.[28] The new stadium was engineered to trap noise and redirect it onto the field. Seattle fans would paint themselves blue and green and drink overpriced stadium beer. They'd get drunk, shout, and force opposing offenses into the most false-start penalties through sheer clamor. Their home field would be the most feared in the sport. Rivals would be afraid of Seattle; football was figurative war.

Pigskin was the pastime that Ivy League schools used to teach teamwork during the Gilded Age; the *Seattle Times* called football and war "GREAT LITTLE PALS" in 1918.[29] Though the sport flowered in liberal cities, its heartland was in the youth fields of rural America. SUV-driving suburbanites bolstered the league's stalwart social base, which cross-pollinated with conservative politics. On his presidential runs in 1968 and 1972, President Nixon weaponized connections with gridiron team owners to reinforce his support in the Sunbelt; in *Pigskin Nation: How the NFL Remade American Politics*, historian Jesse Berrett describes how macho-man-in-chief Ronald Reagan used football imagery "to sell himself as bearer of a reassuring American masculine tradition" during the Cold War.[30] By the early 2000s, warlike football was the most popular game in a country that had been at war—with no formal declaration of it—since 2003.

As the Seahawks took flight under the new regime of head coach Mike Holmgren, "No Iraq War" lawn signs were conspicuous in the Seattle neighborhoods Green Lake and Ballard.[31] In Seattle's Central Area speakers at the 2003 iteration of the annual Martin Luther King Jr. Day march denounced the coming war. All the while, the Pentagon subsidized NFL teams like the local Seahawks, giving them cash benefits for halftime flag salutes and Air Force flyovers.[32] As the United States fought a quixotic "War on Terror" with no end in sight, the Seattle fan refrain "Go Hawks" seemed a double entendre.

After disappointing playoff exits in 2003 and 2004, the Seahawks entered the 2005 season as serious Super Bowl contenders. Running back Shaun Alexander and quarterback Matt Hasselbeck anchored the team's scoring attack behind a punishing front line; Holmgren's innovative version of the "West Coast offense" used tactical passing precision to reinforce the team's ground game. Attacking by land and by air, the Hawks defended their home turf perfectly, going 8–0 at Qwest Field in 2005. Seattle's (department of) defense was anchored by starting lineman Bryce Fisher, an Air Force Academy graduate and active member of the armed reserves during the 2005 season.[33] "Whenever I put on my [Seahawks] uniform, I think about all the people who put on the [military] uniform," Fisher said, as the NFL prepared its Veterans Day celebrations in November 2005. "I've got friends that have been to Baghdad and Afghanistan, and I do my best to honor them."[34]

Fisher totaled nine sacks for the Seahawks in the 2005 season, prompting coaches to comment on his work ethic, a residue, some believed, of his time in the Air Force.[35] References to the defensive end's military discipline were nowhere to be found when he was arrested for assaulting his wife in a dispute over his alleged infidelity. The charges were later dropped.

After compiling an impressive 13–3 regular season record, the Hawks' frontier war simulation escalated when they vanquished the Washington Redskins, and later Carolina, on the way to Super Bowl XL, where the Pittsburgh Steelers awaited them. On paper, the game shouldn't have been close: the Seahawks were the best team in the league, while Pittsburgh was a sixth-seeded wild card that had to win three road games to get to the Super Bowl.

It was played in Detroit, where star Steelers running back Jerome "the Bus" Bettis was from. With Bettis set to retire after the game, Pittsburgh had a potent psychological incentive to send him off on a good note. Worse for Seattle, the short distance from Detroit to Pittsburgh allowed Steelers fans to descend upon the game in droves. Detroit's mayor declared the run-up to the Super Bowl "Jerome Bettis Week."[36] The "neutral field" was stacked against Seattle. At kickoff, ABC play-by-play announcer Al Michaels estimated the game crowd was 80 percent Steelers fans.

Steel City entered the Super Bowl as sentimental favorites over the Emerald City. The national conversation about their chances in the championship game framed Seattle as the more effete team whose "West Coast offense" could be disrupted. The roots of the anti-sissy bias went back to the Reagan-era 1986 NFC Championship Game, when the punishing New York Giants defense made mincemeat of Joe Montana's finesse-first San Francisco 49ers. Twenty years later, if you had to pick a city to win a football game in the also-conservative, anti-urban 2000s, you picked the midwestern one with an industrial pedigree. Seattle was a coastal latte town; Pittsburgh was tougher. It was right there in their names: Emerald was a decorative jewel, somewhat brittle and subject to breakage; steel was hard and functional, America's backbone since the days of the railroad. Frontier Seattle met its maker.

Played Sunday, February 5, 2006, at Ford Field in Detroit, Super Bowl XL was a total farce. In the first quarter, official Bill Leavy flagged Seattle receiver Darrell Jackson for a rare offensive pass interference penalty in the end zone, erasing a touchdown that would have put Seattle up 7–0. With Seattle leading 3–0 in the second quarter, a line judge said Ben Roethlisberger crossed the goal line for a touchdown when replays showed he clearly didn't. As Seattle was driving and Pittsburgh led 14–10 in the fourth quarter, Pittsburgh lineman Clark Haggans—blatantly offsides on the play—baited Seahawks offensive tackle Sean Locklear into a phantom hold, snuffing out a red zone gain that may have led to a go-ahead score for Seattle.[37] Of the one hundred thousand fans polled by ESPN, 61.7 percent believed officiating ruined the game.[38] The Seahawks fell by the final score of 21–10. A liberal city in red America, Seattle had competed in a conservative arena and lost.

After the game the majoritarian view among Seahawks fans was that the game was probably fixed—a belief substantiated by a lengthy shadow history of foul play in professional sports: As the heady Progressive Era gave way to the materialistic 1920s, the 1919 World Series between the Chicago White Sox and the Cincinnati Reds was over before it started. A powerful gambling syndicate coaxed Chicago players to throw the series for Cincinnati, who ended up winning.[39] Later, Dan Moldea's explosive 1989 book *Interference: How Organized Crime Influences Professional Football* revealed deep ties between football players and mafiosos that resulted in scores of rigged games in the mid-twentieth century.[40] A 2007 FBI report uncovered that NBA referee Tim Donaghy systematically fixed basketball games he officiated from at least 2005 through 2007—that is, at the same time the

Seahawks lost the Super Bowl to the Steelers due to dubious officiating.[41]

With Secretary of State Condoleezza Rice watching from the stands and transparently pulling for Pittsburgh, the Steelers' win had the creepy air of conspiratorial inevitability.[42] If the public couldn't have clarity over why precisely it was at war, it would question everything else. In the digital bunker of MySpace groups and in obscure back channels of TheFacebook, fans lamented the gambling interests that they believed convinced the refs to job the Seahawks on the biggest stage possible. Seattleites were paranoid—but that didn't mean everyone wasn't out to get them.

* * *

Success and failure collided. While the Storm stumbled to a pathetic 10–22 record in the 2001–2 WNBA season, Sue Bird's University of Connecticut college squad was literally perfect, compiling a 39–0 record to capture the national championship in spring 2002. After the Storm finished tied with four other teams for the worst record in the league, they won the draft lottery and were given the number one pick in the 2002 WNBA draft. It was a foregone conclusion that they would select Bird, who was by that time the best—if not best-marketed—women's basketball player in the country, a star-in-the-making whose celebrity was boosted by the ESPN media empire in nearby Bristol, Connecticut. Seattle plucked her. "I don't plan on losing," Bird said on draft day.[43]

Born October 16, 1980, in Syosset, New York, Suzanne Brigit Bird brought East Coast basketball excellence to Seattle. Gotham was the city that produced great point guards, floor colonels who conducted the action and served as coaches on court: Bob Cousy, Lenny Wilkens, Kenny Smith, Mark Jackson, Nancy Lieberman. Bird was part of a national title team at Christ the King High School in Queens, where she moved from pampered Long Island after her parents divorced. Hailing from a family of Russian Jews, she was self-aware of the privileges she grew up with as a white person, crediting her young adulthood in New York City for toughening her on and off the court: "Regardless of whether it was hard or easy compared to other people, my upbringing made me self-reliant in this little apartment in Queens."[44]

With four WNBA titles (2004, 2010, 2018, 2020), the Seattle Storm are far and away the most accomplished pro team in the city's sports. Pictured at Westlake Center in 2002, shortly after selecting Connecticut phenom Sue Bird in the draft. Courtesy of the Seattle Municipal Archives, item 130170.

Geographically the biggest borough in New York City, Queens was the most ethnically diverse urban area in the world at the turn of the century, a city unto itself that provoked bigoted remarks from Atlanta Braves pitcher John Rocker in 1999. "It's the most hectic, nerve-racking city," Rocker told *Sports Illustrated*: "Imagine having to take the 7-train next to some kid with purple hair, next to some queer with AIDS, next to some dude who just got out of jail for the fourth time. Asians and Korean and Vietnamese and Indians and Russians and Spanish people. How the hell did they get in this country?"[45] Though pilloried at the time as fringe prejudice, Rocker's remarks forecasted a sea change in American politics. George W. Bush captured the presidency in 2000 as a proponent of strengthening the country's borders, then spawned the Department of Homeland Security and Patriot Act to crack down on immigrants and perceived dissidents after 9/11.

By the time Bird landed in Seattle in April 2002, Republicans controlled the White House, Congress, and thirty-eight of fifty state governor seats, then gained control of the Senate in midterm elections that year. That year Bush had instated a ban on federal funding to family-planning groups that offered abortion counseling, then told an anti-abortion rally a few weeks later in West Virginia: "You're marching on behalf of a noble cause."[46] The conservative shift in American politics followed Bird to progressive Seattle. In her rookie season Bird was the catalyst of the Storm's offense that ranked near the top of the league in total points scored and field goal percentage in 2003. She made a bet with Seattle radio host Mitch Levy that if her assist-to-turnover ratio—a statistical marker of good decision-making in basketball—was lower than 2:1 at the end of the year, Levy would bend her over his knee, spank her, and exhort Bird to yell "harder, daddy, harder" to thousands of listeners on the air. That Bird won the bet did little to quell the controversy surrounding it.

The skeezy wager became the center of controversy.[47] In a scathing July 2003 column Steve Kelley of the *Seattle Times* called Levy "the morning maven of misogyny."[48] Washington State senator Jeanne Kohl-Welles castigated Bird for "feeding into images of violence against women." When ESPN caught wind of the controversy, it became national news. Bird apologized and withdrew her participation in the bet. "I'm embarrassed," she confessed.[49] "When I read the Senator's letter, it made me re-think things." Levy showed no such contrition: "For Kohl-Welles to equate a consensual radio segment that happened to involve a spanking element to violence against women is offensive to any victim of this horrible crime."[50]

In 2004, Bird was selected to her second straight All-Star team, while Seattle center and reigning WNBA Most Valuable Player Lauren Jackson was having another strong campaign. Though Seattle downed the Houston Comets 69–63 on June 18, 2004, for their fifth straight win, the focus of WNBA reporting that day was on a different body of work: Jackson had posed nude in an Australian magazine celebrating athletes competing in the upcoming Olympic games. The photos were due to hit stands in a week. "The Storm have provided Jackson with substantial income and recognition," wrote a commenter on a Storm fan website; "they're entitled to ask for a higher standard."[51]

While some Seattle fans focused on nude photos in a magazine eighty-two hundred miles away, there was little local scrutiny of radio host Mitch Levy's annual "Bigger Dance" tournament. For eight years and running, Levy pitted sixty-four actresses, models, and women athletes against one another in an on-air fantasy tournament to determine who was the most attractive—the "Queen of the Hardwood," as Levy termed the winner. Nor did anyone care when Ichiro Suzuki responded to a 2001 rumor by saying, "If it was true [that a magazine offered me $1 million for nude photos], I'd take the picture myself and send it in."[52] In the face of the double standards, Lauren Jackson was unapologetic: "We work so hard, as athletes, on making our bodies look great."

The uproar around the Storm subsided, but the Storm themselves would not. Seattle romped through the 2004 WNBA playoffs, poaching the Minnesota Lynx in the Western Conference Semifinals and deposing the Sacramento Monarchs in the Western Conference Finals. Awaiting them in the championship round were the Connecticut Sun. Narratively no matchup could sizzle more than a Bird versus Connecticut contest for WNBA supremacy. With the series tied 1–1 and the Storm one home win away from winning the championship, reporter Les Carpenter wrote that "among the cities with three professional sports teams, Seattle's two championships were more than only two: Phoenix and Atlanta."[53] Looking back on a century of sports futility, Carpenter concluded: "When the most logical sports nickname for your town is Loserville, USA, a WNBA title is a pretty big deal." On Tuesday, October 12, 2004, the Seattle Storm shaded the Connecticut Sun to win the 2004 WNBA Championship.

Psyched by her return to Connecticut, Bird had struggled throughout the series, posting eleven assists and ten turnovers in three games. Though she didn't enjoy the benefit of the press attention afforded Bird, Seattle wing Betty Lennox was the best player on either team, scoring 22.3 points per game and winning WNBA Finals MVP honors. Like her superstar University of Connecticut predecessor Rebecca Lobo, Sue Bird was a marketing asset for a league attempting to break into the mainstream—a white woman who was seen as conventionally attractive, contrasting with the hurtful stereotype of "butch" Black women with whom the WNBA had come to be associated.[54] Still early in her career in 2004, Bird later came into her own as one of the greatest women's basketball players of all time. But in the 2004 WNBA Finals, Betty Lennox—a Black woman—carried the team to the title. Ten thousand fans attended the Storm's championship parade downtown on October 15; jersey-wearing fans poured out of downtown businesses and buses. Lennox was on the move, too. A week after winning the championship, she'd board a plane to play basketball in Italy, where player salaries were much higher than in the United States.[55]

To win a Finals MVP is to be the most important player for the most important team at the most important time. But because WNBA player salaries were so low—a reflection of the disparity in resources and attention afforded women's basketball in the United States—many women players were more valued overseas. The WNBA's maximum wage was $132,400 in 2004, with most players making near the league minimum of $51,700. The league's *entire* labor payroll ($19.3 million) was $7.6 million less than the Boston Celtics paid Vin Baker in the 2003–4 NBA season to score 10 points a game.[56]

The Seattle Storm had given Seattle its first big-league championship since the Sonics in 1979. But the work of many women was not done: "You guys are the best," Lennox told the parade crowd in Seattle, her travel plans to her second job already made. "This feels like home."[57]

* * *

By now, the crime's details are well known: winners of the 1979 NBA Championship and a league model for local fan support, the SuperSonics were stolen from Seattle and relocated to Oklahoma City in 2008. We know a lot about the criminals: Clay Bennett, Aubrey McLendon, and Tom Ward were Oklahoma capitalists who bought the team from coffee magnate Howard Schultz with the barely veiled intent of relocating it. After he took control of the Sonics, Bennett clowned Seattle's lame-duck management group by serving them goat testicles at a team dinner. McLendon and Ward formed the anti–gay rights committee Americans United to Preserve Marriage for the 2000 presidential election, then funded the "Swift Boat Veterans for Truth" ads that misrepresented Democratic presidential nominee John Kerry's record of military service in 2004.[58] The relocation of the Sonics was a heist, executed by red state oilmen who pilfered liberal Seattle.

What we don't hear enough about is the motive.

When NBA commissioner David Stern became an accomplice in the relocation of the Seattle SuperSonics, his goal was straightforwardly political. After the November 2, 2004, election in which President Bush prevailed and Republicans increased their majorities in both houses of Congress, Stern consulted with GOP strategist Matthew Dowd. The two thought of ways to bolster the NBA's support among American conservatives.[59] Stern's league was teetering on irrelevancy; low-scoring games with slow paces drove down overall viewership. Some white audiences in particular were alienated by what they considered petulant Black athletes who didn't pay the requisite deference to white spectatorship. When an ugly melee broke out between fans and players in a November 19, 2004, regular season game between the Detroit Pistons and the visiting Indiana Pacers, the league's reputation hit a nadir. The 2007 FBI report revealing crooked refereeing further damaged the NBA brand.

In his book *Bad Sports*, sportswriter Dave Zirin describes how Stern and Dowd acted fast to help the NBA rebound: "Stern met with the 2004 Bush campaign strategist to figure out how to give the league what Stern called 'red state appeal.'"[60] In 2004 the league would disallow defensive players from using their hands to guard opponents, leading to more scoring. In 2005 it would force its players to wear business attire to and from games. Then, in 2006, NBA officials began the search for new red state markets.

Hurricane Katrina gave NBA officials a chance to audition Sunbelt cities for entry into the league. As the 2005–6 NBA season got underway, Kansas City, Louisville, Nashville, and San Diego vied to house the temporarily dislocated New Orleans Hornets. Oklahoma City won out, embracing the brilliant play of young New Orleans–born point guard Chris Paul as if he were a native son. A seed was planted for NBA officials looking to rally basketball fans in conservative areas.[61]

Back in Seattle, Howard Schultz was running his basketball team like he ran his coffee business: with a healthy disrespect for organized labor and a desire to impose himself upon middle management. Schultz dismantled the squad that made a promising run in the 2005 NBA playoffs before selling the team to Clay Bennett and his associates for half a billion dollars. Bruce Schoenfeld of the *New York Times* noted that "with his lifelong Republicanism and partners made rich by fossil fuels, Bennett pushed all the wrong buttons in liberal, health-conscious, ecologically sensitive Seattle."[62] Schultz swore he sold the team to the Oklahoma City group on the understanding that they would keep them in Seattle. Sonic fans could tell they were being played.

Great thefts have not just robbers (the Oklahoma City ownership group), accomplices (David Stern), and motives (opening up a new market in rural America) but also a stolen object of great value. For Bennett and his cohort, that object was not the Seattle Storm. While the WNBA team had been part of the Schultz sale, Bennett sold them in early 2008 to a group of Seattle businesswomen committed to keeping the team in Seattle. Bringing a women's basketball team with a fervent LGBTQ+ fan base to Oklahoma wasn't part of the plan.[63] In Tulsa, former Seattle Seahawks receiver and NFL players' union turncoat Steve Largent had been elected to Congress as a Republican in 1994; he served until 2002, remained a revered figure in the state upon exiting office, and spoke for many an Oklahoman when he said: "No civilization that has ever embraced homosexuality has ever survived."[64]

What the Oklahoma group wanted was the Sonics: a team that had reached an impasse with the NBA over a new basketball arena. The league wanted Seattle fans to shell out public money for a new arena; tired after dolling out arena subsidies for the Mariners and the Seahawks, elected officials in city government and in the Washington State Legislature refused. The Oklahoma City ownership group settled with the City of Seattle to finalize the franchise move, consequently taking possession of the Sonics' 1979 championship trophy, retired jerseys, and stadium banners commemorating conference titles and division wins. The Sonics would be relocating to Oklahoma at the start of the 2008–9 regular season, their name changed to the Thunder. On April 13, 2008, they played their last game in Seattle: a 99–95 victory against the Dallas Mavericks.

That the Sonics were moving was unfathomable. In the book *Hoops Heist*, author Jon Finkel describes how the Sonics had an unusually deep connection with the city's fan base.[65] Several future NBA players that came from Seattle had gone to basketball camps put on by Sonics stars: Jamal Crawford, Isiah Thomas, Nate Robinson, Jason Terry, and Brandon Roy were all gifted scorers. Smaller men who played in a big man's sport, they embodied Seattle's uphill struggle for recognition on the national stage. The Sonics were a basketball guild that elevated local talent through basketball apprenticeships; this connection between town and team was uncommon in the hyper-materialistic world of professional sports. A rookie on the Sonics roster when the team relocated, departed superstar Kevin Durant later mourned the broken bond: "The energy for the Sonics would have been unmatched in pro sports. The fans would have had an up-and-coming team with me, Russell Westbrook, Serge Ibaka, and James Harden. Sometimes I let myself think about what could have been."[66]

While the Oklahoma ownership group planned their relocation, Nick Licata, of the Seattle City Council, said the Sonics contributed "zero cultural and economic value" to the city. It's difficult to imagine a similar statement made about the Washington Huskies, Seahawks, or Mariners, who generated tailgate parties attended by generations of fans and initiated enthused pedestrian and transit trips to and from public stadiums. Although the economic benefits of sports to US cities are usually overstated, it was at least true that these teams created material excitement worth millions in sales taxes, parking fees, and bar and restaurant tabs—not to mention exceptional publicity for Seattle, a benefit identified by officials at the University of Washington a century earlier.[67] A similar dismissal of the Seattle Storm as the one levied by Licata against the Sonics would have drawn blowback from women and LGBTQ+ fans who understood that fair cultural representation of marginalized populations strengthens a city's social fabric; to his credit, Licata was smart enough not to go there.

Under pressure from constituents, the venerable councilmember later apologized for his inflammatory remarks. Many felt that what he meant to say was that because the cultural value of the Sonics skewed disproportionately toward Black Seattleites, the team was worth relinquishing. Back when professional basketball first came to town in 1966, Seattle's sports establishment was slow to embrace the "too-Black" NBA. Over the next four decades, however, the Sonics did as much to foster a feeling of

belonging among still-segregated Black Seattleites as all the minority economic empowerment studies, racial sensitivity curricula for homicidal cops,
and diversity task forces emerging from city hall. To Black city dwellers
enduring waves of gentrifiers in the Central District, the relocation of the
team may have seemed one more example of displacement at a time when
city leaders let economic forces fritter away a Black community that was
forged against all odds. A mom-and-pop small business the SuperSonics
were not; but for a people who had looked to sports as symbols of resilience
and dignity since before the Great Migration—indeed, since the days of
slavery—the team's departure was met with a feeling of real loss. Everywhere
you looked, Seattle seemed a less Black city.

At any rate the Sonics were gone now. Their sale was a proxy battle in the
power struggle between blue coastal cities and America's red state interior.
Parallels to the city's earlier failed rendezvous with the railroad are perhaps
too obvious to not make: the city was shafted again by regional rivals and
distant capitalists. For many years afterward, heartbroken Sonics fans were
reduced to rumormongers, desperately parsing any morsel of gossip that
hinted at the team's return, reproducing the local railroad speculation craze
of the Gilded Age. At parks and in coffee shops—on transit and on social
media—conversations about the departed franchise inspired defeated sighs
and shaking heads: *I still can't believe they let them get away.*

Because it was about politics, it wasn't their fault.

Because it was about politics, it was all their fault.

* * *

Seattle was floundering. After the dot-com bubble bust of
2000, the city lost an infamous Super Bowl to a tougher opponent in 2006.
Crooked oilmen separated fans from their basketball team in 2008, notch-
ing the more conservative Sunbelt another win over its liberal competition.
The Seattle Storm won a championship in 2004 and another six years later,
but the triumphs were widely disparaged by the national sports establishment. In 2010, ESPN sportswriter Bill Simmons described a "Washington
sports malaise," citing the departure of the Sonics, the ascendancy of the

Oklahoma City Thunder, and the fact that "the state's biggest recent sports highlights involved the WNBA."[68] Another recession in 2008 destroyed Washington Mutual, a Seattle-based bank with over forty-three thousand employees that bolstered the city's status as a center of global commerce.[69] Sports were a performance of civic ego; in the 2000s poor Seattle's was bruised. A victim of the tech revolution the city had helped incubate, the *Seattle Post-Intelligencer* became online-only in 2009, taking with it a rich tradition of sports coverage that started with Royal Brougham a century earlier.

The disappointments didn't deter Seattle fans. If anything, the regressive Bush administration activated the double helix of sports and civics in the city—genes that stretched back to the Progressive Era's "City Beautiful" movement, where athletics were a form of civic engagement and a pathway to national recognition. When the placement of a new Major League Soccer franchise in Seattle was announced in 2007, a naming contest provoked thousands of responses from area soccer fans. "A groundswell pushed the name 'Sounders' over the edge," said team owner Joe Roth in April 2008. "I think it shows that we are about democracy and sports."[70]

A part owner of the Sounders, comic Drew Carey met with fans at a Seattle pub in May 2008 to tout the club's innovative management model. The franchise gave fans the power to fire the team's general manager. Municipal ownership of sports franchises was forbidden by all major American sports leagues; Sounders fans had the next best thing.

To American conservatives, Seattle's passion for soccer confirmed how out of touch the "latte liberals" of the left coast really were. "It doesn't matter how you try to sell it to us," said right-winger Glenn Beck in 2010. "We don't want the World Cup and we don't like soccer."[71] Like major cities, soccer embodied exactly the kind of global interconnectedness that conservatives railed against as George W. Bush fought a unilateral "war on terror" in the Middle East. On April 16, 2006, more than fifty-six thousand fans in Seattle went to Qwest Field to watch a friendly between Mexico and China. In a book that hit shelves shortly after the Iraq War started in 2003, pop culture critic Chuck Klosterman complained that "soccer fanatics love to tell you it's the most popular game on earth, as if that proves its value.

The opposite is true. Why should I care that every citizen of Chile and Iran thoughtlessly adores 'futball'?"[72]

Had they paid closer attention, right-wingers who hated soccer might have found a lot to like: the sport was a petri dish of white supremacist revanchism. ESPN reported on players of color in Europe suffering racial slurs in 2006, and the *New York Times* noted ethnocentric views among white Seattle Sounders fans.[73] If conservatives who decried "latte towns" could have conjured their own pro-business, free-marketeering, rugged individualist paradise, they also could have done much worse than Seattle: a city of sundry corporate giants where male chauvinists dreamed of spanking women athletes; a city whose reputation as an antiwar environmentalist utopia was betrayed by a half-dozen military bases in the area; a "he-man" city where men couldn't take more than two years of a woman mayor in 1928 and largely ignored women's basketball. Seattle housed a sexist traditionalism that was right at home in areas of the country thought to be politically regressive. Large swaths of liberal Seattle also rejected soccer; nobody talked about it much on the city's sports radio stations, dominated as they were by coverage of men's football and basketball. These inconvenient truths had no place in the narrative that many conservatives wanted to tell about liberal cities.

Polarized presidential election maps that divided the country's cities and its ruralities distorted reality. "Blue" urban America had always been home to reactionaries and racists; rural America was "red" partially because of widespread voter disenfranchisement of progressive minority voters. Cities were never as progressive as they seemed, nor the countryside ever as conservative. But during America's Bush years, political nuance had gone the way of the Kingdome. Thomas Frank wrote in his 2004 book *What's the Matter with Kansas?* that the "red-state narrative brought majoritarian legitimacy to [George W. Bush], who had lost the popular vote."[74]

American conservatives won federal elections in the early twenty-first century by racking up votes in rural areas, suburban towns, and unincorporated districts. While seizing power, they juked many progressives into believing politics were about finding common ground, not about competing; about feelings, not fighting. "We in coastal metro Blue areas read more books than people in the heartland," wrote David Brooks in

2001, continuing the anti-urban narrative he started with the "latte liberal" stereotype in 1997. "But don't ask us what life in Red America is like. Very few of us could name five NASCAR drivers."[75]

For the previous three decades, Seattle was a boomtown that exemplified America's aspirations for its major cities. Its status as a liberal trendsetter turned into a political liability. In the power struggle between progress and regression, cities were on the defensive. Urban America was losing; Seattle was "Loserville, USA."

Rally

WHO WILL
WIN THE CITY?
2010–2019

The Seahawks and the Obama administration were united in underachievement. A Chicago lawyer raised by a single mother from Seattle, Obama was supposed to institutionalize a sea change in American politics—à la Franklin Delano Roosevelt—by advancing permanent progressive wins for the increasingly liberal, increasingly brown, increasingly urban electorate that voted him into office twice. Super Bowl XLVIII champs, the Seattle Seahawks were supposed to be NFL royalty, a team of labor-friendly upper-management and politically outspoken left-of-center players who showed there was a different way to win in the conservative world of pro-football. Not enough of it materialized. By 2015, Obama's presidency appeared more a cultural achievement than a political one, with the country's first Black president barred from appointing Supreme Court Justices by the hardball tactics of Senate Republicans. Simultaneously, the Seahawks were ignominiously stripped of their title by a team of patriots, putting an end to their football insurgency. The two unfulfilled dynasties—one in sports, the other in politics—were bonded by unmet promise.

When the Seahawks visited the White House in May 2014, three months after slaughtering the Denver Broncos to win the Super Bowl, Obama unfurled a big blue "Twelfth Man" flag for a big "blue" country. The president addressed media members while holding the official flag of Seahawks fandom with the champs. In Seattle he saw something of himself. Speaking to the White House press corps, the president highlighted quarterback Russell Wilson, recognizing in Wilson his own unlikely rise to power: "He's the second African American quarterback to win a Super Bowl. Nobody commented on it, which tells you the progress we've made."[1] A president popular among America's youth, Obama lauded the leadership of boomer Seahawks coach Pete Carroll, who voted for him in 2008 and 2012: "Those of us in leadership positions look at folks who do things the right way. I think Coach Carroll does things the right way." Obama even wanted to be like running back Marshawn Lynch, who skipped the White House hoopla, usually ignored media obligations, and offered absurdist catch phrases (*I'm here so I won't get fined*) and one-word answers (*thankful*) when pressed. "I'm sorry Marshawn Lynch isn't here, because I wanted to say how much I admire his approach to the press," said the president. In the triumph of this faraway Seattle squad to the mainstream of American sport, Obama saw his reflection: "As a guy who was elected president named Barack Obama, I root for the underdogs. Seeing folks overcome the odds excites me. And that's what this team is all about."[2]

As America recovered from the 2008 recession with the underpaid labor of millennial tech and freelance workers, Carroll's 2010 book *Win Forever: Live, Work, and Play Like a Champion* became popular fodder for America's managerial class. The coach had spun his quest to build a formidable football team into a new age manifesto on workplace culture, complete with Post-it note mantras like "either you're competing or you're not" and "competing is better than winning because it lasts longer."[3] An NFL reporter described the environment fostered in Seattle as "refreshing and progressive." Inspired bosses patronized a consulting firm Carroll started as an offshoot of his book. Tech mogul Paul Allen praised Carroll for going "far beyond what makes a great football coach."[4] Back in 1987, Coach Pete was an assistant with the Minnesota Vikings who nearly became the team's starting quarterback when players walked off the job.[5] Almost a strikebreaker, he was now a pathbreaker of twenty-first-century capitalism.

It'd be tempting to call Carroll the second coming of Gil Dobie, both of them football savants who galvanized the city in support of tough teams during times when some feared Seattle had gone soft. Dobie reintroduced Gilded Age grit to party-obsessed students in the Progressive Era; Carroll commanded gridiron respect for the squad from America's biggest latte town. Though the results were the same—stacks and stacks of wins—the methods differed: Dobie led with an iron fist; Carroll, with pom-poms. At Seahawks team practices Coach Pete and his staff blared loud music and played pranks. They held three-point shooting contests, and built an overall climate of mayhem that spilled onto the field on game day.[6] Like the Super-Sonics of the 1990s before them, Seahawks games during the peak of the Pete Carroll era were chaotic and unpredictable, with Seattle overwhelming opponents with crowd noise and competitive entropy. As a measure of their veracity, the Seahawks went sixty-five games in a row, between 2011 and 2015, without losing a game by double digits—the longest-ever such streak in league history.[7]

At the very least, the Seahawks gave Seattle fans three hours a week of feeling like no American city had anything over them; at their best, they transcended sport and implied something political. Other fan bases didn't dress up in their team's colors the Friday before games; very few of them could pack public transit with one another to attend games at a stadium in city limits, and only one other—college fans at Texas A&M—thought to call themselves the "twelfth man" because they genuinely believed they could influence what took place on the field of play, and often did. For a city infamous for its socially awkward, nonconfrontational residents, football scratched an atavistic civic itch, resurrecting a frontier rambunctiousness that had been lost on the road to tech-addled modernity.

The original Seattle Seahawks logo emblazoned a Coast Salish Kwak-waka̱'wakw mask on the side of a silver helmet, making white settler usurpation of Indigenous societies the supertext of the city's participation in big-league pigskin.[8] In this frontier-war simulation—a game centered on securing enemy territory with strength and cunning—there was an implied sense that teams from temperate climates like Seattle weren't as tough; San Francisco coach Bill Walsh's "West Coast offense" of quick passes and precision execution was a deviation from the brutalist vision of Northeastern military officials who popularized football in the Gilded Age. In contrast to the pretty-boy techniques coached by Mike Holmgren when Seattle lost the 2006 Super Bowl to hard-ass Pittsburgh, Pete Carroll's smashmouth style was truer to the spirit of the sport. In 2013, Seattle went 13–3 by running the ball, reducing opposing offenses to rubble, and only launching explosive pass plays where necessary.

"Loserville, USA" was no more. Coastal liberal cities could dominate, and Seattle could be the toughest of them all. During their 2013 Super Bowl season, Seattle's football rivalry with San Francisco pitted America's two paradigmatic postindustrial cities against one another. In the post–World War II period, both cities parlayed federal research and defense grants to build burgeoning tech sectors. By the time a federal judge ruled that Seattle-based Microsoft had engaged in trust-busting against Silicon Valley tech firms in 2011, both the Emerald City and the Bay Area hosted corporate campuses of all the biggest tech companies in the country: Twitter, Google, Microsoft, Facebook, and by 2013, Amazon, which occupied the South Lake Union lots known as the "heart of Seattle" a century earlier. For their thriving computing industries and "high average median income," San Francisco and Seattle topped the list of *Bloomberg* magazine's 2012 "Best Cities in America."[9]

A stout defensive team with a mobile quarterback named Colin Kaepernick, the San Francisco 49ers were a mirror image of Seattle. Though the Seahawks won the NFC West division in 2013, the 49ers remained close in the standings all season. The rivals met in the NFC Championship Game on January 19, 2014, with a trip to the Super Bowl on the line. When defensive back Richard Sherman tipped a Colin Kaepernick pass to teammate Malcolm Smith to end the NFC Championship Game, the rivalry was settled: Seattle was headed back to the Super Bowl, and San Francisco was headed home. Insult was added to injury when, later in the year, a transit official who once worked for the Seattle Department of Transportation colored seats on San Francisco subways in Seahawks' blue and green.[10]

The Seahawks didn't go quietly to the Super Bowl. In a postgame interview with *NFL on Fox* reporter Erin Andrews, Sherman chastised San Francisco for daring to throw the ball in his direction and proclaimed himself the best defensive back in the league in an explosive rant. For two weeks leading up to the Super Bowl, Sherman's boast prompted an uproar about civility in Obama-era America.[11] Some believed that America had become "postracial" with Obama's election; Sherman's cockiness showed that the path to social acceptance for Black athletes still cleaved to the politics of respectability that Obama epitomized. Sherman's "uppity" rant provoked a racial backlash. Football fans took to social media to call him "an ignorant ape," "a jungle monkey," "a fucking gorilla," "a model for today's Taliban Youth," and, predictably, "a n——."[12] Of the insults hurled, "thug" seemed the most insidious because it managed to retain all the ugly racial subtext of more straightforward slurs, while remaining socially permissible.

A communications major who graduated from Stanford, Sherman pounced. "The reason it bothers me is because 'thug' is an accepted way of calling somebody the n-word," he explained, his words reprinted by *Time* magazine, who named him one of the "100 Most Influential People" in 2014.[13] Sherman referenced a 2012 game between the New Jersey Devils and the New York Rangers, in which the predominantly white teams fought before the game even began, highlighting racial double standards in sports coverage: "Can a guy on a football field just talking to people be a thug? There was a hockey game where they didn't even play hockey." Sherman and the Seahawks had the last word in the discussion: on February 2, 2014, they dismantled Denver in the Super Bowl by 35 points.

The Seahawks were the champions—of the NFL and of the idea that a football team could win while standing for on-field excellence and standing for something more. On May 21, 2014, they went to see Obama.

While the Seahawks were a new kind of football team, Obama seemed a new kind of Democrat. During his 2008 campaign the senator from Illinois used social media to rally young voters, wowed crowds with his soaring rhetoric, and played basketball on the campaign trail to appeal to his urban base. Where Seattle had demonstrated a different way to win games, the president showed a different way to win elections: by energizing blocs of diverse city dwellers and reform-minded ruralities, such that wasting energy trying to convert right-wingers with watered-down policy proposals would be unnecessary. "Progressive people of color now comprise 23 percent of all voters, and progressive Whites account for 28 percent," wrote Obama campaign operative Steve Phillips in his 2016 book *Brown Is the New White*. "America has a progressive multiracial majority that has the power to reshape American priorities."[14]

Diverse big cities like Seattle and San Francisco powered America into a heady new progressive period. The movement was led by a president whose bohemian mother spent her young adulthood in Seattle, going to basketball games, dancing at sock hops, and discussing communism in University District coffee shops in the 1950s and 1960s. Something of the youthful

JFK aura surrounded Stanley Ann Dunham's son, who was reelected to the presidency for a second time on November 6, 2012—the same day that Washington State voters approved legalizing marijuana and same-sex marriage. Two years later, in June 2014, with the Seahawks still basking in their Super Bowl win, Seattle became the first major city in the country to adopt a fifteen-dollar-per-hour minimum wage.[15] Sports, politics, and the new progressive movement met when the Seattle Seahawks visited the White House in May 2014.

During the White House press event, the president celebrated Seattle's loud fans, its lucrative tech industry, its forward-thinking city dwellers, and the social progress their football team embodied. Within a year, however, both the Seahawks' bid to repeat as champions and Obama's presidential agenda would be in shambles.

Seattle stumbled to a 3–3 start to its 2014 campaign, took three games in a row against mediocre competition, then dropped to 6–4 after running back Marshawn Lynch failed to convert a short fourth down in Kansas City on November 16, 2014—one of five times that season when Lynch faltered in high-leverage short yardage situations behind Seattle's shaky offensive line.[16] The Seahawks regained championship form and made it back to the playoffs as the best team in the conference. In January 2015 they beat the Carolina Panthers to advance to the NFC Championship Game, then played one of the wildest games in NFL history: a 28–22 overtime win against the Green Bay Packers, in which Seattle rallied from a 16-point third-quarter deficit to advance to the Super Bowl. Awaiting the Seahawks in the championship game was an opponent that was everything they were not.

If the Seahawks were emblematic of Obama-era America, the New England Patriots were their conservative counterparts: buttoned-down, lacking Seattle's sociopolitical braggadocio, completely comfortable in the Bush White House, which they had visited three times after winning Super Bowls in 2002, 2004, and 2005. Befitting of their status as the representative American sports team of the Patriot Act era, New England was caught illegally surveilling opponents in 2007.[17] New England embodied the conservative tide that Obama had overcome in 2008; they were the kind of dull establishmentarian drones that Pete Carroll never wanted his team to become. To be the first repeat Super Bowl Champions since New England a decade earlier, the progressive Seahawks would have to defeat a team infamous for its repressed work atmosphere. In a rare act of self-expression permitted by Patriots management, a red MAKE AMERICA GREAT AGAIN cap was spotted in Tom Brady's locker in 2015.

Played February 1, 2015, at University of Phoenix Stadium in Glendale, Arizona, Super Bowl XLIX was a back-and-forth affair between two proud teams, with New England taking a 7–0 lead in the first quarter, Seattle storming back to tie, the Patriots going ahead 14–7, and Seattle ending the first half with a Russell Wilson strike to tie the game. Despite losing two key defensive starters to injury, Seattle built a 10-point lead in the third quarter but failed to put the game out of reach when Patriots cornerback Malcolm Butler broke up a critical third down conversion deep in New England territory. Seattle's depleted defense gave up two fourth-quarter touchdowns. Down four, the Seahawks had two minutes to try to win the title. Russell Wilson threw Seattle onto New England's five-yard line, zipping a crafty wheel-route reception to Marshawn Lynch and a miracle pitch to Jermaine Kearse, who gained possession of the ball after a spectacular juggling catch. Wilson handed the ball to Lynch, who would have walked into the end zone were it not for a last-ditch tackle made by a Patriots linebacker lying on the ground. With the ball on New England's one-yard line on second down and the clock dwindling, statisticians placed Seattle's win probability at 73.8 percent.[18]

In the week leading up to the Super Bowl, Patriots coach Bill Belichick praised Pete Carroll for getting his teams to "compete relentlessly as well as any organization I've ever observed."[19] Belichick had replaced Carroll in New England after Coach Pete was fired there in 1999. The firing prompted a period of self-reflection that resulted in the concoction of the *Win Forever* philosophy and the eventual assembly of the juggernaut Seahawks. Carroll was going to stick it to his old team. He would call in a pass play. If it fell incomplete, the clock would stop, saving the team a time-out. Seattle would win its second Super Bowl title after Russell Wilson dropped back to deliver a touchdown slant pass to Seattle receiver Ricardo Lockett. Except Malcolm Butler intercepted it. New England took possession and won the Super Bowl. Marshawn Lynch laughed at the Seattle coaching staff while red, white, and blue confetti fell from the sky. A competitor to his core, Pete Carroll had done battle with common sense and lost.

Once the icon of an ascendant liberal city, the Seattle Seahawks became a symbol of self-sabotage. Lynch was a local folk hero and national icon, a power runner whose vicious steamrolling of flailing defenders was legendary. In 2014, *USA Today* reported that while he was in his mother's womb, Lynch fed on two placentas due to a possible twin who never developed, making him an exceptionally strong child and a terrifying running back.[20] Even casual football fans understood the lunacy of not seeing if the man could run three feet to win a Super Bowl. Though Wilson had given Lynch the ball on the play before the calamitous interception, luminary Seattle writers Sherman Alexie and Ijeoma Oluo speculated that Seahawks management wanted the more clean-cut Wilson—not the dreadlocked Lynch—to get credit for the win. If the Seahawks couldn't have a white Super Bowl–winning quarterback, the line of argumentation went, they would have one who white audiences were more comfortable with.[21] Russell Wilson was clean-cut, well-spoken, lighter-skinned; before the NFC Championship game against San Francisco, memes circulated comparing him favorably to the tattooed, corn-rowed Colin Kaepernick. *Of course* management wanted Wilson, and not the unapologetically Black Marshawn Lynch, to be the hero, the reasoning went. *Of course.*

That this conspiracy theory was spun with little basis in fact wasn't the point. The point was that the "postracial" fantasy of Obama's presidency had deflated to such an extent that many now believed structural racism to be an indestructible force in American life—a force that would haunt the country on television and in locker rooms, on the field and in workplaces, on the one-yard line and even in progressive places like Seattle. Just as their Super Bowl victory a year earlier was hailed as progress, so too did Seattle's excruciating loss become a postmortem on political regression.

After Obama's 2008 win, Republicans in the House and Senate played stall and delay, blocking, filibustering, and watering-down policy advents by Democrats who had majority control of the Senate and Congress. In 2010 the so-called Tea Party flank of anti-government supporters helped Republicans take control of Congress, who then commanded the US Senate in 2014. By this time, the Obama coalition largely dissipated. Disillusioned progressives took to increasingly radical activity like the Occupy Wall Street protests of 2011, where activists squatted in the financial districts of major cities to protest enduring postrecession wealth inequalities. In addition, Black Lives Matter protests began as the spectacle of extrajudicial killings of Black youths was amplified on social media after the 2012 murder of Trayvon Martin. In 2013, Seattle voters dissatisfied with the slow pace of progressive change elected economics professor Kshama Sawant to city council: an avowed socialist who saw Democrats as an equally insidious obstacle to economic justice as Republicans. With the dreams of robust Democrat governance deflating by the day, Obama's second term concluded with Republicans blocking him from appointing a Supreme Court nominee to replace the deceased Justice Antonin Scalia. If the Seahawks were the back-to-back champs that could have been, Obama was the FDR who never was.

With the rudderless Obama administration licensing permits for offshore drilling in May 2015, hundreds of Seattle activists in kayaks demonstrated against a Shell Oil drilling rig making its way to the Yukon through the city's port. National media took a break from ridiculing the Seahawks to gawk. Environmental magazine *Mother Jones* praised Seattle as a "progressive city taking a dramatic stand."[22] Athletic triumph had returned to Seattle: the colorful sporty "kayaktivists" held a line that their president would not. Still, the city had been let down. Once champs, the Seahawks were a dynasty undelivered. A promise unfulfilled. Looking back, it's no wonder Obama saw himself in them.

* * *

Vitriol poured in from all four corners of the internet. In May 2016 a Bay Area investor obsessed with bringing men's professional basketball back to Seattle had attained the urban acreage needed to build a new arena. He would pay for it himself. All that was needed was a perfunctory vote from Seattle City Council to vacate a useless strip of pavement for the stadium's construction.[23] Area unions, afraid of losing jobs near the Seattle waterfront, pressured the city's nine-member city council to vote "no." To the shock of even arena opponents who believed the vote would

Champs after their dominant 43–8 win over the Denver Broncos in Super Bowl XLVIII, the Seattle Seahawks visited the Obama White House in May 2014. Obama saw himself in this team, which hailed from the city where his mother came of age in the 1950s. Alamy Stock Photo.

be a slam dunk, Seattle lawmakers disapproved of the street vacation. The 5–4 vote cleaved along gendered lines, with the city council's four male members voting in approval, and its five women members voting "no." Consequently, misogynistic hate speech rained in liberal Seattle.

Angry tweets about the city council's five women proliferated, the messages too specific, the profile names and pictures too personal, to be the work of bots.[24] One post tagged the accounts of the councilmembers who disapproved of the street vacation and cursed "These 5 dumb bitches voted no on sonics." At that time the most moderate politician in city government, Sally Bagshaw was elsewhere called a "socialist shitbag." Another post about the vote read "and people want a woman to be president." All that stood between Seattle, ostensibly a liberal bastion, and America's growing conservative movement was the ninety-four-foot length of a basketball court. "Since you voted no on the Arena, I'm voting yes for Trump," read one of the tweets.

* * *

How "progressive" was Seattle—honestly—if it incubated the family fortune of the most regressive president in recent memory? Born March 14, 1869, in the Rhineland region of what became Germany, Frederick Trump moved to Seattle in 1891 after reading that the city was a nice place to make a buck in real estate.[25] Seattle progressives objected to the concentration of gambling and sex work in Pioneer Square but had no issue with opportunistic speculators who treated the city as a takable piece of cheap carrion. Trump opened a brothel on Second Avenue and Washington Street, then flipped his profits into a purchase of forty acres of Seattle-area land from the Northern Pacific Railway.[26] He opened several more establishments on that property, amassed a small fortune, then parlayed it into stores that capitalized on miners making their way through Seattle to the Yukon after gold was discovered there in 1896. Wary of Seattle reformers who cracked down on vice in the red-light district, Trump liquidated his real estate holdings before settling in New York City at the turn of the century. He perished in the 1918 influenza pandemic. The family fortune survived Grandaddy Trump, eventually landing in the hands of his grandson, Queens real estate baron Donald J. Trump, who was elected president of the United States on November 8, 2016.

Back in 1989, Trump had been a character in the story of urban conservatism, placing a full-page ad in the *New York Times* calling for the execution of five Black youths who were falsely accused of brutalizing a Central Park jogger. Though Trump hailed from the largest liberal city in the country, his New York was not the New York of children frolicking by uncorked fire hydrants in public housing developments—not the New York of stickball games played on the streets of Black, Jewish, and Puerto Rican neighborhoods; nor the New York of Sue Bird's empowerment as a young woman on the asphalt basketball courts of Queens.[27] Trump's New York was the New York of racial reaction; the New York where urban planner Robert Moses built low overpasses on roads to local parks so buses couldn't bring poor people there.[28] It was the New York where a mob of angry white people attacked Black children riding bikes through the recently integrated neighborhood of Rosedale in 1975; the New York of an angry NYPD riot in 1992, birthed by a racist backlash to the election of the city's first Black mayor. The New York where Mayor Rudy Giuliani escalated Richard Nixon's War on Drugs. The New York of America's forty-fifth president was a place where many agreed with Atlanta Braves pitcher John Rocker's incendiary 1999 comments about queers and immigrants, subway riders and non-English speakers.[29]

Five days after taking office on January 20, 2017, Trump issued an executive order threatening to terminate federal funding to all cities that refused to comply with federal immigration officials.[30] The list of these "sanctuary cities" included almost every major municipality in the country; Seattle was one of the first to be established after its city council declared it a "city of refuge" for immigrants in January 1986. Though reactionary Seattle voters launched a successful initiative to rescind the declaration shortly afterward, the city successfully reiterated its sanctuary status in 2003. In response to Trump's 2017 executive order, rival liberal cities put their differences aside. Seattle and San Francisco were two of the sundry American urbanities to sue the Trump administration over its targeting of sanctuary cities.[31] The teamwork extended from the courts to the fields.

During the 2016 presidential election, San Francisco 49ers quarterback Colin Kaepernick knelt during the national anthem to protest police brutality. Several Seattle Seahawks joined in support, including defensive end Michael Bennett, who later took to giving the Black Power salute during games.[32] If the Seahawks couldn't be a dynasty, they would join the insurgency. Five days after Trump's election in November 2016, they traveled to New England for *Sunday Night Football*; in their first meeting since the catastrophic Super Bowl XLIX, they defeated the Patriots, whose coach had written a letter of congratulations to Trump and whose quarterback was golfing buddies with the president-elect. With *The Guardian* declaring Seattle "the most outspoken team in the NFL," the Hawks were riding high on glowing press coverage; lineman Cliff Avril used postgame press conferences to further relief efforts for Hurricane Sandy, and receiver Doug Baldwin campaigned for a statewide police accountability bill in the Washington State Legislature. *Rolling Stone* billed the team "the Social Justice

Warriors" of the league in 2017.[33] In response, the Facebook page "Vets for Trump" generated a widely circulated fake image of Michael Bennett torching the American flag while the Seahawks locker room celebrated.[34] Seattle's reputation as a progressive bastion—long overblown, to be sure—was nonetheless furthered by its professional football team.

As president, Trump turned the arena of sport into a proxy battle in his larger contest with urban America, most of whose residents didn't vote for him in the 2016 election. He called NFL players who knelt for the national anthem "sons of bitches," demanding the league expel them. When Steph Curry expressed discomfort with visiting Trump's White House, Trump rescinded the invitation and didn't invite the Golden State Warriors in 2018. He did the same to the Seattle Storm when they captured the 2018 WNBA title. When the US women's national soccer team won the World Cup in June 2019, Sue Bird's partner—Seattleite and midfielder Megan Rapinoe—made it plain: "I'm not going to the fucking White House."[35]

Since Teddy Roosevelt during the Progressive Era, most US presidents used sports to polish their public personas, manipulating the ableist expectations of American spectatorship to appear fit to lead.[36] While guiding the country through depression and world war, Franklin Delano Roosevelt hid that he was wheelchair-chair bound so as not to seem vulnerable. JFK brandished an image of spry exuberance while concealing lifelong health issues stemming largely from back injuries he sustained as a college football player. Later, as pundits roasted him about his weight, Bill Clinton took up jogging. Obama sank three-pointers for flashing cameras; in the 2008 presidential primary against Hillary Clinton, he benefited from the sexist perception that women didn't have the strength to command the country. For his part, President Trump overstated his athletic triumphs, lying to whomever would listen about being scouted as a prized baseball player. He maintained a lifelong affinity for sports that superseded fandom and bordered on fixation: if he couldn't box, bat, or play ball, he'd buy sports teams, host heavyweight fights at his hotel, and use the *Rocky III* anthem "Eye of the Tiger" as his walk-on music at campaign rallies in 2016. As president, it irked him that the country's most popular athletes represented cities whose voters rejected him at the ballot box.

While in office, Trump explained his hostility to major cities by saying "they're Democrat run, they're stupidly run."[37] As Seattle had allowed Trump's grandfather to start the family business there, perhaps he had a point.

* * *

Mayor Jenny Durkan presided over a deeply divided city. Although she prevailed over urban planner Cary Moon in the November 7, 2017, election by twelve and a half points, precinct data showed a stark contrast in the candidates' respective bases of support. Moon carried most of Seattle's dense urban demographics, areas with higher concentrations of young and working-class people and almost all of left-leaning Capitol Hill and the University District.[38] Durkan, by contrast, won wealthier precincts with waterfront views—affluent areas that typically had higher turnout and more moderate voters. Trump's vote share in Seattle was small, but greater concentrations of it were in areas Durkan carried, including her home neighborhood of Laurelhurst. Although Durkan and Moon were both Democrats, the political geography of the 2017 election replicated FDR-era redlining maps that separated areas of wealth and capital investment from those of comparative poverty and neglect. In an effort to paper over Seattle's divides, Mayor Durkan pivoted to sports.

Born May 19, 1958, Jenny Anne Durkan had played high school basketball in nearby Bellevue and once worked as a statistician for the Notre Dame women's basketball team. In an interview given shortly after she became Seattle's mayor, she recalled growing up in Seattle as the Super-Sonics raised the spirits of a recession-racked community, saying "professional sports teams knit together different parts of the fabric of the city."[39] During her term as mayor, Durkan appeared at press conferences in Sonics T-shirts and participated in NCAA basketball tournament bracket competitions. She lambasted the Major League Baseball Hall of Fame when it didn't approve Edgar Martinez's candidacy in January 2018, and she hyped National Girls and Women in Sports Day a month later with a giddy Twitter video, wearing a Storm jersey. When a Seattle ownership group hoping to bring the National Hockey League filed its application to the league in February 2018, Durkan celebrated, then celebrated some more when the application was approved later in the year. An open lesbian, Durkan's embrace of sport was a callback to the late 1940s, when LGBTQ+ Seattleites built a vibrant culture around athletics before the reinstitution of retrenched gender roles in the 1950s.[40]

But as a titular Democrat, Durkan was a conservative in the urban political context. Her candidacy was backed by corporate spending from Seattle companies that opposed the fifteen-dollar minimum wage hike and resisted the implementation of a city-owned internet utility.[41] Seattle's business establishment expected a return on their investment. The mayor delivered: Durkan did her best to sabotage taxes on major Seattle corporations and repeatedly moved to shrink social services in the city. Her fiscal conservatism prompted labor-backed Teresa Mosqueda and socialist Kshama Sawant of the city council to criticize her for implementing "austerity policies."[42] When the Durkan administration defunded the city's "Sports Court Restoration Program," the Seattle Metro Pickleball Association wrote Durkan a pointed letter: "Physical activity is essential for quality of life and longevity. Why is it not receiving the attention it deserves?"[43]

The pride of progressive Seattle had long been its playgrounds and parks, paved in the Progressive Era, updated by the Forward Thrust campaign in 1968, and praised by *Sports Illustrated* and *Time* magazines decades later. An original purpose of these playfields was to increase proximity between Seattle's rich and poor as a way of diffusing class conflict. Increasingly in the 2010s, these playgrounds housed homeless residents who were displaced from stable shelter by rising rents.[44] The spike in homelessness overlapped with terrifying stories of random assaults occurring in Seattle greenways. In March 2017, Seattle jogger Kelly Herron was attacked in a public washroom, screaming "Not today, motherfucker!" when a man attempted to rape her, and staving him off with tactics she learned in a self-defense class. In October 2018 another woman runner near Green Lake was assaulted, prompting her to ask, of Seattle officials, "How many people are going to be attacked before you do something to handle homelessness?"[45]

The Seattle Mariners addressed the problem of homelessness by making a bad situation worse. With housing advocates clamoring for more funding for shelters and social services to meet the overlapping issues of homelessness, street harassment, and mental health support, the Mariners organization in September 2018 successfully lobbied the King County Council for $135 million in repairs to Safeco Field, usurping funds that would have gone toward affordable housing.[46] By this time the team had become synonymous not just with bad baseball but also bad politics. As the "Me Too" movement against sexual harassment hit social media, mainstream press outlets, and whisper networks across the country, a 2018 investigation revealed that camera operators for the Mariners' regional television network had filmed scantily clad fans in the Safeco Field stands, archiving the salacious finds in a shareable folder for later access.[47]

If Seattle couldn't count on the Mariners, maybe they could count on their government. A 2018 study by the McKinsey consulting firm estimated that the Seattle area would need upward of $450 million in public funds annually for a decade to end homelessness. But when Seattle activists successfully lobbied Seattle City Council to ratify a corporate tax in June 2018, Mayor Durkan broke state law by texting with councilmembers to coordinate a repeal of it.[48] Like Ole Hanson, Durkan had a knack for nabbing headlines; *Time* magazine elevated her when she told Trump, "My city isn't afraid of immigrants" in October 2018.[49] The mayor neglected to mention that the city's residents once rallied to overturn the city's sanctuary city status.

Under Durkan's term Seattle would introduce its own brand of xenophobia, with many claiming the city's homeless weren't "from" the area and only moved to the Puget Sound region to take advantage of services offered to transients. Cynics coined the term "Freeattle."[50] A March 2017 survey revealed that nearly 70 percent of homeless residents in King County lived in the area when they became homeless and that half of all homeless residents in Seattle lived there for at least five years. More than a third of homeless Seattle-area residents had attended college, and over 40 percent were employed.[51] But in the rush to wield nativist sentiments and meritocratic myths against the city's homeless, facts were ignored. Just as Trump's rhetoric weaponized the issue of immigration, turning it into a Trojan horse to decry welfare spending of any kind, homelessness in Seattle became a catchall conversation about who "belonged" in Seattle and who didn't.

While Trump's agenda was disseminated with cable news propaganda on Fox News and right-wing media like Breitbart, stigmas about the homeless in Seattle were driven by conservative blogs like *Safe Seattle*; the editorial slant of the *Seattle Times* argued against the use of progressive taxation to end homelessness.[52] The pro-Trump company Sinclair took over one of the city's local news stations in 2018, broadcasting garish propaganda that made homeless Seattleites seem necessarily prone to criminal activity. The 2019 Seattle City Council candidate Christopher Rufo made criminalizing the homeless a core part of his platform, then worked with the Trump administration to ban federal agencies from partaking in diversity training.[53] Conservatism took its place alongside computing and coffee as Seattle's most visible exports.

Early in his term, President Trump launched an unprecedented attack on America's national parks, reducing protections for approximately thirty-five million acres of public land. The president's privatization of communal reserves had a parallel in sweeps the Durkan administration conducted of homeless encampments in Seattle parks.[54] Durkan spent $10 million annually to rid city greenways of Seattleites who had no place else to go; in so doing, her office replicated a strategy that had been a proven failure since the 1930s, and blew many millions of dollars that could have been spent on actual housing.[55]

Liberal Seattle could have been a refuge from hostile political winds. But a city in competition with itself could scarcely give anyone else shelter.

* * *

The arrival of the National Hockey League (NHL) in Seattle kick-started a chain of events that led me to enter the foray of local politics. After the NHL's Board of Governors approved a local ownership group's application for a Seattle NHL franchise, Rob Johnson of Seattle City Council District 4 vacated his seat in November 2018 to take a job with the team. The councilmember's trade of politics for sport popped the cork on Seattle's 2019 election cycle, with city council races shaping up as a clash between Mayor Durkan's Chamber of Commerce and candidates who objected to the direction Seattle's business establishment was taking the city in. I was one of fifty-six candidates who vied to represent one of Seattle's seven city council districts, announcing my run for the seat vacated by Johnson in the alt-weekly tabloid *The Stranger* on November 23, 2018.

My district included the northeast Seattle neighborhoods of Wedgwood, the University District, and Sand Point, where Seattle police had killed a pregnant Black mother named Charleena Lyles in June 2017.

Politics are the arena where conflicting group interests are settled. Recalling a book I read as a history student at the University of Washington—Henri Lefebvre's 1968 "Right to the City," a manifesto about reclaiming cities from the grips of finance capital—I made our campaign's slogan "FIGHTING FOR YOUR RIGHT TO THE CITY."[56] And the fight was real. District 4 had some of the wealthiest, most racially homogenous neighborhoods in Seattle, areas that might have hesitated to vote for a card-carrying member of the Democratic Socialists of America, and a Black one at that. Late in the campaign a yard sign with my image on it was defaced with the n-word.[57]

During the primary my campaign was endorsed against by nearly every sitting federal, state, and city elected official in Seattle, with many believing I was too much of a radical to advance to a general election and in any case not capable of running a serious campaign. To win, we would have to seize any advantage we could. As the August primary approached and the hot sun of another summer beset by climate change beat down on Seattle, my campaign doubled down on door knocking. We routinely turned out dozens and dozens of volunteers in city parks who believed that Seattle could be the progressive city it said it was. Playgrounds planted during the age of reform were a staging point for our ground attack. Thanks to the efforts of these volunteers and our campaign staff—the first in Seattle electoral history to unionize—we advanced past the August 6, 2019, primary and into the general election.

Ultimately, I came up a few points short in November. Because of my campaign stance on paying for public housing by taxing large corporations, our campaign was outspent one hundred to one in corporate independent expenditures—some of them by the ownership group of the Seattle Mariners.[58] On election night, Tuesday, November 5, 2019, our campaign trailed by sixteen points; late ballots narrowed the final margin of defeat to four. Though we narrowly lost the election, our campaign rallied areas with renters and students to pay closer attention to local politics; not an easy task when rising rents and stagnating wages make it difficult on many to spend time on civic engagement. In addition, I was proud of how we competed in areas typically thought of as moderate, if not conservative. On a platform devoted to building affordable housing by repealing Seattle's restrictive zoning laws, we won twenty-nine of thirty-one precincts in Wallingford, a once-segregated neighborhood long believed to be categorically resistant to the construction of affordable housing.[59]

After the campaign Christopher Rufo took to the *New York Post* to clutch his pearls: "Socialist city council candidate Shaun Scott argued that the city must 'disinvest from the police state' and 'build towards a world where nobody is criminalized for being poor.' At a debate hosted by the Seattle Police Union, Scott blasted officers for their 'entrenched ties to institutional racism.' One might dismiss such proclamations as part of a fringe movement, but advocates of these views are gaining political momentum."[60]

Rufo was right about one thing: momentum was growing for the idea of reimagining public safety. Variations on the idea of using police funding to bolster human services have appeared throughout history, reiterated by policymakers and political figures who didn't believe more police necessarily meant safer communities. In 1924, Seattle mayor Bertha Landes told the city's police chief "the police department has lost the confidence of the people. Taxpayers should not pay the salaries of men who should be removed from the force."[61] In 1958 urban planner Jane Jacobs asserted that "no quantity of policemen can enforce civilization where informal community self-policing falls to pieces."[62] In 2005, former Seattle Police chief Norm Stamper argued for "using the money now being squandered on cops to finance new public policies and educate and rehabilitate."[63] Before long, reactionaries like Rufo would see exactly how much "political momentum" police accountability via police divestment really had in urban America. In the meantime, I poured over precinct data, searching for clues about how and why I had come up short.

* * *

A city is a competition. Who will win it? During the city council campaign, land-use activists brought it to my attention that private golf courses in Seattle enjoyed huge tax subsidies and that public golf courses had bigger budgets than critical city bureaucracies.[64] As of 2019, if the Sand Point Country Club in northeast Seattle paid the same land taxes that area homeowners do on their property there, its annual tax bill would grow from $36,507 to $2.85 million. Similar figures exist for all private Seattle golf clubs; the Broadmoor Country Club in Madison Park gets an annual tax subsidy of $6.8 million. That's lost revenue that could be used on civilianized 911 response, earthquake retrofitting, housing, and more. In addition, the four public golf courses operated by the City of Seattle totaled 528 acres of city-owned land; many housing advocates and environmentalists wondered whether these expansive courses could be converted into sustainable affordable housing developments with plush parks and trees for low- and middle-income residents.[65]

Seattleites don't have to look too far for a better way to use the hundreds of acres of city land currently being usurped by golf. In 1947 the University of Washington recast a nine-hole golf course to build the UW School of Medicine. "They could've preserved some of the course, but that's progress," recalled a medical student who hit the fairway when he wasn't hitting the books.[66] If the area south of Lake Union is the heart of Seattle and Pioneer Square is its gut, the University District is the mind—a place where big ideas radiate outward and collegiate optimism pushes the city to be better than before. The "U-District" was established in the Progressive Era as a release from the downtown business blocks; its original name was "Brooklyn." The University District is a city within a city, connected to the rest of Seattle by subways, by bike lanes, by brain waves.

Conceptually the college districts of major cities are among the most coveted urban designs in the United States. They're dense ecosystems where residential units collide with commercial storefronts, street clatter with spaces of quiet contemplation. This kind of cityscape has become increasingly trendy as the fiscal and moral costs of automobile-centric lifestyles in US suburbs have escalated. Tech and industrial science corporations often brand their workspaces as "campuses," presenting them as futuristic fairgrounds free from history. In reality, they mimic college contours that have existed for centuries. As it turns out, corporate America has little to offer in the way of improving upon what Marxist-urbanist Mike Davis has called "the quasi-socialist paradises of university campuses."[67] Fitting for a hub of research in the sciences and humanities, the University District is a laboratory for the urban experiment, showing what cities value by what they decide to cheer.

As Gil Dobie began his run of excellence in autumn 1908, the University of Washington's *Washington Alumnus* publication wrote that "the North-west [has] just woken up to the fact that championship teams advertised the college in a unique and effective way." A century later, in 2013, the school completed a $280 million renovation of Husky Stadium, followed by the opening of two U-District subway stations that were the result of a transit measure King County voters approved in 2008.[68] The weekly parade of foot traffic to and from Husky football games in autumn—to and from blooming on-campus cherry blossoms in spring—increased on newly paved walkways and pedestrian bridges. Sports and outdoor spaces advertised UW beautifully, broadcasting it as an oasis apart from the rest of the neoliberal city. In his 2021 book *In the Shadow of the Ivory Tower: How Universities Are Plundering Our Cities*, historian Davarian L. Baldwin writes that "the university has shifted from being one noble part of the city to serving as a model for the city itself."[69]

If Baldwin is right, then the "model city" in America is one where free labor builds and pays for everything. College football was a lucrative game worth more to UW than its players would ever see. In 2019 the university reported $133.8 million in total revenue from its Athletics Department; most of it ($84 million) came from media rights and tickets sales generated by Husky football, which—in addition to underpaid academic employees who struck for higher wages in 2019—directly subsidized research worth $1.3 billion to the American economy.[70] As pathways to prosperity were few and far between for economically marginalized populations under neoliberalism, sports were a way out of poverty, creating a biopolitical regime where athletes from disproportionately poor backgrounds sacrificed their bodies to the altar of college sports. In the same way that privileged Americans with blood disorders benefit from the sold plasma of the destitute to stay alive, college athletics programs are similarly vampiric, sucking life and health from football players pursuing the distant dream of sports stardom.[71]

Seeing the tremendous value generated by uncompensated college athletes, a Republican in the Washington State Legislature introduced a bill in 2019 to allow college athletes to be paid: "Everybody is getting extremely wealthy off of this system, except for the college athletes themselves," said Drew Stokesbary, a GOP politician representing the Seattle suburb of Auburn.[72] Stokesbary faced opposition from a Democrat and self-professed progressive whose district included Seattle neighborhoods near Husky Stadium. The rep argued that if a student executed research that brought in money for the university, that student would not be paid—hence, student athletes who provide revenue for the university shouldn't either.[73]

In Washington State's Democrat-controlled House of Representatives, the argument that labor exploitation in one place excused it in another proved compelling. The bill to abolish student athlete serfdom was defeated.

With progressives like these, did American cities need conservatives?

18th Inning

LIFE AND BREATH
IN THE FOREVER CITY

When the Seattle Mariners played the Houston Astros in Game Three of the American League Division Series (ALDS) on October 15, 2022, the game took place during the autumn of humankind. Sunny commentary from TBS broadcasters reassured television audiences that it was a "picture perfect day in Seattle," but that picture was polluted by yellow wildfire smoke drifting in from Bolt Creek. The "Air Quality Index"—an Orwellian stat that West Coast residents had only gotten used to checking in recent years—measured 161 when the game started.[1] That was categorically "unhealthy" for the general public, but the mass health hazard didn't dissuade Mariners team officials from opening T-Mobile Park's retractable roof, further exposing a capacity crowd of forty-eight thousand to toxic haze. Of planetary decay brought on by torrents of carbon from cars, US military activity, and corporate polluters, Mariners fans had a pristine view.

The Coast Salish peoples who stewarded these lands for millennia before white settlement knew well enough to strategically ignite select patches of area greenwood, because small tactical blazes prevented natural brush fires from doing too much damage. Under the industrial management of major timber corporations, area forests were more prone to unproductive wildfires than public woodlands.[2] The civilization that whites grifted upon Native land was made to burn. Seattleites lunged for the gasoline.

While making headlines as the head of a "green" city, Mayor Jenny Durkan never followed through on her 2017 campaign promise to build a comprehensive bike network in the city as an alternative to automobile travel; her office even canceled bike lanes already in construction.[3] When the aging West Seattle Bridge closed for repairs in 2020, area elected officials lobbied for federal funds to reopen it but didn't add any rail, biking, wheelchair, or pedestrian pathways on its new surface.[4] Many organized homeowners went on as they had for decades, fighting urban density that would reduce carbon emissions by reducing the length of commutes city dwellers made in cars. Data from the 2020 census revealed Seattle's pro-environmentalist reputation to be largely fraudulent: the city sprawled more than Los Angeles and Miami.[5] And though the Amazon corporation had bought and repurposed KeyArena—renaming it and its Coast Salish rainhat-inspired roof Climate Pledge Arena—the company was among the largest polluters on the planet. With TBS announcers not mentioning the source of the filthy mist that clouded the on-field action between the Astros and Mariners in October 2022, many viewers were unaware that something was seriously wrong in Seattle.

In the twenty-first century the struggle to reverse the worst impacts of climate change has been daunting and steep. Odds have mounted, morale has been low, and defeat seems much more likely than victory. Few understand the moral fiber required to sustain a fight like that better than Seattle Mariners fans. Since the 9/11 fall of 2001, the M's missed the playoffs every year, making them the only team in the four major American sports leagues to do so for that long—twenty-one years. Seattle didn't appear on ESPN's *Sunday Night Baseball* broadcast for twelve years between 2004 and 2016, a testament to their terribleness.[6] On June 19 the Mariners' 2022 campaign seemed doomed. Seattle sat near the cellar of the American League West standings at 29–39. In a stunning turnaround, they went 25–6 between June 21 and July 27, won fourteen games in a row during that stretch, and concluded the season 61–33 to make the playoffs. A world beleaguered by rising seas needed resilient mariners, and Seattle had theirs.

From my eighth-floor University District apartment—the brick fortress Malloy, constructed during Seattle's 1920s building boom—I could hear it all: cheers emanating from the dingy sports bar across the street after the thirteen walk-off hits the Mariners slapped in 2022; cars honking when Seattle eliminated Toronto in the American League Wild Card round; the alarming cough of the resident in the next unit as wildfire smoke intensified;

work calls on Zoom derailed by score updates and discussions about the team. Was there a surer sign that the end times had arrived than Seattleites honestly believing the Mariners could win the World Series?

As it had during the miracle season of 1995, baseball fever swept Seattle. The new contagion was more welcome than the other one that still hadn't subsided. In March 2020 the COVID-19 pandemic unplugged civic connection in most American cities, cloistering Seattleites into quarantine with the rest of the country. When public gatherings resumed, they were smothered in a thick layer of social anxiety, the inevitable result of many people feeling for two years that their bodies were the vessels of societal collapse. The influenza pandemic of 1918 caused the first recorded instances of the "Seattle Freeze" of standoffish Seattleites; the COVID-19 pandemic left many city dwellers craving collective dopamine.[7]

Smaller foreshocks anticipated the larger quake of support for the Mariners. On Saturday, April 16, 2022, the NHL Kraken, the Sounders, and the Mariners all played home games, turning Seattle's recently expanded subway into a public feeder system for privately owned sports leagues. Seattle fans rooted for Sue Bird during her final WNBA season as the Storm made a deep playoff push in summer 2022. In September, Seahawks fans rained boos on Denver Broncos quarterback Russell Wilson—the most accomplished player in Seattle football history—when he returned to Seattle after being traded earlier in the year. Though some Seattle spectators had a vicious streak, as when they hurled racial slurs at Warren Moon in the 1970s, they could be magnanimous as well. At WNBA playoff games in September 2022, fans graciously cheered the visiting Las Vegas Aces during player introductions.[8] But baseball had been the sport most closely tied to the city's boiling ambition ever since the 1870s, when Seattleites traveled with their team to games against competitors for the railroad. Mariners fandom unlocked Seattle chauvinism.

After the Mariners beat Toronto to advance to play the Houston Astros, some Seattle fans were full of themselves. In Game Two of the first-to-two series in Canada, the M's erased a seven-run deficit to win 10–9; Seattle fans taunted their Toronto counterparts on social media and in the press, puncturing whatever positive underdog aura they may have had going into their ALDS showdown with the Astros. An iota of success had revealed many Seattle baseball fans to be as cutthroat as everybody else, their decades of futility failing to impart them with the pleasant countenance expected of perennial losers. After twenty years of playoff starvation, Mariners fans felt entitled to their pound of flesh. They sought it in Houston, a city it had maintained sometimes subtle, sometimes explicit sports and civics rivalries with since the 1980s.

Back in 2017, the Houston Astros had won the World Series with the help of systematic cheating; in the cutthroat world of professional sports, the team was doing business as business was done. Baseball tends to invoke tear-jerker sentimentality from its followers—seen clearly, it's a crassly material-istic sport, prone to periodic moral panics about steroids and rule-bending, and always beholden to big money. In the twenty-one seasons comprising 2002 through 2022, when the Mariners finally made the playoffs after last appearing in 2001, eighty-four teams played in baseball's League Champion-ship rounds: sixty-three of them had payrolls above the league average. Of the twenty-one champs crowned in this period, seventeen had above-average spending on player salaries, and ten were in the top ten. In 2022 the mighty Houston Astros had the league's ninth largest payroll ($194.1 million). By contrast, the Mariners' comparatively meager spending on player salaries ($128.7 million) ranked twenty-first of thirty teams.[9] The end of most un-derdog stories are written with the same pens that sign checks; Seattle had little chance against one of the best teams money could buy.

Established (unknown at the time) on top of one of the largest petro-leum reservoirs on the planet, Houston was the luckiest city in the United States; in the 2022 ALDS against the Mariners, it showed. In Game One of the first-to-three series played in Houston, Seattle raced out to a 4–0 start, then took a 7–3 lead into the bottom of the eighth. The Astros scored two runs in their half of the inning; when Mariners manager Scott Servais inexplicably allowed struggling pitcher Robbie Ray to face one of the most potent hitters in the game, slugger Yordan Alvarez blasted a three-run walk-off homer in the ninth. Game Two followed a familiar script, with Seattle taking a 2–1 lead that was erased in the sixth by a two-run dinger from Alvarez. Down 0–2 and heading back to Seattle after dropping two games they should have won, the Mariners counted on their home-field advantage in T-Mobile Park to stave off elimination.

For the October 14 game in Seattle, Mariners fans packed Pioneer Square an hour before airtime. Pearl Jam guitarist Mike McCready played the national anthem, and Mariners legend Félix Hernández threw out the opening pitch. All of it was blanketed by thick wildfire smoke that lingered all day and all night. What followed for the next six hours and twenty-two minutes was the most excruciating baseball game in the sport's modern history: a scoreless marathon broken open on a one-run shot by Astros shortstop Jeremy Peña in the top of the eighteenth. When the Mariners failed to answer in their half of the inning, their fate was sealed. Houston advanced to the American League Championship Series, on the way to winning the World Series.

In recent years record numbers of Major League Baseball games have been canceled due to inclement weather—yet another example of the human-made impact of climate change. That Game Three between the Mariners and Astros was even played forecasted a dreary future. The spectacle of a predominantly Latin American labor force going to work under these conditions was a clear articulation of the late capitalist social contract: come pandemic or deadly pollution, city dwellers who could afford the price of admission expected their strawberries to be picked, their food delivered, their raspberry macchiatos with a shot of espresso served, their game-winning homers hit.

A display of human endurance during climate collapse, the Mariners' 2022 playoff run was in any case well-timed. Had Seattle waited another two decades to make the playoffs, there may not have been much of a planet left to play on.

* * *

Urban America is the country's respiratory system, inhaling people, labor, and raw materials, then exhaling commodities, symbols, and ideas. When urban areas become congested, nothing moves; when they sneeze, the country falls ill. In February 2020 a Seattle-area resident died of a mysterious respiratory malady that was making its way through the country. This person is believed to be the first US casualty of the illness, until subsequent autopsies revealed an earlier death in Kansas on January 9, 2020—the same day that the World Health Organization announced a spate of pneumonia-like cases in the Wuhan region of China.[10] Though some people began to scrub their groceries and mail, believing the infection bred on surfaces, a more accurate profile of the virus gradually emerged: it spreads primarily through respiratory droplets that linger in the air. Tight spaces like office cubicles, elevators, and enclosed sports stadiums facilitate its proliferation among human hosts.[11] Per capita fatalities of the virus were greater in more sparsely populated areas of the country; caseloads accumulated more rapidly in big cities. Epidemiologists understood the disease to be the result of a novel instantiation of coronavirus called SARS-COV-2, and believed the first outbreak occurred in December 2019.[12] As a result, it was named COVID-19.

Because they bring people together, sports were the canary in the coal mine for the social disruption caused by COVID-19. On March 11, 2020, a game between the Oklahoma City Thunder and the visiting Utah Jazz was abruptly canceled, with news breaking just before the game that Utah center Rudy Gobert had tested positive for COVID-19. As a packed house at Chesapeake Arena waited anxiously for the game to start, the stadium public address announcer took to the mic: "Due to unforeseen circumstances the game has been postponed. We are all safe."[13]

But we weren't all safe. The intensive care units of hospitals in major cities soon became packed with patients in need of intubation. As COVID-19 attacked the human vascular system, those who contracted even mild cases reported lingering health effects: trouble concentrating, shortness of breath, inability to achieve an erection. Nor was the game between Oklahoma City and Utah "postponed." It would never be played. In spring 2020 shelter-in-place orders flowed from state and local governments trying to stop the pandemic's spread; the 2019–20 NBA season was delayed, and seasons of other major sports leagues followed. Just as the premature end of the 1919 Stanley Cup Championship in Seattle was a flash point in the influenza pandemic a century earlier, the game played by the relocated Seattle basketball team in Oklahoma City announced a new global contagion.

Even the terrorist attacks of September 11, 2001, couldn't stop pro-sports ticket sales and advertising revenue. Whatever halted America's sports calendar had to be a serious threat to the way of life that our games were often at the center of. And for many, that's exactly what COVID-19 was.

It emptied sports bars and cafés, cleared spaces of civic gathering, quieted once-clamoring cosmopolitan cities. But in the same way that Plato once wrote that "every city is divided into a city of the poor and a city of the rich," there were two pandemics: one for the 63.4 million "white-collar" professional, technical, and managerial workers who comprised 43 percent of the US labor force in 2020; and another pandemic for the country's 1.3 million food delivery workers, its 1.7 million rideshare drivers, its 2.7 million grocery store employees, its 24.3 million laborers in education and health services.[14] Though both of these labor contingents were concentrated largely in urban America, only one had the luxury of commuting to work via teleconferencing software. Despite company miscreants who deliberately misclassified many laborers as managers in order to deny them union benefits, a more or less stark divide existed in the American workforce, separating capitalists, supervisors who sided with them, and workers who generated all the value.

Make no mistake: with the exception of global elites whose wealth increased greatly because of a rise in media streaming and in-home purchases during quarantine, COVID-19 hurt everybody.[15] But the anxieties and aspirations of America's more privileged labor cohort swiftly became shorthand for the country's general pandemic experience. The trope of quarantine bread-baking and Zoom mishaps defined the times, as if millions of others hadn't gone on tending to the sick, shuttling around passengers, ringing up groceries, and delivering food while others worked from home. In May 2020, for example, 73 percent of workers in managerial occupations teleconferenced, compared to 7 percent of service workers.[16] Behind only Austin, Seattle saw the second largest increase in the utilization of food-delivery apps in 2020–21, with hurried cyclists for DoorDash and Postmates bobbing in and out of city bike lanes.

The COVID-19 pandemic exacerbated existing class tensions in American cities. During quarantine, telecommuting customers whose only in-person social interaction in a given day was with the local barista came to expect the requisite pleasantries and prompt service. They were disappointed to find harried coffee slingers who weren't in the mood. In a plot twist, service workers often managed those who wanted to speak to the manager, asking angry customers to wear masks and social distance. In the early 2020s the perfect storm of pandemic, short-tempered customers and low pay created a crisis in the labor market—described by economists as "the great resignation"—and sparked a wave of worker organization in fields long thought to be immune to unionization: newspapers, nonprofits, and political campaigns, among others.[17] Starbucks's earlier union-busting history was reanimated when Howard Schultz returned as the company's CEO to fight the wave of workers organizing at his company's stores in 2021. Millennial and Gen-Z baristas in Seattle who had mostly known Schultz as the bastard billionaire who let the Sonics escape to Oklahoma City had a new reason to revile him. At a Starbucks picket line in Seattle's University District in August 2022, a worker wearing mini-guillotines as earrings carried a sign that read "FIRST THE SUPERSONICS, NOW THIS?"[18]

* * *

The NBA has long been a window into US labor relations in ways that football and baseball are not—a sport where labor switches teams more freely than in more traditional leagues, and individual performances impact games with an immediacy not seen elsewhere. With no hats or helmets to hide behind, sweaty basketball players go to work in jerseys and shorts that don't extend past the knees. Like pedestrians sauntering past a construction site, fans can see how hard the richest unionized workers in the world are working, and on what. Off the court, NBA players often make front-office decisions, recruit their friends to come play with them, and are generally empowered to an extent not seen in America's other sports leagues.

In their 2018 book *Managerial Capitalism*, economists Gérard Duménil and Dominique Lévy wrote that "the rise of the managerial classes conveys new systems of thought—ways of life, morals, social behaviors."[19] Professional basketball is an epiphenomenon of late-stage capitalism—a period where freelancers, temps, Instagram influencers, Etsy sellers, YouTube fitness gurus, Twitter "grind bros," and SoundCloud rappers operate as businesses unto themselves, making the marketing and bureaucratic responsibilities once handled by major corporations the entire basis of their online personas. To be sure, "hustlers" had existed in American cities for decades:

teenage Sick's Stadium concession stand worker William Nass referred to himself as one while describing his time peddling peanuts and popcorn to Seattle crowds in the 1940s.[20] But with the decline of traditional nine-to-five jobs, the onset of corporate outsourcing, and the breakdown of traditional kindship networks during deindustrialization, hustlers moved from the margins of American society to somewhere nearer the center. The NBA bolsters the neoliberal fantasy that through superhuman individual effort and deep-seated distrust of one's peers, great wealth and status can be attained. Consequently, the most popular players tend to be scoring guards who play not just one-on-five but one-on-nine—that is, ballers who overcome both the structural failings of their own teams and also opposing defenses to step back and fade away from everyone else.

In a country where self-monetization is culture—a 1099 tax form a personality—central concerns for NBA fans include scheduling, workload management, and contracts. The price and movement of labor is followed by NBA media as closely as actual games. Glorified human resource conflicts between team management and employees make headlines. Fans have become familiar with rotational diagnostics like the "plus-minus," which allow pundits to measure an individual player's productivity relative to their peers. Through 2023, a top-line sponsor of basketball writer Bill Simmons's podcast—the most downloaded sports podcast of all time—was Indeed .com, a hiring website. Professional basketball is a pastime for millions who spend their work lives on admin tasks, supervisor check-ins, performance evaluations, and hiring panels. The spectacle of professional basketball is postindustrial capitalism gazing at itself.

In basketball games played in the pandemic-proof bubble the NBA established in Orlando, fans teleconferenced "into" the games, their faces displayed on courtside digital screens in a clumsy tech promotion sponsored by Microsoft.[21] In the 2020–21 season Milwaukee Bucks center Giannis Antetokounmpo's life story became the stuff of a Disney movie, a meritocratic fairy tale about a starving Nigerian-Greco youth who fashioned himself into a champion, persevering through pain and fatigue in a season defined by debilitating injuries to players.[22] During a pandemic that many didn't survive, Antetokounmpo symbolized survival of the fittest. Sports media praised him for seemingly never resting, for not exercising the power of free agency to play for another team—in short, for being a model employee.

If pandemic basketball typified US labor relations, it also reproduced the disparities therein. The sibling league to the NBA, the WNBA also played the remainder of their interrupted 2020 season in a COVID-safe campus in Orlando in 2020; its players made significantly less money than their male counterparts for enduring the same inconvenience. Because many WNBA players were single mothers and primary caregivers, the league was forced to allow children who had no other caretakers into the closed-off Orlando campus.[23] As women workers in all fields are more likely to put in "second shifts" of housework—with male partners unwilling or unlikely to help pick up the slack, even and especially as these responsibilities increased during quarantine—the WNBA mirrored a core inequity of capitalism.

After the Sue Bird–led Seattle Storm won yet another WNBA Championship in 2020—their fourth in sixteen years—a graphic circulated by *Fadeaway World* revealed a tremendous wage gap: Bird had won as many championships as LeBron James in the same amount of seasons but made 187 times less in salary that year ($215,000 to James's $37.4 million). Bird's win bonus for being on the team that won the 2020 WNBA title was $11,356. For James's equivalent accomplishment in the NBA, the figure was $370,000.[24] Both Bird and James lived lives of conspicuous privilege, earning more in social acclaim and riches than most wage laborers could ever dream of. That deep inequity followed them even into utopia, which didn't bode well for those left behind.

* * *

Just as ideas vary on how progressive movements start, not all sports observers believe in momentum. Some statisticians hold that events are just events and don't necessarily add up to a winning wave. Common sense suggests otherwise. A ball rolls out of bounds during a basketball game, resulting in a turnover; the other team scores. The crowd cheers, igniting confidence where previously there was none. A missed shot leads to another basket. A sense of inevitability builds. Politically, matters unfold in much the same way: a precipitating event ignites public awareness. Conversations start. Protests push an agenda that only used to be whispered in private. At this point affairs can go in one of two ways: continued wins that ripple outward in changed economic conditions, changed laws, and changed behavior; alternatively, a conservative response can stifle what once seemed promising.

During the civil rights summer of 2020, the feeling in Seattle was that a window of opportunity had opened to curtail police abuses. For a century starting with its inception in 1869, as detailed in Christopher T. Bayley's book *Seattle Justice*, the Seattle Police Department was patently corrupt, operating as a protection racket until reformers waged a systematic effort to weed out police corruption in the 1970s. During the Progressive Era, Seattle cops sold licenses to establishments that sold sex work and alcohol, and badgered businesses that didn't pay bribes. In the post–World War II period, when establishments with pinball machines became a high-stakes front for criminal enterprise in Seattle, police continued selectively enforcing the law, shielding mafiosos who handed over the requisite bribes.[25] As early as 1926, the Seattle Police Department brought shame on the city, with the *New York Times* referring to it as "a citadel of entrenched evils" after Mayor Landes suggested defunding them.[26] Even after city reformers ended Seattle's police payoff system in the 1970s, tragic headlines of slain minority Seattleites were a frequent occurrence in Seattle. From the 1980s on, civil asset forfeiture laws allowed city cops to take and sell the belongings of Seattleites merely suspected of being involved in the drug trade. Norm Stamper, Seattle Police chief from 1994 to 2000, denounced the practice in his 2006 exposé about the culture of racism, misogyny, and violence in his former department. Seattle cops in 2012 were placed under a federal probe that lasted a decade because of the department's habit of using force unconstitutionally.[27] If Seattleites couldn't get justice in the courts or at city hall for a century of police abuse, they would seek it in the streets.

Tens of thousands of Seattleites protested in the summer of 2020, demanding that their elected officials direct funds from the city's bloated police budget into housing, childcare, and other human services. They would avenge Seattleites—Seattleites of all colors—who had grave concerns about police misdeeds near Capitol Hill's Cal Anderson Park ever since police criminalized youth of color who played baseball there in the 1900s. Some Seattleites seized the East Precinct near the park and established a "Capitol Hill Autonomous Zone" to watch abolitionist films and play stickball in. They said a city didn't need overpolicing—or policing at all—to be safe. Almost as quickly as it emerged, however, their movement spawned a backlash.

At the height of the summer protests in 2020, members of the Seattle City Council pledged to defund the city's police department by 50 percent, but they declined to follow through when the weather turned and Seattle-ites stopped protesting. In the November 2021 elections, candidates who pledged to uphold overinvestment in Seattle's traditional model of policing swept their races in open seats against abolitionist and police reformist opponents, capturing the mayor's office and an at-large city council seat.[28] In the race for Seattle city attorney, a onetime registered Republican and Trump supporter defeated abolitionist Democrat Nicole Thomas-Kennedy. A former linebacker at the University of Washington in the 1970s, Bruce Harrell was elected mayor of Seattle after campaigning on the absurd pledge to celebrate every week that the Seattle Police Department didn't kill a Black person. The movement for police accountability had not only stalled but was reversed to such an extent that its opponents rode the backlash to power. Where had the momentum gone?

Seattle historian Roger Sale said in his 1976 book *Seattle, Past to Present* that "the failure of progressive politics lies in the failure of reformers to realize the chances they had to build a political base strong enough to fight interests that held power."[29] Though he was speaking of the original Progressive Era, his words reverberate through many decades of progressive travail. Over and over in Seattle history, one sees progressives self-defeat by underestimating their own strength, potential run after potential run left in scoring position. Part of what made the 2021 Seattle elections so disheartening was the sense of missed opportunity. Leftist candidates had been handed a historic mandate by the civil rights protests of 2020. They faced significant headwind from right-wing media committed to making them look like scary radicals. They weren't elected.

In 2019, I had run for city council as an abolitionist and also came up short, a year before the 2020 movement for police accountability bubbled over into the streets. Sitting with defeat, I realized it was easier to blame the electorate, the political landscape, and other circumstances outside of my control than it was to self-assess. I forced myself to review precinct data. A trend emerged: with the exception of the Wallingford precincts (a neighborhood in north Seattle), we won against all odds; areas where the campaign did well generally had lower voter turnout than those where it did poorly.[30] Additional time spent among our campaign's natural base could have helped bridge the losing gap of four percentage points. Now, as in the past, latent left-of-center blocs have the potential to transform our cities.

In February 2023, with the city mired in what seemed a counterprogressive period of sociopolitical reaction, millennial and Gen-Z organizers in the House Our Neighbors coalition notched an improbable win: in a low-turnout special election, they convinced 57 percent of voting Seattleites to establish a public development authority to build public housing in the city. Opponents attacked the initiative as unrealistic and unfunded; they neglected to mention it would be paid for with the same mechanism—civic bonds—that had built many of Seattle's sports facilities. The *Seattle Times* opposed the plan; the Initiative 135 campaign proved the paper wrong.[31] Obstinate as ever, business interests in the city went on boosting privatized spectacles over public works. With Initiative 135 set to appear on Seattle ballots, Mayor Harrell proposed taking money from the city's affordable housing revenue source and using it to boost sports tourism with the 2023 MLB All-Star Game and FIFA World Cup matches.[32]

If the city's history with the 1995 NCAA Final Four was any indication—when city police destroyed a homeless encampment and arrested antipoverty protestors—Seattle would prepare for these celebrations by attempting to sweep its issues under the rug. As they always had, Seattle sports simulated the city's political climate, sometimes symbolizing progress and other times substantiating regression.

* * *

Seattleites should want to believe in progress. The idea that society moves inexorably in the direction of its own improvement is soothing. Bad things happen; people learn from them and make changes. They harbor memory of the time before reform, and promise to never return there. "We draw comfort from the idea that history is an autonomous moral force that can motivate action and set straight the record of human misdeeds," historian Joan Wallach Scott writes.[33] But what if it doesn't work this way? What if, as Scott ponders, "history [is] a process of contention and conflict, a story of struggles for power, with no sharp boundaries between past, present, and future"?[34] This would mean that past progressive gains could be undone. Mistakes could be repeated. People forget.

Seattle's original progressive agenda at the turn of the twentieth century included environmental conservation, visionary urban planning, and closing the gap somewhat between the rich and the poor. Over time, groups excluded by the first progressives insisted on inclusion, adding to the agenda racial justice, worker rights, gender equity, the protection of sexual minorities. Wins were secured, rolled back, and reinforced. In politics, nobody wins forever. Ground can be lost, resetting social conditions that had been improved, and reopening questions that had already been settled. I've tried to illustrate in this book not the inevitability of progressive defeat but rather the repeated failure of a specific approach to reform: the approach that mortgages the long-term success of progressivism in favor of half measures that fail to inspire excitement, that reproduce social inequities, and that are more susceptible to defeat. The rise and fall of the cycling movement in the United States is a case in point.

Bikers transformed urban America in the age of reform. Seattle cyclists spearheaded paved streets, spurred some of the city's first licensing and public space bureaucracies, and advanced the then-radical proposal of taxing city dwellers to pay for roads. But riding clubs were often segregated, were slow to accept women riders, and were often ableist.[35] As a result, reactionaries could falsely portray them as out-of-touch elites, then push anti-cycling sentiment as a Trojan horse to deflate the expansion of government action that biking represented. An anti-tax activist in 1897 denounced privileged riders for benefiting from taxing "shop girls, laborers, and impoverished invalids."[36] Biking's real and perceived exclusivity weakened it politically, exposing riders to car activists who continue shaping city terrain. The devastating impact is seen most clearly in Seattle's disproportionately Black and brown neighborhoods, where sidewalks are scant, protected bike lanes are few and far between, and preventable pedestrian deaths occur more frequently than elsewhere in the city. "Progressive" exclusivity harms everybody, and no one more than the excluded.

Seattle institutions that have survived rightward political pendulum swings show that progressives win when they decide to create institutions that last. The public parks and libraries that Seattleites built during the

Progressive Era can be policed, but they can't be pulled out of the ground. With nowhere to go and nothing to do during the COVID-19 quarantine, Seattleites flocked increasingly to the playgrounds that progressives established during the age of reform. If they had to be rebuilt in later years, many of these institutions would be fought tooth and nail by some of the same people who use them. Even Seattle's moderates and conservatives make use of the public beaches, public health-care centers, and public park improvements built by the New Deal in the 1930s. That these progressive improvements provoked a backlash shouldn't prevent us from building more.

Why did Robert "Firebug" Driscoll burn down Seattle's baseball stadium in 1932? What exactly made it an appealing target for white supremacist violence, its wooden stands the bane of a prolific arsonist who decided to incinerate them? Driscoll was a lumber worker who wanted more from a society that gave other white loggers tremendous benefits; he detested Black and Asian Seattleites who had jobs. A biographical sketch of Driscoll compiled by the Seattle Fire Department after his arrest indicates that he hated having to share space with racial minorities in integrated homeless encampments, where downtrodden men of all races got together to listen to Seattle baseball on the radio.[37] Firebug wanted to inflict as much pain as possible on the society that had cast him aside. He hit Seattle where he thought it would hurt most.

Firebug charred trains and industrial tracts to disrupt Seattle commerce and destroy its ambition. He burned schools, apartment complexes, and service centers for the disabled, hating that Seattle gave shelter and a safety net to others while seemingly denying them to him. Driscoll burned down Seattle's baseball stadium because it gave the city joy; Seattleites got together there. More gathered around radios, listening closely as the melodic delivery of announcer Leo Lassen lifted them from their troubles during the Great Depression. Driscoll couldn't stand it. Because he was suffering, everyone else had to. Baseball had to burn.

Seattle public safety officials could arrest Driscoll. They could sentence him to five-to-ten years in Walla Walla Penitentiary, and they could monitor him after his sentence was over to make sure he behaved himself. But they couldn't smother his combustible prejudice, the perpetual flame that made him set fire to Seattle's social fabric—the flame seen elsewhere in segregated neighborhoods, in golf courses that were off-limits to Seattle minorities, in racist policing. That fire smoldered in a sizable 1930s Nazi-sympathizer movement that had at least sixteen hundred members in Seattle in 1939, rekindling the KKK resurgence of a decade earlier.[38] The fire burned when hateful Seattleites voted down the city's 1964 housing desegregation measure; it burned on and on when Seattleites opposed school integration in 1978, rescinded Seattle's sanctuary city status in 1986, and stood by as Black churches fell to arson in the mid-1990s. This fire spawned local arch-conservative Christopher Rufo; it could be a "progressive" fire that criminalized sex workers, the homeless, and LGBTQ+ Seattleites but had no problem with heartless capitalists like Frederick Trump Sr. building their fortunes there.

Firebugs were everywhere in Seattle—some expressed themselves with tinder and flame, others with ballots and city ordinances. "I realize a man should live like the rest of decent society," wrote Driscoll to Seattle officials from prison; "I should have retaliated lawfully."

Some would have it that the proper response to a Firebug—that is, to the threat of targeted hate, mass shooters, and organized racists who command great power and influence—is to give up on the idea of a shared civic destiny, besieged as it is by threats on all sides. This viewpoint is evident mostly on Seattle's left-of-center, where timid half measures are frequently allowed to masquerade as progress, and demographics that would transform the city are often hesitant to compete, scared of the heartbreak they believe to be inevitable. They prove themselves right by proving themselves right: self-defeatism reinforces itself, creating the conditions it needs to keep on self-defeating. Where fire can't take out a great society directly, it does so through fear that prevents anything from ever getting made, ever being built, ever happening.

The way to stamp out the fire that feeds on exclusion is with more shared spaces like the baseball stadium that angered Firebug. It's with the integrated city he couldn't tolerate. It's with strong, inclusive unions that raise the standard of living of all workers and encourage solidarity, and with social safety net protections that keep people from falling into poverty and alienation. It's with collaborative institutions that are even enjoyed by people who claim to oppose them.

Seahawks Stadium (in front of Safeco Field) stands on artificial tideland forged by Seattle engineers at the turn of the twentieth century to make way for the railroad. Courtesy of the Seattle Municipal Archives, item 145124.

In 2022 the Washington State Legislature passed the Move Washington transit package, unlocking $4.3 billion in new spending for biking, mass transit, and accessible pedestrian improvements in a state where most individual counties vote Republican and where roughly 40 percent of the general population does the same.[39] Within weeks of the environmental subsidy's passage, funding applications made by small towns in conservative areas fueled more than $457 million worth of total requests—over double the amount of the previous biennium. Move Washington was designed to advance "non-car modes of travel"; it found a political base in some of the most car-dependent, conservative areas of the state.

Even when Seattle doesn't live up to its own inclusive pretentions, those

T-Mobile Park (known earlier as Safeco Field) is among the most resplendent ballparks in American sport. The combination of modern engineering, diverse crowds, and civic spirit points to what Seattle might exemplify, if only it could get out of its own way. Courtesy of the Seattle Municipal Archives, item 105420.

Formerly Seattle Center Coliseum (and later KeyArena), Amazon renovated and renamed this facility Climate Pledge Arena in 2020. The arena debuted during the 1962 World's Fair. Its architecture was inspired by woven Coast Salish hats that defray the infamous Seattle rain. Image courtesy of Sea Cow, via Creative Commons (tinyurl.com/4ndsy7sb).

pretentions resonate elsewhere. In late 2022, observers noted the explosive rise nationally of pickleball, calling attention to "its potential to bring diverse populations together around the common goal of recreation and fitness."[40] Is it any wonder that the game originated in scenic Bainbridge Island, from which the Seattle skyline can be seen on a sunny day? Grass-roots support exists everywhere for the uncommon mix of outdoor spaces and urban amenity that defines Seattle—a heritage seen in Progressive Era bike paths, city trails and playgrounds, and publicly subsidized sports.

The Seattle Seahawks, Mariners, and Sounders were all made possible by public elections for new stadiums. The Seattle Storm won all their pre-2020 championships in the once-public facility inhabited by the Seattle Kraken during the 2023 Stanley Cup playoffs. University of Washington football is straightforwardly state property. Inevitably during nationally televised games in Seattle featuring any of these teams, commentators call attention to the city's immaculate scenery and "game-day atmosphere." Droves of fans near the football, soccer, and baseball stadiums in Pioneer Square spill onto Royal Brougham Way, sauntering on the street named for Seattle's sports godfather in the 1970s. The culture of college-like enthusiasm for professional sports in Seattle is the result of having four major athletic facilities all in city limits, all near primary transit hubs of greater or lesser size, all in some of the most accessible neighborhoods in the city. Fans watch sports to see normal human limits defied; in Seattle those defied limits include inherited bad ideas of what a city should look like.

A forever city is still achievable—not as a dull errand into an uncertain wilderness, but as a joyous exhibition authored by people united in pursuit of common purpose. The game plan for permanent progressive victory has been laid out over a long legacy of lesson-worthy losses and enduring wins. To take from Seattle the civic riches handed down by activists past would be to take what makes the city a city at all. But if faded glories are all we have to look forward to, generations hence will look upon Seattle's Climate Pledge Arena like we do the dusted aqueducts of ancient Rome.

Unfinished bike lanes won't age as well as the Colosseum.

ACKNOWLEDGMENTS

Though conceived and written largely in isolation during the 2020–22 pandemic years, this book is the by-product of a dedicated team of editorial and production staff at the University of Washington Press and true friends who made me feel a little less alone while researching and writing it.

I'm grateful to Andrew Berzanskis, former acquisitions editor at the University of Washington Press, who spotted my leftist diatribes in Seattle publications and on social media in 2018 and invited me to submit a manuscript for a book proposal. After its acceptance, Andrew challenged me to craft a narrative voice that would hopefully stand the test of time. Heeding his advice, I searched out and revisited authors whose prose could serve as inspiration. Paging through Tom Wolfe's *Bonfire of the Vanities*, Mike Davis's *City of Quartz*, Albert Camus's *The Plague*, Isabel Wilkerson's *Caste*, David Halberstam's *The Breaks of the Game*, and Seth Wickersham's *It's Better to Be Feared*, I've tried—reaching, stealing—to assemble my own style from theirs.

After I generated the first draft, Mike Baccam of UW Press provided indispensable narrative guidance, encouraging me to amplify aspects of this story that had to do with Seattle's competitions with other cities. A midwesterner, Mike offered periodic ribbing about the greater glories of Windy City sports—a very small price to pay for a greatly improved story. He was a terrific accomplice and consummate professional, helping to guide me through the book's editorial and production process.

I'm indebted to library workers at the Seattle Municipal Archives and UW libraries for their stewardship of Seattle's expansive storehouse of public archival materials. In May 2021, Joe at Special Collections in the Seattle Public Library provided a page-to-page scan of an obscure volume about early biking in Seattle. In February 2021, Jeanie Fisher at the Seattle Municipal Archives scanned and relayed the city's extensive file on Robert "Firebug" Driscoll. In December 2021, Allee Monheim, public service librarian at the UW Special Collections, procured issues of *Boeing News* and *Boeing Magazine,* making possible sections of this book that were once only a glimmer of an idea. In addition, keepers of the UW microfilm collection—past, present, and future—are keepers of our shared civic past.

Through spring and summer of 2022, Erica Zucco of KING 5 News fed me sundry essays and articles that expanded my range as a writer, shaking me a bit out of the pallid academic clichés upon which it is often too easy to rely. Alongside James Gregory, Quintard Taylor, Trevor Griffey, and Knute Berger, David B. Williams is one of the dozen or so most rigorous and important writers of Seattle's history whom I've had the chance to speak with and learn from. I look forward to the continued contributions of Taha Ebrahimi and Amanda Cummings, whose scholarship made key additions to this book's narrative about sports and its intersection with politics in Progressive Era Seattle.

I don't know that I'll ever cross paths again with the Seattle rando I noticed wearing the sweatshirt with an image of the imploding Kingdome on it on University Way on November 8, 2022—but if I ever do, I should like to thank them immensely. After passing them while crossing the street, their shirt made me realize there was something worth investigating about the haunting spectacle of the Kingdome's implosion.

I thank my parents for encouraging me, at a very young age, to explore my love of sports with words. While a youngster in Queens, New York, in the early 1990s, my mom urged me to hold my own in debates with the men in my family about the many shortcomings of the New York Knicks. Later, after moving to Seattle with my dad in May 1992, I fell in love with the city's sports while traversing to and from UW football games at Husky Stadium, Seahawks games at the Kingdome, and Sonics playoff contests at KeyArena. I spent countless hours talking with my dad about these teams and how they played, listening to sports radio with him, learning how to read the standings and read between the lines of mainstream sports coverage, and hearing him talk about how sports were politically coded entertainment. Marshawn Lynch said it best: "I'm thankful."

NOTES

Introduction

1. "Ambitious Dog," *Puget Sound Dispatch*, July 18, 1872, 1, column 6.

2. Murry Morgan, *Skid Road: An Informal Portrait of Seattle* (Seattle: University of Washington Press, 2018), 67.

3. Heather McInstosh, "Northern Pacific Railroad and Seattle Development," History Link, https://historylink.org/File/1734 (accessed September 2, 2022). All dollar figures that appear in the first, second, and third parts of this book are adjusted forward for inflation in 2022 dollars. Dollar figures cited in the fourth part are reprinted without adjustment from their source.

4. John Caldbick, "Washington Territorial Legislature Merges Tacoma City and New Tacoma to Take Effect on January 7, 1884," HistoryLink, https://historylink.org/File/5062 (accessed September 2, 2022).

5. Morgan, *Skid Road*, 67.

6. Frederick Brown, "Cows in the Commons, Dogs on the Lawn: A History of Animals in Seattle" (PhD diss., University of Washington, 2010), 56–58.

7. Brown, "Cows in the Commons, Dogs on the Lawn," 56–58.

8. Morgan, *Skid Road*, 73. In *Too High and Too Steep* (Seattle: University of Washington Press, 2015), natural historian David B. Williams relays that the brief attempt at a citizen-railroad only made it as far as Renton—that is, a distance of about fourteen miles. Details about the "dinky" Seattle mill come from John Caldbick, "Henry Yesler's steam-powered Seattle sawmill cuts its first lumber in 1853," HistoryLink, https://www.historylink.org/file/760 (accessed April 8, 2023).

9. Scott Cline, "'To Foster Honorable Pasttimes': Baseball as Civic Endeavor in 1880s Seattle," *Pacific Northwest Quarterly* 87, no. 4 (Fall 1996): 171–79.

10. Cline, "'To Foster Honorable Pasttimes.'"

11. As mentioned earlier, "New York, Alki" was the first name given to the settlement that became Seattle—translated from the Chinook language, it means "New York, eventually."

12. Cline, "'To Foster Honorable Pasttimes.'"

13. Cited in Cline, "'To Foster Honorable Pasttimes.'"

14. Shaun Scott, "Durkan, Seattle Police, and the Undermining of Civil Liberties," *Crosscut,* July 15, 2020, https://tinyurl.com/2e2xkcpj.

15. Samuel Stein, *Capital City: Gentrification and the Real Estate State* (New York: Verso Books, 2019), 118–23.

16. Paul Goldberger, *Ballpark: Baseball in the American City* (New York: Knopf, 2019), 9.

17. Ole Hanson, "Anarchists Tried Revolution in Seattle, but Never Got to First Base," *New York Times*, February 9, 1919, 1.

18. "Times Terrors Chuckle as They Accept Challenge of P.I. Bunch," *Seattle Times*, June 21, 1913, 9; "Times Rings in a Big Leaguer," *Seattle Post-Intelligencer*, June 27, 1913, 13; "Umpires Favoritism Gives Pirates Tie with Terrors," *Seattle Times*, June 30, 1913, 14. Account of the Seattle Potlatch riot of 1913 can be heard on a 1970–71 series of radio lectures delivered by Seattle historian Roger Sale—see Part 18, https://tinyurl.com/me6nwk3j (accessed December 31, 2022).

19. Julia Budlong, "What Happened in Seattle," *The Nation*, August 29, 1928, 197–98.

20. Arthur M. Schlesinger Jr., *The Cycles of American History* (New York: Houghton Mifflin, 1987), loc. 4845, Kindle.

21. Schlesinger, loc. 74, Kindle.

22. Roger Sale, *Seattle, Past to Present* (Seattle: University of Washington Press, 1976); James Lyons, *Selling Seattle: Representing Contemporary Urban America* (London: Wallflower Press, 2004); Fred Moody, *Seattle and the Demons of Ambition: A Love Story*, 1st ed. (New York: St. Martin's Press, 2003). The citation for Sale being "a devout Sonics fan" is seen in David Shields's book *Black Planet* (New York: Crown, 1999), in which Shields details going to games with Sale, who reported on the team for *Seattle Weekly* and other publications (Shields, loc. 331, Kindle).

23. Sale, *Seattle, Past to Present*, 299.

24. Terry Anne Scott, ed., *Seattle Sports: Play, Identity, and Pursuit in the Emerald City* (Fayetteville: University of Arkansas Press, 2020).

25. Morgan, *Skid Road*, 104–5. All population statistics sourced from the US Census (https://tinyurl.com/2p8a3tr6).

26. Robert E. Ficken and Charles P. LeWarne, *Washington: A Centennial History* (Seattle: University of Washington Press, 1988), 29–48.

27. Moody, *Seattle and the Demons of Ambition*, 59.

1st Inning

1. Ross Reynolds, "Does the Soviet of Washington Deserve Its Lefty Reputation?," http://archive.kuow.org/post/does-soviet-washington-deserve-its-lefty-reputation (accessed September 2, 2022).

2. Murry Morgan, *Skid Road: An Informal Portrait of Seattle* (Seattle: University of Washington Press, 2018), 115.

3. "Annexed Cities," Seattle Municipal Archives, http://www.seattle.gov/cityarchives/exhibits-and-education/online-exhibits/annexed-cities (accessed September 2, 2022).

4. "The Heart of Seattle," *Seattle Republican*, July 5, 1907.

5. "The Heart of Seattle."

6. Bruce Englehardt, "Our Subway Plan, Rejected 105 Years Ago," *Seattle Transit Blog*,

March 7, 2017, https://seattletransitblog.com/2017/03/07/bogue-plan/; Eric Scigliano, "Seattle That Might Have Been," *Seattle Times*, September 17, 1972, 182.

7. "Seattle That Might Have Been."

8. Coll Thrush, *Native Seattle: Histories from the Crossing-Over Place* (Seattle: University of Washington Press, 2007), 214–55.

9. Bill MacKay, "When the Indians Tied the Redskins Three All," *Sports Illustrated*, May 6, 1958; Ben Pickman, "As Lacrosse Ascends, Reckoning with Its Past," *Sports Illustrated*, September 17, 2021. Bil Gilbert, "Sports Were Essential to the Life of the Early North American Indian," *Sports Illustrated*, December 1, 1986.

10. Coll Thrush, "The Lushootseed Peoples of Puget Sound Country," Digital Collections, UW Libraries, https://tinyurl.com/hdbn4jcx (accessed December 26, 2022).

11. Carlos Schwantes, "The Concept of the Wageworkers' Frontier: A Framework," *Western Historical Quarterly* 18, no. 1 (January 1987): 42; "Billiard Table," *Seattle Weekly Gazette*, April 19, 1865, 2, column 1; "Poker," *Puget Sound Dispatch*, April 22, 1875, 1, column 4; "Horse Race," *Puget Sound Dispatch*, June, 24, 1876, 5, column 5; "Walking Match," *Puget Sound Weekly Argus*, December 4, 1879, 4, column 3.

12. "No Cases in Police Court," *Puget Sound Dispatch*, August 26, 1875, 1, column 2.

13. "Roller Skating," *Puget Sound Dispatch*, March 7, 1872, 3, column 2.

14. Morgan, *Skid Road*, 120.

15. Mildred Andrews, "Sisters of Providence opened Seattle's first hospital on August 2, 1878," HistoryLink, December 8, 1998, https://tinyurl.com/mmrsdya8; Greg Lange and Cassandra Tate, "Legislature Incorporates the Town of Seattle for the First Time on January 14, 1865," HistoryLink, https://www.historylink.org/file/168 (accessed September 2, 2022): "The trustees met for the first time on January 28, 1865. Over the next two years, the trustees adopted a total of 14 ordinances, beginning with one that implemented a municipal tax (possibly a source of resentment that led to the eventual dissolution of Seattle's first municipal government)."

16. Cited in Richard Hofstadter, *Social Darwinism in American Thought*, rev. ed. (Boston: Beacon Press, 1955), 44.

17. Cited in Clarence B. Bagley, *History of Seattle, Volume 1: From the Earliest Settlement to the Early 20th Century* (Loschberg: Jazzybee Verlag, 2017 [1913]), 406.

18. Louis Moore, *I Fight for a Living: Boxing and the Battle for Black Manhood, 1880–1915* (Champaign: University of Illinois Press, 2017), 9.

19. Morgan, *Skid Road*, 80–82; Alan J. Stein, "Lynch Mob Hangs Three Men in Seattle on January 18, 1882," HistoryLink, https://historylink.org/File/1965 (accessed September 2, 2022).

20. Paul Dorpat, "The Dark Day of Mob Rule and Lynching as Sport in Seattle," *Seattle Times*, July 18, 2014.

21. Frank B. Cameron, *Bicycling in Seattle, 1879–1904* (self-published in 1982); Erika Lee, *The Making of Asian America: A History* (New York: Simon & Schuster, 2015), 94.

22. As reported in "New Women's Superstitions," *Seattle Times*, April 6, 1896.

23. James Longhurst, *Bike Battles: A History of Sharing the American Road* (Seattle: University of Washington Press, 2015), 37.

24. Cameron, *Bicycling in Seattle, 1879–1904*; Frederick Brown, "Cows in the Commons, Dogs on the Lawn: A History of Animals in Seattle" (PhD diss., University of Washington, 2010), 92.

25. Evan Friss, *The Cycling City: Bicycles and Urban America* (Chicago: University of Chicago Press, 2015), 103; "Build Bicycle Paths," *San Francisco Call*, August 4, 1897.

26. Jennifer Ott, *Olmsted in Seattle: Creating a Park System for a Modern City* (Seattle: University of Washington Press, 2019).

27. Cited in "Document 23. Seattle Parks," Center for the Study of the Pacific Northwest, https://tinyurl.com/y9m2pzyb (accessed June 20, 2022): "Parks are Nature's innocent and holy inspirations, and in them are whispers of peace and joy. Parks are the breathing lungs and beating hearts of great cities; the multitudes, their circulating blood rushing hither and thither, performing the functions of life and usefulness, and when the lungs are freshened and purified, they reinvigorate the whole system through the pulsating beats of these life-centers, where rich and poor mingle to inhale the unalloyed, God-given perfumes to body, mind and soul."

28. "Let Us Make a Beautiful City of Seattle," *Seattle Post-Intelligencer*, September 21, 1902, 40.

29. "Need of Civic Center Emphasized," *Seattle Times*, February 14, 1912, 5.

30. "Lester Apartments intended to be the world's largest brothel on Beacon Hill," University of Washington Special Collections, https://tinyurl.com/4xr7muwd (accessed April 8, 2022); "A Red Light History of Seattle," *Seattle Met*, January 29, 2010, https://tinyurl.com/2p993x6s.

31. "Cotterill, George Fletcher (1865–1958)," HistoryLink, https://www.historylink.org/file/2709 (accessed September 2, 2022).

32. Robert D. Putnam and Shaylyn Romney Garrett, *The Upswing: How We Came Together a Century Ago and How We Can Do It Again* (London: Swift Press, 2020), 112.

33. Cited in Michael E. McGerr, *A Fierce Discontent: The Rise and Fall of the Progressive Movement in America, 1870–1920* (New York: Free Press, 2003), loc. 1265, Kindle.

34. "House Committee Urges Race Track Bill for Passage," *Seattle Post-Intelligencer*, January 27, 1909, 3.

35. Thomas C. Leonard, *Illiberal Reformers: Race, Eugenics and American Economics in the Progressive Era* (Princeton, NJ: Princeton University Press, 2016), xiii.

36. Taha Ebrahimi, "Cal Anderson Park's Surprising Past: A Forgotten History Haunting Our Present," Capitol Hill Historical Society, capitolhillpast.org, September 17, 2020.

37. Ebrahimi, "Cal Anderson Park's Surprising Past."

38. "Cotterill, George Fletcher (1865–1958)," HistoryLink, https://www.historylink.org/file/2709 (accessed July 5, 2022).

39. Cited in "Seattle That Might Have Been."

40. Roger Sale, *Seattle, Past to Present* (Seattle: University of Washington Press, 1976), 132–37.

41. McGerr, *Fierce Discontent,* loc. 1251, Kindle: "Rejecting socialism and individualism alike, the great majority of the middle class wanted something in between the two doctrines, which Richard T. Ely labeled 'the golden mean.'"

42. "I Cure Men," *Seattle Times*, December 17, 1905, 62.

43. Alan J. Stein, "Chief Joseph Watches a University of Washington Football Game and Gives a Speech in Seattle on November 20, 1903," HistoryLink, https://www.historylink .org/File/10286 (accessed December 26, 2022); "Chief Joseph," *Seattle Times*, November 18, 1903, 4; "Joseph Continues His Fight," *Seattle Times*, November 20, 1903, 8; "Joseph Tells His Story," *Seattle Times*, November 21, 1903, 7; "Joseph Has a Hard Day," *Seattle Post-Intelligencer*, November 21, 1903, 1.

44. Robert Ketcherside, "Capitol Hill Historical Society | 13th and Jefferson Park— Part 1: Opening Day 1895," *Capitol Hill Seattle Blog*, January 27, 2019, https://tinyurl.com /v2th4h4v; "Duffy, 1901, Husky, Is Still 'Around' at Right End," *Seattle Times*, November 5, 1961, 128.

45. "What's the Matter with Washington Athletics," *Washington Alumnus*, 1908, 10.

46. Tanaka Keiko, "Early Telephone Use in Seattle, 1880s–1920s," *Pacific Northwest Quarterly* 92, no. 4 (Fall 2001), 190–202.

47. Lynn Borland, *Gilmour Dobie: Pursuit of Perfection* (Frisco: Tribute Publishing, 2010), loc. 224, Kindle; Lynn Borland, "Legendary Coach Gil Dobie's Only Loss at Washington: His Legacy," *Seattle Times*, November 20, 2010, https://www.seattletimes.com /sports/uw-huskies/legendary-coach-gil-dobies-only-loss-at-washington-his-legacy/.

48. Robert S. Welch, "The Loser Who Won," *Columbia* 1, no. 3 (Fall 1987), https:// tinyurl.com/38c9vnhk.

49. Cited in Borland, *Gilmour Dobie*, loc. 4369, 4152, Kindle.

50. "Pennant Goes Up Tomorrow at Seattle's New Ball Park," *Seattle Times*, September 16, 1913, 17.

51. Paul Goldberger, *Ballpark: Baseball in the American City* (New York: Alfred A. Knopf, 2015), 67.

52. Goldberger, *Ballpark*, 99.

53. Julia Dallas, "100 Years Later, Progress for 'Evergreen State' to Become Washington's Official Nickname," KIRO 7, February 20, 2023, https://tinyurl.com/2jm56tr5.

54. Lyndsie Bourgon, *Tree Thieves: Crime and Survival in North America's Woods* (New York: Hachette Books, 2022), 22.

55. Robert E. Ficken and Charles P. LeWarne, *Washington: A Centennial History* (Seattle: University of Washington Press, 1988), 36 (for citation about Ballard and shingle manufacturing); Megan Asaka, *Seattle from the Margins: Exclusion, Erasure, and the Making of a Pacific Coast City* (Seattle: University of Washington Press, 2022), 77 (for citation about high proportion of loggers in the Washington State workforce in 1910).

56. Tom Gierasimczuk, "How a Team in Seattle, of All Places, Changed Hockey Forever," *New York Times*, March 27, 2017.

57. "Hockey Will Make Bow to Seattle Fans When Victoria Plays Locals," *Seattle Post-Intelligencer*, December 7, 1915, 9; "Hockey Makes Hit with Seattle Fans," *Seattle Times*, December 8, 1915; Portis Baxter, "Seattle Beats Victoria in Opening Hockey Game of Season at the Arena," *Seattle Post-Intelligencer*, December 8, 1915, 9.

58. "Big Ice Arena Opens Tonight," *Seattle Times*, November 12, 1915, 18; "Arena Opens with Crowd of Skaters," *Seattle Times*, November 13, 1915, 7; "Seattle N.A.A.C.P. Branch Holds Annual Meeting," *Northwest Enterprise*, January 8, 1931, 8.

59. Asaka, *Seattle from the Margins*, 93.

60. Cited in Asaka, *Seattle from the Margins*.

61. Danielle McCreadie, "New documentary explores the Mi'kmaq origins of hockey," *CityNews Halifax*, https://tinyurl.com/35m4unur, February 10, 2019; Natasha Girshin, "The Forgotten Indigenous Roots of Hockey," *Back Sports Page*, August 1, 2022, https://tinyurl.com/fehdfp7k.

62. "Agitation over Forward Pass Fails to Interest Gil Dobie," *New York Times*, December 28, 1924, 92; Phil Langan, "Gloomy Gil Dobie All-Time Pessimist," *The Heights*, November 30, 1956, 8.

63. Travis Patterson, "Patrick Brothers Who Shaped Modern Hockey Also Tried, but Failed, to Remove Violence," *Victoria News*, September 20, 2020; Taylor McKee, "Born of a Spirit That Knows No Conquering: Innovation, Contestation, and Representation in the P.C.H.A., 1911–1924" (PhD diss., University of Western Ontario, 2020).

64. "Teddy Roosevelt and the Institution of the Forward Pass," *SBNation*, December 15, 2018, https://www.sbnation.com/2018/12/15/18139338/teddy-roosevelt-forward-passinvented.

65. "Hockey Fans Protest," *Seattle Post-Intelligencer*, March 25, 1917, 25.

66. "City's Biggest Sporting Event Ready to Start," *Seattle Post-Intelligencer*, March 15, 1918, 27; Kevin Ticen, *When It Mattered Most: The Forgotten Story of America's First Stanley Cup Champions* (Seattle: Clyde Hill Publishing, 2019).

67. "Seattle, Washington and the 1918–1919 Influenza Epidemic," *The American Influenza Epidemic of 1918: A Digital Encyclopedia*, https: //tinyurl.com/bde7v7zk (accessed July 5, 2022); "Everybody Tries to Look Happy Despite Masks," *Seattle Times*, October 30, 1918, 1.

68. David Wilma, "World War I in Washington," HistoryLink, August 20, 2004; Erik Lacitis, "As Coronavirus Spreads in 2020, Here's How Seattle Handled the 1918 Flu That Killed 1,513 People," *Seattle Times*, March 13, 2020.

69. Karen Given, "A Cautionary Tale: Spanish Flu and the 1919 Stanley Cup Final," WBUR, https://www.wbur.org/onlyagame/2020/03/27/spanish-flu-seattle-metropolitans-1919-stanley-cup (accessed July 5, 2022).

70. "Tack Quarantine Signs on Many Seattle Doors," *Seattle Post-Intelligencer*, April 2, 1919, 1; "Great Series Ends without Victor Named," *Seattle Post-Intelligencer*, April 2, 1919, 15.

71. "Seattle, Washington and the 1918–1919 Influenza Epidemic."

2nd Inning

1. Amanda Lane Cummings, "War, Pandemic, and Seattle Baseball in 1918," *Lookout Landing*, August 5, 2020, https://tinyurl.com/5ytxvm96.

2. "New League Plays Opening Game Today," *Seattle Daily Times*, May 12, 1918, 72.

3. "Beginning Today," *Seattle Daily Times*, June 27, 1915, 18.

4. "'Birth of a Nation'—Clemmer," *Seattle Daily Times*, June 28, 1915, 10.

5. "Bernard Shaw on Film and Play," *Seattle Post-Intelligencer*, June 18, 1915, 6.

6. Alexis Clark, "How 'The Birth of a Nation' Revived the Ku Klux Klan," *History*, https://www.history.com/news/kkk-birth-of-a-nation-film (accessed June 22, 2022).

7. Clark, "How 'The Birth of a Nation' Revived the Ku Klux Klan."

8. "In the Society Editor's Mail," *Seattle Daily Times*, November 3, 1918, 38: "I presume, my dear, you were one of many who behind the disguise of 'flu' masks resembled the famous Ku Klux Klan."

9. Lornet Turnbull, "UW Project Sheds Light on Ku Klux Klan as Force in the State," *Seattle Times*, November 13, 2008, https://tinyurl.com/bdeh5pmm.

10. Trevor Griffey, "Ku Klux Klan in Seattle," Seattle Civil Rights and Labor History Project, University of Washington, https://depts.washington.edu/civilr/kkk_seattle.htm (accessed June 22, 2022).

11. Trevor Griffey, "KKK Super Rallies in Washington State, 1923–1924," Seattle Civil Rights and Labor History Project, University of Washington, https://depts.washington .edu/civilr/kkk_rallies.htm (accessed December 27, 2022).

12. Linda Gordon, *The Second Coming of the KKK: The Ku Klux Klan of the 1920s and the American Political Tradition* (New York: W. W. Norton, 2017), 21.

13. Kenneth T. Jackson, *The Ku Klux Klan in the City, 1915–1930* (Oxford: Oxford University Press, 1967), 10.

14. Gordon, *Second Coming of the KKK*, 85.

15. Felix Harcourt, *Ku Klux Kulture: America and the Klan in the 1920s* (Champaign: University of Chicago Press, 2017), 165.

16. Tim Wiles, "Night Games Gave Access to Baseball to Millions," *National Baseball Hall of Fame*, https://tinyurl.com/5tuvsjyu (accessed December 27, 2022).

17. Harcourt, *Ku Klux Kulture*, 165.

18. Ole Hanson, *Americanism versus Bolshevism* (Garden City, NJ: Doubleday, 1920), 3, manuscript available at https://tinyurl.com/4f5cpu6y (accessed December 27, 2022).

19. Josephine Ensign, *Skid Road: On the Frontier of Health and Homelessness in an American City* (Baltimore, MD: Johns Hopkins University Press), 19.

20. W. C. Rucker, "More 'Eugenic Laws,'" *Journal of Heredity* 6 (1915): 219–26. Additional summary of eugenics laws in Washington State and beyond compiled by Lutz Kelber, associate professor of sociology at the University of Vermont, https://tinyurl.com /yva6vwj6 (accessed December 27, 2022).

21. This slur was used gratuitously in Seattle media for decades, from the nineteenth century until the mid-twentieth, often supplanted by other unfortunate descriptors such as "retard." In 1899, Seattle audiences were rapt at the story of a disabled newsboy—called a "cripple" in the *Seattle Times*—who trekked to the Alaska Yukon to sell newspapers ("Is a Brave Lad," *Seattle Daily Times*, December 1, 1899, 8).

22. "Hanson, Ole Thorsteinsson (1874–1940)," HistoryLink, https://www.historylink .org/File/11101 (accessed December 27, 2022); "Improving Slowly," *Seattle Daily Times*, March 31, 1919, 16.

23. Hanson, *Americanism versus Bolshevism*, 3.

24. Count conducted by searching online file of Hanson's 1920 memoir, *Americanism versus Bolshevism*, https://tinyurl.com/nhbvux5k (accessed December 27, 2022).

25. Hanson in "Proclamation," *Seattle Star*, February 7, 1919, 1.

26. Hanson, *Americanism versus Bolshevism*, 24: "It was because of a desire on their part to foment hatred, suspicion, and discontent to such a degree that the workers would first make impossible demand; then call a general strike, establish a soviet, and start the flame

of revolution in this country, with the hope and plan of the ultimate destruction of the Government and the establishment in its stead of bolshevism, pure and undefiled, with its consequent red terror and tyranny."

27. "Ole Hanson, Fighter; His Record Proves It," *New York Times*, February 9, 1919, 1; "Ole Hanson on the Job!," *McClure's*, April 1919; "Seattle to Enforce Law," *Los Angeles Times*, February 7, 1919, 11; "Soldiers Guard Seattle Plants," *Atlanta Constitution*, February 8, 1919, 1.

28. Sheila M. Shown, "The National Press and the Seattle General Strike," Seattle General Strike Project, University of Washington, https://depts.washington.edu/labhist/strike /shown.shtml (accessed December 27, 2022).

29. Ole Hanson, "Anarchists Tried Revolution in Seattle, but Never Got to First Base," *New York Times*, February 9, 1919, 1.

30. "Mayor Going South," *Seattle Times*, March 16, 1919, 11; "Sudden Fame Robs Seattle Mayor of Rest," *Seattle Times*, March 26, 1919, 1.

31. David Eskenazi, "Wayback Machine: Genesis of Husky Stadium," *SportspressNW*, https://tinyurl.com/5dxamcwj (accessed June 22, 2022).

32. "Repairs Badly Needed to Elliott Avenue," *Seattle Times*, November 28, 1920, 33; for the construction of Montlake Bridge, see "Triumph for Clean Sport," *Seattle Times*, November 28, 1920, 20.

33. David B. Williams, *Too High and Too Steep: Reshaping Seattle's Topography* (Seattle: University of Washington Press, 2015).

34. Richard C. Berner, *Seattle 1921–1940: From Boom to Bust* (Chicago: Charles Press, 1991), 276; "87 Eat Dinner in Snow," *Seattle Daily Times*, March 6, 1916, 22; the slur "Rastus waiter" appears in *The Mountaineer* 14 (1921). Mountaineer establishing a golf course in Berner, *Seattle, 1921–1940*, 270.

35. John J. Caldbick, "Seattle 'More Homes Bureau' Housing Campaign Kicks Off on September 3, 1918," HistoryLink, August 17, 2009, https://www.historylink.org/File/9109; "Park Board Is Raising Money for New Links," *Seattle Times*, September 12, 1920, 33.

36. "Racial Restrictive Covenants: Neighborhood by Neighborhood Restrictions across King County," Seattle Civil Rights and Labor History Project, University of Washington, https://depts.washington.edu/civilr/covenants.htm (accessed June 22, 2022).

37. The advertisement appears in the following editions of *Seattle Times*: February 20, 1927, 56; March 13, 1927, 26; March 20, 1927; March 27, 1927, 67; April 3, 1927, 17.

38. See the Seattle Civil Rights and Labor History Project, http://depts.washington .edu/civilr/index.htm (accessed June 22, 2022).

39. Richard Rothstein, *The Color of Law: A Forgotten History of How Our Government Segregated America* (New York: Liverlight Publishing, 2017), 60.

40. For details, see the Seattle Civil Rights and Labor History Project, http://depts .washington.edu/civilr/index.htm (accessed June 22, 2022).

41. Rothstein, *Color of Law*, 48; Ben Ross, "One Man Zoned Huge Swaths of Our Region for Sprawl, Cars, and Exclusion," *Greater Greater Washington*, https://ggwash.org /view/70408/harland-bartholomew-the-man-who-zoned-washington-dc (accessed June 22, 2022).

42. Berner, *Seattle, 1921–1940*, 270.

43. Farah Jasmine Griffin, *Who Set You Flowin'?: The African-American Migration Narrative* (Oxford, UK: Oxford University Press, 1995), loc. 156, Kindle.

44. Quintard Taylor, *The Forging of a Black Community: Seattle's Central District, from 1870 through the Civil Rights Era* (Seattle: University of Washington Press, 1994), 56.

45. Langston Hughes, "One-Way Ticket Woodcuts," by Jacob Lawrence (New York: Alfred A. Knopf), 60.

46. James N. Gregory, "Remember Seattle's Segregated History," *Seattle Post-Intelligencer*, December 11, 2006.

47. Lyle Kenai Wilson, *Sunday Afternoons at Garfield Park: Seattle's Black Baseball Teams, 1911–1951* (Seattle: Lowell Printing & Publisher, 1997), 2.

48. Wilson, *Sunday Afternoons at Garfield Park*, 15.

49. Paul Avrich, *Sacco and Vanzetti: The Anarchist Background* (Princeton, NJ: Princeton University Press, 1991), 140–43, 147, 149–56, 181–95.

50. "Lynchings: By Year and Race," http://law2.umkc.edu/faculty/projects/ftrials/shipp/lynchingyear.html (accessed June 22, 2022).

51. Severyns's autobiography as cited in Shaun Scott, "Seattle Police Had a Chance to Prove Abolitionists Wrong. They Didn't," *Crosscut,* May 25, 2021, https://tinyurl.com/yc386xky.

52. Quoted in Wilson, *Sunday Afternoons at Garfield Park*, 5.

53. Wilson, *Sunday Afternoons at Garfield Park*, 5.

54. Wilson, *Sunday Afternoons at Garfield Park*, iii.

55. Kenneth T. Jackson, *Crabgrass Frontier: The Suburbanization of the United States* (New York: Oxford University Press, 1985), loc. 3357, Kindle.

56. Quoted in Wilson, *Sunday Afternoons at Garfield Park*, 2.

57. "Neighbors to Get Acquainted, Seattleites Urged to 'Thaw,'" *Seattle Daily Times*, March 26, 1920, 1.

58. "Neighbors to Get Acquainted."

59. "Neighbors to Get Acquainted."

60. Keynes, quoted in Nathan Miller, *New World Coming: The 1920s and the Making of Modern America* (Boston: Da Capo Press, 1994), 60.

61. Erika Lee, *America for Americans: A History of Xenophobia in the United States* (New York: Basic Books, 2021), 113.

62. James R. Walker, *Crack of the Bat: A History of Baseball on the Radio* (Lincoln: University of Nebraska Press, 2015).

63. Roger Sale, *Seattle, Past to Present* (Seattle: University of Washington Press, 1976), 141.

64. Feliks Banel, "Husky Stadium Has Long History beyond Football," KUOW .org, August 30, 2013, https://kuow.org/stories/husky-stadium-has-long-history-beyond -football/.

65. Hanson, *Americanism versus Bolshevism*, 5; Berner, *Seattle, 1921–1940*, 179, for statistics about Seattle real estate in the 1920s.

66. "New Malloy Apt. Big Achievement in District Bldg.," *University District Herald*, August 10, 1928, 1, 7.

67. Rothstein, *Color of Law*, 38.

68. Sandra Haarsager, *Bertha Knight Landes of Seattle: Big-City Mayor* (Norman: University of Oklahoma Press, 1994), 110–15, 169 (on park cleanup), 99 (on bowling alleys).

69. Haarsager, *Bertha Knight Landes of Seattle*, 110.

70. Haarsager, *Bertha Knight Landes of Seattle*, 111.

71. Tiffany Lewis, "Municipal Housekeeping in the American West: Bertha Knight Landes's Entrance into Politics," *Rhetoric and Public Affairs* 14, no. 3 (Fall 2011): 465–91.

72. Haarsager, *Bertha Knight Landes of Seattle*, 169, for Landes on pedestrian safety; Haarsager, *Bertha Knight Landes of Seattle*, 160 (on "Wilsonian apartment").

73. Haarsager, *Bertha Knight Landes of Seattle*, 155.

74. Lewis, "Municipal Housekeeping in the American West," 479.

75. "Seattle Ably Run by Woman Mayor," *New York Times*, July 4, 1926.

76. "Seattle Ably Run by Woman Mayor."

77. Julia Budlong, "What Happened in Seattle," *The Nation*, August 29, 1928, 197–98.

78. Haarsager, *Bertha Knight Landes of Seattle*, 213. Frank Edwards had taken a meeting with the KKK during his campaign, and—when discovered—issued a statement clarifying that he wasn't a member.

79. Anna Louise Strong, *I Change Worlds: The Remaking of an American* (New York: Henry Holt, 1935), 53.

80. Strong, *I Change Worlds*, 57.

3rd Inning

1. All quotes and information about Robert Driscoll fires culled from Seattle Municipal Archives collection "Fire Investigation—Arson—Robert Driscoll," container 96/3, and from sundry Seattle newspaper articles: "Industrial Tract Razed by Flames," *Seattle Times*, June 9, 1931, 1; "4,000 Chicks Lose Lives in Night Blaze," *Seattle Times*, June 9, 1931, 5; "Ballpark Destroyed in Mystery Night Fire," *Seattle Times*, July 5, 1932, 1; "Suspect in Church Fire under Quiz," *Seattle Times*, May 4, 1935, 1; "Church Firebug Admits Lighting 100 Blazes Here," *Seattle Times*, May 6, 1935, 1; "$300,000 Damage Laid to Firebug," *Seattle Times*, May 7, 1935, 3. All figures—that is, those indicating the cost of damages caused by Firebug—are inflation-adjusted to 2022 dollars.

2. Brad Holden, *Seattle Prohibition: Bootleggers, Rumrunners, and Graft in the Queen City* (Charleston, SC: The History Press, 2019), 107: "In November of that year, Washington State residents headed to the polls to vote on Washington State Initiative 61, which, if passed, would repeal all state liquor laws. The Eighteenth Amendment had not yet been repealed, and national law always holds power over state law. So the initiative was seen as more of a mandate to support the repeal of the amendment. By a huge margin, Initiative 61 passed, with voters making it clear that they were ready for alcohol to be decriminalized."

3. Jane Ziegelman and Andrew Coe, *A Square Meal: A Culinary History of the Great Depression* (New York: Harper, 2016), 151. Text quotes socialist journalist Oscar Ameringer, who traveled to Seattle during the early 1930s: "In the State of Washington I was told that the forest fires raging in that region all summer and fall were caused by unemployed timber workers and bankrupt farmers in an endeavor to earn a few honest dollars as fire fighters.

The last thing I saw on the night I left Seattle was numbers of women searching for scraps of food in the refuse piles of the principle market of that city."

4. Lucie Levine, "The 1936 'Summer of Pools': When Robert Moses and the WPA Cooled Off NYC," *6sqft*, https://www.6sqft.com/the-1936-summer-of-pools-when-robert -moses-and-the-wpa-cooled-off-nyc/ (accessed June 23, 2022).

5. "Text of Speech at Bonneville," *Seattle Daily Times*, August 4, 1934, 3. See also "Candidate Calls City's Reception Greatest on Trip," *Seattle Daily Times*, September 20, 1932, 1.

6. "1932 Expansion of Play Areas Is Widespread," *Seattle Daily Times*, January 3, 1932, 24.

7. "Golden Gardens Park Improvements—Seattle WA," *Living New Deal*, https://living newdeal.org/projects/golden-gardens-park-improvements-seattle-wa/ (accessed June 23, 2022).

8. Details about income tax repeal culled from historian Phil Roberts's 1990 University of Washington dissertation, "Of Rain and Revenue: The Politics of Taxation in the State of Washington, 1862–1940." For discussion of the coalition, see 238–39.

9. David Eskenazi, "Wayback Machine: The Washington Athletic Club," *SportspressNW*, October 29, 2013.

10. Biographical details about Culliton from Roberts, "Of Rain and Revenue," 228; "Cullitons Win Bowling Title," *Seattle Daily Times*, April 6, 1933.

11. Roberts, "Of Rain and Revenue," 236–38.

12. Roberts, "Of Rain and Revenue," 257–58.

13. William C. Rhoden, *Forty Million Dollar Slaves: The Rise, Fall, and Redemption of the Black Athlete* (New York: Three Rivers, 2006), 52–57.

14. Kat Eschner, "Was the First Battle of Bull Run Really 'The Picnic Battle'?," *Smithsonian Magazine*, July 21, 2017.

15. Esther Hall Mumford, *Seattle's Black Victorians: 1852–1901* (Seattle: Anansi Press, 1980), 25.

16. Kipling cited in James Ross Gardner, "A Brief History of Seattle in Three Disasters," *Seattle Met*, July 13, 2020.

17. Dan Raley, *Pitchers of Beer: The Story of the Seattle Rainiers* (Lincoln: University of Nebraska Press, 2012), loc. 33–80, Kindle.

18. "Klepper Fires Johnny Bassler," *Seattle Daily Times*, September 20, 1937, 1.

19. "Aerial Duel of Water and Fire Amuses," *Seattle Daily Times*, June 9, 1931, 5.

20. See Maureen Smith's stellar essay, "Helene Madison, Aquatics Queen—Seattle's First Sports Hero," in Terry Anne Scott, ed., *Seattle Sports: Play, Identity, and Pursuit in the Emerald City* (Fayetteville: University of Arkansas Press, 2020), 181.

21. "Seattle Sports Heroes Are Pushed into Background by Young Swimmer's Feats," *Seattle Daily Times*, March 16, 1930, 21.

22. Smith, "Helene Madison, Aquatics Queen," 185.

23. Eskenazi, "Wayback Machine."

24. Brian Harris, "Seattle Sports Scene: 1932," Great Depression in Washington State, Civil Rights and Labor History Consortium, University of Washington, https://depts .washington.edu/depress/sports_depression.shtml (accessed June 23, 2022).

25. Smith, "Helene Madison, Aquatics Queen," 96.

26. Smith, "Helene Madison, Aquatics Queen," 198.

27. David B. Williams, *Homewaters: A Human and Natural History of Puget Sound* (Seattle: University of Washington Press, 2021), 12.

28. Williams, *Homewaters*, 9.

29. Williams, *Homewaters*, 34.

30. Smith, "Helene Madison, Aquatics Queen," 199.

31. Jack Hewins, "'Invisible Mermaid' Begins Biggest Fight," *Seattle Times*, December 13, 1968, 79; Jack Hewins, "Helene Madison Recuperating," *Seattle Times*, January 3, 1969; Don Duncan, "Helene Madison Succumbs at 57," *Seattle Times*, November 26, 1970, 26.

32. Don Duncan, "Funds Lacking, Helene Madison May Miss Trip to Hall of Fame," *Seattle Times*, December 15, 1966, 78.

33. Daniel James Brown, *The Boys in the Boat: Nine Americans and Their Epic Quest for Gold at the 1936 Berlin Olympics* (New York: Penguin Books, 2014), 135–37.

34. Julia Park, "'The Boys in the Boat': What Clooney's Film Has to Get Right," *UW Daily*, April 6, 2023, https://tinyurl.com/uf8k8ubn.

35. Bruce G. Miller, "The Great Race of 1941: A Coast Salish Public Relations Coup," *Pacific Northwest Quarterly* 89, no. 3 (Summer 1998): 127–35.

36. "Yes, Sir, City's Pastime Haven Opens Monday," *Seattle Times*, September 24, 1933, 7.

37. Josephine Ensign, *Skid Road: On the Frontier of Health and Homelessness in an American City* (Baltimore, MD: Johns Hopkins University Press, 2021), 126–29.

38. Maurice MacDonald, "The Firebug—What Impels Him in His Destructive Operations," *Seattle Daily Times*, April 28, 1957, 123.

39. Samuel O. Regalado, "'Play Ball!': Baseball and Seattle's Japanese-American Courier League, 1928–1941," *Pacific Northwest Quarterly* 87, no. 1 (Winter 1995–96): 29–37; Shelley Lee, "'That Splendid Medium of Free Play': Japanese American Sports in Seattle during the Interwar Years," in Scott, *Seattle Sports*, 109.

40. "Jap Team Closes Tour Here," *Seattle Daily Times*, June 6, 1905, 11.

41. "Jap Team Closes Tour Here"; Regalado, "'Play Ball!'"

42. Richard C. Berner, *Seattle Transformed: World War II to Cold War* (Charles City: Charles Press, 1991), 23, 29.

43. "Minidoka," *Densho Encyclopedia*, https://tinyurl.com/yc4vp3h6 (accessed June 25, 2002); "Minidoka Irrigator," *Densho Encyclopedia*, https://tinyurl.com/4557exuu (accessed June 25, 2002).

44. "Work Starts on Nine-Hole Course," *Minidoka Irrigator*, April 10, 1943, 7; "Hunt, Merchants Remain Victorious," *Minidoka Irrigator*, July 21, 1943, 7.

Concession Stand

1. André Peñalver, "Brewing Up Bases: A Story of Labor, Beer, and the All-American Pastime," *Columbia* 33, no. 2 (Summer 2019): 6.

2. Peñalver, "Brewing Up Bases."

3. Murray Morgan, *Skid Road: An Informal Portrait of Seattle* (Seattle: University of Washington Press, 2018), 232.

4. Morgan, *Skid Road*, 234.

5. Morgan, *Skid Road*, 270.

6. Thomas I. Palley, "The Forces Making for an Economic Collapse," *The Atlantic*, July 1, 1996, https://tinyurl.com/2p88vz7r.

7. "Baseball's Organization Men," *Sports Illustrated*, June 23, 1958: "The history of big league baseball shimmers with the memory of managers whose vibrant personalities dominated ball parks like the crackle of peanut shells and the scent of hot franks. In today's baseball, as in other great industries, this is the age of the organization man." Alfred Wright, "The New Managers," *Sports Illustrated*, April 9, 1956.

8. David Halberstam, *The Breaks of the Game* (New York: Knopf, 1981), 180.

4th Inning

1. Details about Kropf's story combined from sundry Seattle newspapers: "For Boys Only? Preps Object to Girl Foe," *Seattle Times*, April 30, 1947, 18; "Girl on Team; Match Off," *Seattle Post-Intelligencer*, May 1, 1947, 1; "Bremerton Refuses to Meet Tacoma Gal," *Seattle Times*, May 11, 1947, 32; Emmett Watson, "Marilyn Earns Prep Berth; Some Boy Foes Won't Play," *Seattle Times*, May 18, 1947, 30; Bill Scholle, "Bill Scholle: Female Tennis Star Overcame Taboos in the 1940s," *East Bay Times*, April 29, 2009, https://tinyurl .com/2xb4st77.

2. "Everett Keeps No-Girl Stand," *Seattle Times*, May 1, 1947, 19.

3. "Well, Lincoln? These Girls Play Football," *Seattle Times*, June 5, 1947, 17.

4. Emmett Watson, "Marilyn Earns Prep Berth," *Seattle Times*, May 18, 1947, 30.

5. "Marilyn Earns Prep Berth."

6. "Marilyn Earns Prep Berth."

7. "What's the Matter with Washington Athletics," *Washington Alumnus*, 1908, 12.

8. Cited in Roger Sale, *Seattle, Past to Present* (Seattle: University of Washington Press, 1976), 72–73.

9. Sale, *Seattle, Past to Present*, 72–73. In fairness, Sale seemed to be riffing on Beaton's language.

10. John C. Putman, *Class and Gender Politics in Progressive-Era Seattle* (Reno: University of Nevada Press, 2008), 75.

11. "Negro Woman on Seattle's Force," *Seattle Times*, January 21, 1914, 7; "Program for Negro Health Week Planned," *Seattle Daily Times*, March 22, 1947, 3.

12. "Women, Labor, and World War II," *Oregon Encyclopedia*, https://tinyurl.com /472kkesr (accessed June 24, 2022). Statistics about divorce rate taken from "100 Years of Marriage and Divorce Statistics, United States, 1867–1967," provided by the National Vital Statistics System, taken from Jennifer Betts, "Historical Divorce Rate Statistics," July 10, 2018, https://tinyurl.com/55zcyhnm.

13. Quintard Taylor, *The Forging of a Black Community: Seattle's Central District from 1870 through the Civil Rights Era* (Seattle: University of Washington Press, 1994), 69–73.

14. "Doghouse Team Blows Up in Ninth," *Seattle Post-Intelligencer*, August 29, 1938, 11; "Pacific Play in Spokane Tonight," *Seattle Post-Intelligencer*, August 29, 1939, 15.

15. Taylor, *Forging of a Black Community*, 164–65.

16. Anne Stych, "'Josie the Riveter,' Who Helped Integrate Boeing during World War II, Dies," *Chicago Business Journal*, December 19, 2016, https://tinyurl.com/2n3zs6k7.

17. Marilyn E. Hegarty, *Victory Girls, Khaki-Wackies, and Patriotutes: The Regulation of Female Sexuality during World War II* (New York: New York University Press, 2008), 99; Josh Levin, *The Queen: The Forgotten Life behind an American Myth* (New York: Little, Brown, 2019), 216.

18. Don Paulson and Roger Simpson, *An Evening at the Garden of Allah: A Gay Cabaret in Seattle* (New York: Columbia University Press, 1996), 13.

19. Paulson and Simpson, *Evening at the Garden of Allah*, 15.

20. Quoted in Paulson and Simpson, *Evening at the Garden of Allah*, 60–64.

21. Quoted in Paulson and Simpson, *Evening at the Garden of Allah*, 11, 60–64.

22. "Seattle Municipal Group Urges County Park Board," *Seattle Post-Intelligencer*, March 26, 1949, 14; "Park Hoop Play to Open," *Seattle Post-Intelligencer*, 27.

23. "Scholars and Pabst Tied," *Seattle Post-Intelligencer*, 24; Paulson and Simpson, *Evening at the Garden of Allah*, 62.

24. Paulson and Simpson, *Evening at the Garden of Allah*, 2.

25. Gary Atkins, *Gay Seattle: Stories of Exile and Belonging* (Seattle: University of Washington Press, 2003), 7, 23, 28–29.

26. Peter Boag, *Re-Dressing America's Frontier Past* (Oakland: University of California Press, 2011), 23–30.

27. Atkins, *Gay Seattle*, 37.

28. Edward L. Glaeser and David M. Cutler, *The Survival of the City: Human Flourishing in an Age of Isolation* (New York: Penguin Press, 2021), 1: "If cities are the absence of physical space between people, then the social distancing that began in March 2020 is the rapid-fire deurbanization of our world." Mimi Sheller, *Mobility Justice: The Politics of Movement in the Age of Extremes* (New York: Verso, 2018).

29. "Cyclists to Turn on Speed," *Seattle Post-Intelligencer*, July 20, 1947, 94; Frank Lynch, "Husband or Motorcycle?," *Seattle Post-Intelligencer*, October 10, 1947, 23; "Picture's in the Paper," *Seattle Post-Intelligencer*, October 22, 1947, 13.

30. Julie Davidow, "Motor Maids Were 'Nice Kids,'" *Seattle Post-Intelligencer*, September 27, 2003, https://www.seattlepi.com/seattlenews/article/Motor-Maids-were-nice-kids-1125518.php.

31. Frank Lynch, "Husband or Motorcycle?," *Seattle Post-Intelligencer*, October 10, 1947, 23.

32. "'Gloomy Gil' Had Nine Perfect Seasons at UW," *Seattle Daily Times*, December 24, 1948, 14; William Coyle, "'The Spell of Gil Dobie,'" *Seattle Daily Times*, December 30, 1948, 15.

33. Cited in Lynn Borland, *Gilmour Dobie: Pursuit of Perfect* (Frisco, TX: Tribute Publishing, 2010), loc. 5618, Kindle.

34. "Fly ATA," advertisement, *Seattle Times*, September 22, 1949, 4; Royal Brougham, "'Gophers' Power Beats Washington," *Seattle Post-Intelligencer*, September 25, 1949, 1; Royal Brougham, "Gophers Rout UW, 48–20," *Seattle Post-Intelligencer*, September 25, 1949, 14; Royal Brougham, "Gophers Wallop Young Huskies," *Seattle Post-Intelligencer*, September 25, 1949, 18.

35. "Air Power and American Independence," *Boeing Magazine*, August 1947, 4.

36. "Progress Depends on Research," *Boeing Magazine*, July 1947; "Progress Is a Two-Letter Word," *Boeing Magazine*, July 1946, 6.

37. "Biography of a Gladiator," *Boeing Magazine*, March 1947, 3.

38. "Husky Special," *Boeing Magazine*, October 1949.

39. "We Had to Strike," *Aero Mechanic*, April 22, 1948, 4.

40. Polly Reed Myers, *Capitalist Family Values: Gender, Work, and Corporate Culture at Boeing* (Lincoln: University of Nebraska Press, 2015), 53.

41. "Keep 'Em Rolling Bud," *Aero Mechanic*, September 9, 1948, 3; "Wrestlers Join AFL, *Aero Mechanic*, January 31, 1946; "This Guide Knows the Way," *Aero Mechanic*, March 28, 1946.

42. "The Motorcycle Squad," *Aero Mechanic*, April 29, 1948.

43. "Ashamed," *Aero Mechanic*, September 16, 1948.

44. "Do People Expect Too Much of Doctors during Epidemic," *Aero Mechanic*, April 11, 1946.

45. Lee Lowenfish and Tony Lupien, *The Imperfect Diamond: The Story of Baseball's Reserve System and the Men Who Fought to Change It* (New York: Stein and Day, 1980), 82.

46. Lowenfish and Lupien, *Imperfect Diamond*, 30, 35, and 82.

47. "Niemiec Case on Trial, Rights of Ball Players under Service Act to Be Tested," *New York Times*, June 15, 1946, 14.

48. Niemiec v. Seattle Rainier Baseball Club, 67 F. Supp. 705 (W.D. Wash. 1946).

49. Ira Katznelson, *When Affirmative Action Was White: An Untold History of Racial Inequality in Twentieth-Century America* (New York: W. W. Norton, 2005), 114.

50. Dave Eskenazi, "Wayback Machine: Seattle Steelheads' Short Life," *SportspressNW*, https://tinyurl.com/mry99j5m (accessed June 24, 2022).

51. "Racial Tolerance Pays Off Big in Sports Field," *Seattle Post-Intelligencer*, November 22, 1946, 6.

5th Inning

1. Quintard Taylor, *The Forging of a Black Community, Seattle's Central District from 1870 through the Civil Rights Era*, 2nd ed. (Seattle: University of Washington Press, 2022), 208.

2. Taylor, *Forging of a Black Community*, 192, is source for subsequent quotes about Black citizens and stereotypes of criminality.

3. Roger Sale, *Seattle, Past to Present* (Seattle: University of Washington Press, 1976), 217–18.

4. Sarah Gilbert, "A History of Seattle's African-American Community—in Pictures," *The Guardian*, February 9, 2018, https://tinyurl.com/ycqcg7b3.

5. William C. Rhoden, *Forty Million Dollar Slaves: The Rise, Fall, and Redemption of the Black Athlete* (New York: Three Rivers Press, 2006), 55.

6. Amy Louise Wood, *Lynching and Spectacle: Witnessing Racial Violence in America, 1890–1940* (Chapel Hill: University of North Carolina Press, 2009); Vincent Woodward, *The Delectable Negro: Human Consumption and Homoeroticism within U.S. Slave Culture* (New York: New York University Press, 2014).

7. Michelle Newblom, "Traveling Back in Time to Seattle University's Sports Hall of Fame," *The Spectator*, February 7, 2018, https://tinyurl.com/y67v64su.

8. Dan Raley, "Baylor, Seattle U Scoring Machine, Was Toast of Town in 1950s," *Seattle Post-Intelligencer*, February 12, 2008, https://tinyurl.com/yxf48ddr.

9. Bill Simmons, *The Book of Basketball: The NBA According to the Sports Guy* (New York: Ballantine Books, 2009), 553.

10. Knute Berger, "Seattle Needs a New Nickname," *Crosscut*, February 2014, https://crosscut.com/2014/02/seattle-needs-new-nickname-knute-berker.

11. Patterson quote comes from a 1985 television special *Once a Star*, https://tinyurl.com/bdbxurdn (accessed August 29, 2020).

12. Figures compiled from substantiated Wikipedia entries detailing heavyweight fighting reigns by date.

13. Carlos Bulosan, *America Is in the Heart* (New York: Penguin Books, 2019), 104; "Larry Doby's Symbolic Left Hook," *Ebony*, September 1957, 51.

14. Martin Kane, "The Man the System Could Not Beat," *Sports Illustrated*, December 10, 1956, https://tinyurl.com/yxm6rj7n. Oddsmakers had Moore as a 12–5 favorite initially, before the betting line set in at 8–5 by the night of the fight. In an interview Mike Tyson described boxing as "communism" because of the syndicates and mob bosses who tightly controlled who was allowed to rise through the sport's ranks (see "Mike Tyson Presents the Heavyweights," YouTube, https://tinyurl.com/y5279xru [accessed December 28, 2022]).

15. Robert A. Beauregard, *Voices of Decline: The Postwar Fate of US Cities* (Oxfordshire: Routledge Press, 1933).

16. Beauregard, *Voices of Decline*, 90.

17. Beauregard, *Voices of Decline*, 86.

18. Jeffrey Craig Sanders, *Seattle and the Roots of Urban Sustainability* (Seattle: University of Washington Press, 2010), loc. 350, Kindle.

19. Figures taken from the US decennial Census.

20. James N. Gregory, "Remembering Seattle's Segregated History," *Seattle Post-Intelligencer*, December 11, 2016, https://tinyurl.com/y4r62ft6; Marcie Sillman, "Here's Why Old Seattle Is OBSESSED with Hydroplanes," KUOW, August 4, 2016, https://tinyurl.com/y2q495nb; David Neiwart, *Strawberry Days: How Internment Destroyed a Japanese American Community* (New York: St. Martin's Press, 2015), 6.

21. "Harold Mills (1953–)," BlackPast.org, February 26, 2008, https://tinyurl.com/yj5r8s2x.

22. "Five Things to Know about Seafair's Hydroplane Races," KING5, March 11, 2019, https://tinyurl.com/y6dxdnvq.

23. "Racial Restrictive Covenants," Seattle Civil Rights and Labor History Project, https://tinyurl.com/y3q7q3x8 (accessed August 28, 2020).

24. David Eskenazi, "Wayback Machine: Elgin Baylor's Run at Seattle U," *SportspressNW*, March 22, 2021, https://tinyurl.com/y59owotl.

25. Jon Hale, "Kentucky Basketball: Adolph Rupp Defends Record on Race," *Courier Journal*, July 30, 2020, https://tinyurl.com/yxgflny4.

26. Chris Surovick, "The Day College Basketball Changed Forever," *Bleacher Report*, May 19, 2010, https://tinyurl.com/y6q9dky5.

27. Terry Mosher, "Seattle U's Dream Season and the Legacy of Racism," *Kitsap Sun*, July 20, 2020, https://tinyurl.com/y4oy7pul.

28. See Seattle sportswriter Emmett Watson's *Digressions of a Native Son* (Seattle: Pacific Institute, 1982). The book contains a wonderful essay, "Long Shot Pete," which details the racial and financial dynamics at play in the Patterson-Rademacher fight.

29. Watson, *Digressions of a Native Son.*

30. Edward P. F. Eagan, "An Open Letter to Pete Rademacher," *Sports Illustrated*, August 19, 1957, https://tinyurl.com/y5zh3058.

31. Martin Kane, "The Champ Meets a Veep," *Sports Illustrated*, August 19, 1957.

32. Alan Levy, *Floyd Patterson: Boxer and a Gentleman* (Jefferson, NC: McFarland, 2008), 69–71.

33. The phrase was historically used to describe impudent white challengers who try to take down Black champions. See Louis Moore, *I Fight for a Living: Boxing and the Battle for Black Manhood, 1880–1915* (Chicago: University of Illinois Press, 2017).

34. "Rademacher's Dream Nearly Came True," *Los Angeles Times*, August 9, 1987, https://tinyurl.com/y33gvobo; Richard Sandomir, "Pete Rademacher, 1956 Olympic Boxing Champion, Dies at 91," *New York Times*, June 11, 2020, https://tinyurl.com/y5gghw02.

35. A. S. Young, "Is Floyd Patterson Betraying Boxing?," *Jet*, September 5, 1957, 54, https://tinyurl.com/432xykt3.

36. Craig Smith, "Patterson Recalls 1957 Frightful Fight in Seattle—Ex-Champ Admits Taking Rademacher Too Lightly," *Seattle Times*, February 5, 1994, https://tinyurl.com/yxwt7yet.

37. The newsreel is viewable at the HistoricFilms.com archive, https://tinyurl.com/yxfa65cx (accessed August 29, 2020).

38. Levy, *Floyd Patterson*, 69–71.

39. Watson, *Digressions of a Native Son,* 107–10.

40. Frank Litsky, "Floyd Patterson, 71, Good-Guy Heavyweight Champion, Dies," *New York Times*, May 12, 2006, https://tinyurl.com/y4cmhb59.

41. Helen O'Neill, "Floyd Patterson—Ex-Champ Shadowboxes with His Past," *Seattle Times*, July 26, 1998, https://tinyurl.com/y6g8pyow.

42. Litsky, "Floyd Patterson, 71, Good-Guy Heavyweight Champion, Dies."

43. Patterson as quoted in Floyd Patterson, "In Defense of Cassius Clay," *Esquire*, August 1, 1966.

44. "Floyd Patterson: The Champion He Wants to Be," *Jet Magazine*, December 20, 1956, 52–55.

45. Floyd Patterson (as told to Allan Morrison), "My Greatest Ambition," *Ebony*, March 1957, 59–62.

46. The newsreel is available from the criticalpast.com archive, "Floyd Patterson Trains for Fight with Pete Rademacher," https://tinyurl.com/y6khpw2a (accessed August 29, 2020).

47. Watson, *Digressions of a Native Son,* 111.

48. The fight in its entirety can be viewed on YouTube, "Floyd Patterson vs Pete Rademacher 22/8/1957," https://www.youtube.com/watch?v=3NUKNkblQD0 (accessed August 29, 2020).

49. Mosher, "Seattle U's Dream Season."

50. Mosher, "Seattle U's Dream Season."

51. Mosher, "Seattle U's Dream Season."

52. Mosher, "Seattle U's Dream Season."

53. Eskenazi, "Wayback Machine: Elgin Baylor's Run at Seattle U."

54. Jeremiah Tax, "The Old Master Outfoxed Them," *Sports Illustrated*, March 31, 1958, https://tinyurl.com/y41898eg.

55. Eskenazi, "Wayback Machine: Elgin Baylor's Run at Seattle U."

56. Filip Trivic, "Elgin Baylor Served in the Army and Played on Weekends," *Basketball Network*, August 29, 2019, https://tinyurl.com/y3php6fl.

57. Mosher, "Seattle U's Dream Season."

58. Doug Fischer, "Pete Rademacher: The Most Ambitious Pro Debut of All Time," *The Ring*, October 10, 2019, https://tinyurl.com/y6zs2old.

59. Oates quoted in Joyce Carol Oates, "Kid Dynamite: Mike Tyson Is the Most Exciting Heavyweight Fighter since Muhammad Ali," *Life*, March 1987, https://tinyurl.com/y53hxalo.

60. Royal Brougham, "Patterson KOs Pete in Sixth," *Seattle Post-Intelligencer,* August 23, 1957, 1.

61. Cassandra Tate, "Elvis Shakes up Seattle on September 1, 1957," HistoryLink, July 10, 2001, https://tinyurl.com/y4eq5csn.

62. Cheryl I. Harris, "Whiteness as Property," *Harvard Law Review* 106, no. 8 (1993): 1707–91.

63. Josh Cohen, "Rectifying Seattle's Racist Past Requires a Denser Future, Says Report," *Crosscut*, December 12, 2018, https://tinyurl.com/y3xw8zc7.

64. Gregory, "Remembering Seattle's Segregated History."

65. See Jennifer Taylor's excellent essay, "The 1965 Freedom Patrols and the Origins of Seattle's Police Accountability Movement," Seattle Civil Rights and Labor History Project, https://tinyurl.com/y45nsa55 (accessed August 29, 2020).

66. Kimmy Yam, "How Bruce Lee Became a Symbol of Solidarity with the Black Community," *NBC News*, June 11, 2020, https://tinyurl.com/tzwsft4k.

6th Inning

1. Jeffrey Craig Sanders, *Seattle and the Roots of Urban Sustainability* (Seattle: University of Washington Press, 2010), loc. 695, Kindle; see "Dumping on the U-Dub," in the University of Washington's alumni magazine, *Columns*, March 1996, https://tinyurl.com/yyzecjnp. HistoryLink's entry on the subject, "Union Bay Natural Area (Seattle)," January 2, 2013, https://tinyurl.com/yxj65xku, is also helpful; "Landfill of Old a Problem of New," *The Daily,* April 29, 2002, https://tinyurl.com/y36kgkcr.

2. See the documentary *When Seattle Invented the Future: The 1962 World's Fair*, which aired in 2012 on Seattle's PBS affiliate, KCTS 9.

3. "Puget Sound Emerging as Megalopolis," *Los Angeles Times*, February 12, 1967.

4. This speech was delivered January 21, 1966, to the anniversary luncheon of the Seattle Junior Chamber of Commerce and is available at University of Washington Special Collections.

5. Matthew Klingle, *Emerald City: An Environmental History of Seattle* (Seattle: University of Washington, 2007), 219–20.

6. Jon Solomon, "Significance of Texas Western's 1966 NCAA Title Not Realized at First," CBS Sports, February 26, 2016, https://tinyurl.com/y5e067m2.

7. John Owen, "Franchise in NBA Pending," *Seattle Post-Intelligencer*, December 16, 1966, 1; "State: Not a Time for Rapid Transit," *Seattle Post-Intelligencer*, December 16, 1966, 1.

8. "A Look at the Sonics' 39 Seasons in Seattle," *Seattle Times*, July 19, 2006, https://tinyurl.com/y3yhnhns; Thomas Aiello, *Hoops: A Cultural History of Basketball in America* (Washington, DC: Rowman & Littlefield, 2021), 160.

9. Hy Zimmerman, "No More Oshkosh; Seattle among Elite," *Seattle Times*, December 22, 1966, 19.

10. Hy Zimmerman, "A Coat on the Vote; New Orleans Swings," *Seattle Times*, November 10, 1966, 44.

11. Brian Floyd, "Seattle's Floating Stadium and What Could Have Been," *SB Nation Seattle*, March 2, 2011, https://seattle.sbnation.com/seattle-mariners/2011/3/2/2026022/seattle-floating-stadium-kingdome-safeco-field; "That Time Seattle Almost Built a Football Stadium on Water," *Curbed*, February 4, 2016.

12. In 2018, I wrote about Forward Thrust in a four-part essay series for *The Urbanist*, https://tinyurl.com/yuuu36wx (accessed August 29, 2020). Much of my analysis and research in this chapter—unless otherwise cited—draws on that material. In addition, Bill Mullins's essay "The Persistence of Progressivism: James Ellis and the Forward Thrust Campaign," Center for the Study of the Pacific Northwest, University of Washington, https://tinyurl.com/wxrbum4 (accessed August 29, 2020), is indispensable.

13. See Seattle writer Larry Coffman's obituary of Jim Ellis, who passed away in October 2019, "Jim Ellis: Precious Memories," *MarketingNW,* October 24, 2019, https://tinyurl.com/yxkmp18g.

14. See my 2018 essay series about Forward Thrust in *The Urbanist*, https://www.theurbanist.org/category/civics-and-culture/ballot-measures/forward-thrust/.

15. Shelby Scates, "Voters Still Hesitant about Forward Thrust," *Seattle Post-Intelligencer*, January 1, 1968, 1.

16. "Pro Exhibition Brings Out No Real Football," *Seattle Daily Times,* February 1, 1926, 1.

17. "Can Seattle Come Out and Play Now," *Seattle Post-Intelligencer*, February 13, 1968.

18. Emmett Watson, "This, Our City," *Seattle Post-Intelligencer,* February 1, 1968, 2.

19. Unless otherwise cited, all quotations in this paragraph are in my 2018 Forward Thrust essay series in *The Urbanist*.

20. Citations for all quotations, as well as the electoral figures in this chapter, are provided in my 2018 Forward Thrust essay series in *The Urbanist*.

21. Cited in Roger Sale, *Seattle, Past to Present* (Seattle: University of Washington Press, 1976), 212–15.

22. Williams H. Mullins, *Becoming Big League: Seattle, the Pilots, and Stadium Politics* (Seattle: University of Washington Press, 2013), loc. 1570, Kindle.

23. John Garrity, "Anne Sander, Née Quast: Still Winning at 52," *Sports Illustrated*, December 11, 1989.

24. Mile-run world record progressions are cataloged on a Wikipedia page, "Mile run world record progression," https://tinyurl.com/5yb33m74 (accessed August 29, 2020).

25. A 1971 Seattle Public Schools Archives photo, published as part of a KUOW article on recess time, captures Black youth playing double-dutch; see Ann Dornfeld, "Seattle Kids Used to Get 95 Minutes of Lunch and Recess," KUOW, October 1, 2015, https://tinyurl.com/y6h6y9kl.

26. *What Is So Great about Seattle?* can be watched in its entirety on YouTube, https://tinyurl.com/y5790ybn (accessed August 29, 2020).

27. Sanders, *Seattle and the Roots of Urban Sustainability,* loc. 585, Kindle.

28. Judson Jeffries as quoted in Aaron Dixon, *My People Are Rising* (Chicago: Haymarket Books, 2012), loc. 79, Kindle.

29. Coll Thrush, *Native Seattle: Histories from the Crossing-Over Place* (Seattle: University of Washington Press, 2007), 188.

30. Thrush, *Native Seattle,* 189.

31. Statistics from James Gregory, "Mapping Race in Seattle/King County, 1920–2010," Civil Rights and Labor History Consortium, University of Washington, https://tinyurl.com/y7sbf6xt (accessed August 20, 2020).

32. See my essay series about Forward Thrust in *The Urbanist*.

33. See Yuxin Zheng's essay, "Trauma and Silence in *No-No Boy*: An Interdisciplinary Reading," *Inquiries Journal* 11, no. 10 (2019), https://tinyurl.com/y28aowlf: "Okada also hints at possible ways that trauma would affect future generations. For example, the three young girls watching a baseball game seem to imply the young generations' Americanization, which is actually a realistic reflection of some Nisei parents' efforts to have their children 'blend into the mainstream.'" John Okada, *No-Noy Boy* (Seattle: University of Washington Press, 1957).

34. "Luke, Wing (1925–1965)," HistoryLink, January 25, 1999, https://tinyurl.com/y2w3yxvb.

35. See "The Seattle Open Housing Campaign, 1959–1968," Seattle Municipal Archives, https://tinyurl.com/y6gbvneb (accessed August 30, 2020).

36. See my essay series about Forward Thrust in *The Urbanist*.

37. Mullins, *Becoming Big League,* loc. 1983, Kindle.

38. Owen quoted in Mullins, *Becoming Big League,* loc. 2700, Kindle.

39. Mullins, *Becoming Big League,* loc. 2695, Kindle.

40. Mullins, *Becoming Big League,* loc. 2225, Kindle.

41. Jim Bouton, *Ball Four* (New York: Rosetta Books, 1970), loc. 2708, Kindle.

42. Roger Sale, *Seattle, Past to Present* (Seattle: University of Washington Press, 1976), 283.

43. Michelle Baruchman, "Jim Ellis, Who Preserved Washington's Nature and Spearheaded Public Works, Dies at 98," *Seattle Times,* October 22, 2019, https://tinyurl.com/y2enpyrp; see Mullins, "Persistence of Progressivism."

44. Michelle Alexander, *The New Jim Crow: Mass Incarceration in the Age of Colorblindness* (New York: New Press, 2012), 47: "During the [1968 presidential election], both the Republican candidate, Richard Nixon, and the independent segregationist candidate, George Wallace, made 'law and order' a central theme of their campaigns, and together they collected 57 percent of the vote. Nixon dedicated seventeen speeches solely to the topic of law and order, and one of his television ads called on voters to reject the lawlessness of civil rights activists."

45. "1968 Presidential General Election Results in Washington," uselectionatlas.org, https://tinyurl.com/y4kj753m (accessed August 30, 2020).

46. Mullins, "Persistence of Progressivism."

47. Mullins, "Persistence of Progressivism."

48. At least two books focus on the topic of police corruption in Seattle: Christopher T. Bayley, *Seattle Justice: The Rise and Fall of the Police Payoff System in Seattle* (Seattle: Sasquatch Books, 2015); Rick Anderson, *Seattle Vice: Strippers, Prostitution, Dirty Money, and Crooked Cops in the Emerald City* (Seattle: Sasquatch Books, 2010).

49. "Boeing Bust (1969–1971)," HistoryLink, December 16, 2019, https://tinyurl.com/y5yzp5ag; Janes Jacobs, *Cities and the Wealth of Nations: Principles of Economic Life* (New York: Random House Books, 1985), 185; Mullins, "Persistence of Progressivism"; Sharon Boswell and Lorraine McConaghy, "Lights Out, Seattle," *Seattle Times*, November 3, 1996.

50. Royal Brougham, "Morning After, It Could Happen Here," *Seattle Post-Intelligencer*, January 21, 1968, 55.

51. Mullins, "Persistence of Progressivism."

52. "Another City Chooses Progress," *Seattle Times*, November 3, 1965, 52.

7th-Inning Stretch

1. Steve Rudman, "Shoe Express," *Seattle Post-Intelligencer*, November 19, 1976, 32.

2. "Runners Plan 26-Mile Race," *Seattle Times*, November 13, 1970, 62; "Shull Wins 1st Seattle Marathon," *Seattle Times*, November 16, 1970, 47.

3. Dorothea Nordstrand, "Pioneer Women of Seattle," HistoryLink, December 5, 2005, https://www.historylink.org/File/7540.

4. "A Long Race on a Cold Day," *Seattle Times*, November 30, 1975, 3; Craig Smith, "Stonkus Secretive about Strategy for Seattle Marathon," *Seattle Times*, November 23, 1977, 63; Sherry Stripling, "Glad Wins Marathon in Record Time," *Seattle Times*, November 27, 1977, 123; "Seattle Marathon Special," *Seattle Times*, November 15, 1978, 119; "1,950 Runners Ready for Today's Seattle Marathon," *Seattle Times*, November 26, 1978, 57; "Record Field Set for Seattle Marathon," *Seattle Times*, November 22, 1979, 140; "Paraplegic Trikers in Marathon," *Seattle Post-Intelligencer*, November 23, 1977, 14.

5. Kirk Smith, "Green Lake Rules to Stand," *Seattle Post-Intelligencer*, April 8, 1977, 3; T. Clarence Cleangarden, "The Lake Is a Haiku," *Seattle Post-Intelligencer*, April 3, 1977, 67.

6. "Long Race on a Cold Day," 3.

7. "Trust in Government: 1958–2015," US Politics & Policy, Pew Research Center, November 23, 2015, https://www.pewresearch.org/politics/2015/11/23/1-trust-in-government-1958–2015/.

8. Drew DeSilver, "For Most U.S. Workers, Real Wages Have Barely Budged in Decades," Pew Research Center, https://www.pewresearch.org/fact-tank/2018/08/07/for-most-us-workers-real-wages-have-barely-budged-for-decades/ (accessed June 26, 2022).

9. Jane Leavy and Susan Okie, "The Runner: Phenomenon of the 70s," *Washington Post*, September 30, 1979.

7th Inning

1. Royal Brougham, "Team of the Year?," *Seattle Post-Intelligencer*, October 24, 1948, 22.

2. Emmett Watson, "R.B.—R.I.P.," *Seattle Post-Intelligencer*, October 31, 1978, 12; Dab Raley, "The Life and Times of Royal Brougham," *Seattle Post-Intelligencer*, October 29, 2003, 35; "Stricken at Seahawks Game, Royal Brougham Dies," *Seattle Post-Intelligencer*, October 30, 1978, 1; Don Tewkesbury, "Hundreds from All Walks in Farewell to Brougham," *Seattle Post-Intelligencer*, November 4, 1978, 1.

3. Eric L. Flom, "Brougham, Royal (1894–1978)," HistoryLink, August 22, 2005, https://www.historylink.org/file/3423.

4. Steve Raible, *Tales from the Seattle Seahawks Sideline* (New York: Constable & Robinson, 2013), 76.

5. Emmett Watson, "R.B.—RIP," *Seattle Post-Intelligencer*, October 31, 1978, 12.

6. Marc J. Spears and Gary Washburn, *The Spencer Haywood Rule: Battles, Basketball, and the Making of an American Iconoclast* (Chicago: Triumph Books, 2020), 116.

7. David Halberstam, *The Breaks of the Game*, 1st ed. (New York: Knopf, 1981), 100.

8. Roy E. Brownell II, "The Ambivalent Legacy of the 1977 NBA Finals," NASSH Conference Panel Presentation, May 25, 2019, Boise, Idaho; Halberstam, *Breaks of the Game*, 20.

9. Brownell, "Ambivalent Legacy of the 1977 NBA Finals."

10. Halberstam, *Breaks of the Game*, 178.

11. On Lenny Wilkens receiving hate mail in Seattle, see Frank Deford, "Sweety Cakes Runs the Sonics," *Sports Illustrated*, November, 24, 1969, https://tinyurl.com/bdf25k3u. Citation for Wilkens supporting Haywood in Spears and Washburn, *Spencer Haywood Rule*, 101.

12. Curry Kirkpatrick, "Down to One Last Collision," *Sports Illustrated*, June 12, 1978; Curry Kirkpatrick, "The Sonics Keep Their Garde Up," *Sports Illustrated*, November 13, 1978; Curry Kirkpatrick, "It's Washington (City) vs. Washington (State), by George," *Sports Illustrated*, April 16, 1979; John Papanek, "It Was Seattle, Handily," *Sports Illustrated*, June 11, 1979.

13. This history is detailed in SI Staff, "How Far Have We Come?," *Sports Illustrated*, August 5, 1991, https://tinyurl.com/35zfx7rw.

14. Halberstam, *Breaks of the Game*, 182.

15. "Mail," *Seattle Post-Intelligencer*, June 4, 1978, 103; Michael Sweeney and Don Tewkesbury, "Playoffs Score $350,000 for City," *Seattle Post-Intelligencer*, June 9, 1978, 8; Karen West, "Sonics Drown Out Alki Public Meeting," *Seattle Post-Intelligencer*, June 3, 1978, 6; Don Tewkesbury, "Seventh Game in Playoff to Profit Bars," *Seattle Post-Intelligencer*, June 5, 1978, 1.

16. Curry Kirkpatrick, "Ready for a Sonic Boom," *Sports Illustrated*, May 22, 1978.

17. "A Decade in the City by the Sound," *Seattle Medium*, October 8, 1976, 8.

18. Walt Evans, "Playoff Money Was Split Less Habegger," *Seattle Times,* June 30, 1978, 10; Walt Evans, "Boy, Was That a Dome Idea," *Seattle Times,* May 31, 1978, 10; "Black Community Night," *Seattle Medium*, January 31, 1979, 3. The case could be made that the Portland Blazers were the first team to embody this dynamic, but there's a crucial difference: the Sonics were a mostly Black team, the Blazers a mostly white one—therefore, Seattle's

team forecasted the racial dynamics of NBA marketing in future years in ways that the Blazers did not.

19. David B. Williams, *Too High and Too Steep* (Seattle: University of Washington Press, 2019), 94; information about elected officials pulling up railroad spikes from a Kingdome retrospective aired by KING 5 News on the occasion of the building's implosion in the year 2000—"Kingdome Retrospective," YouTube, https://www.youtube.com/watch?v=t6fv5nedBG0&t=27s (accessed December 31, 2022).

20. Royal Brougham, "Rose Bowl Flashback," *Seattle Post-Intelligencer*, December 31, 1977, 16.

21. Warren Moon and Don Yaeger, *Never Give Up on Your Dream: My Journey* (Boston: Da Capo Press, 2009), 47.

22. Moon as quoted in Joe Jares, "A Perfect Moon Shot for the Huskies," *Sports Illustrated*, January 8, 1978: "This pressure is nothing to me after what I've been through the last three years. I can say that I only felt really comfortable playing the last four home games of this season. I guess that's why I played some of my best games on the road."

23. Sportswriter Jack Olsen's *Sports Illustrated* exposé "The Black Athlete: A Shameful Story" ran in the summer of 1968. It was later self-published as an e-book form: Jack Olsen, *The Black Athlete: A Shameful Story* (Crime Rant Books, 2015), 105 (for quotas), 81 (for penalties on interracial dating).

24. "Sophisticated Institutional Racism," *The Facts*, January 7, 1971, 6; Greg Bishop "At Long Last, Peace for Three UW Players," *Seattle Times*, November 6, 2006, https://tinyurl.com/5cx66r8m.

25. Moon and Yaeger, *Never Give Up on Your Dream*, 47.

26. "College Athletes Find a Friend," *Ebony*, December 1975, 103.

27. Todd Warnick, "A Loss Huskies Should Try to Forget," *UW Daily*, September 28, 1976: "Yet to hang the noose around quarterback Warren Moon's neck would be ridiculous. He had an average day and missed some passes and had some dropped."

28. I'm not related to Tyree Scott—at least, not genetically; see William H. Mullins, *Becoming Big League: Seattle, the Pilots, and Stadium Politics* (Seattle: University of Washington Press, 2013), loc. 4367, Kindle; "Blacks Set Sea-Tac Protest," *Seattle Times*, November 5, 1969, 61.

29. Carol Anderson, *White Rage: The Unspoken Truth of Our Racial Divide* (New York: Bloomsbury, 2016), 5.

30. "Judge Rejects Discrimination Charge," *UW Daily*, October 1, 1976, 1.

31. "Does Reverse Discrimination Exist?," *UW Daily*, September 28, 1977.

32. "Finding the Man in Moon," *UW Daily*, September 27, 1976.

33. Roy Blount Jr., "Pittsburgh's Black Quarterback," *Sports Illustrated*, September 23, 1974; Mark Mulvoy, "Twinkle, Twinkle, and Pffft," *Sports Illustrated*, August 11, 1975; Robert H. Boyle, "The Brutal Trip Down," *Sports Illustrated*, November 5, 1979.

34. A photograph of this rally is in the archives of Seattle's Museum of History and Industry (MOHAI), 2000.107.185.36.01.

35. Fred Moody, *Seattle and the Demons of Ambition: A Love Story*, 1st ed. (New York: St. Martin's Press, 2003), 87–88.

36. Moon and Yaeger, *Never Give Up on Your Dream*, 48.

37. "Sonics Party Over," *Seattle Post-Intelligencer*, June 8, 1978, 16; John Papanek, "There's an Ill Wind Blowing for the NBA," *Sports Illustrated*, February 26, 1979.

38. James Reston, "Sports and Politics," *New York Times*, May 14, 1978, E19, https://tinyurl.com/ycypse9w.

39. Curry Kirkpatrick, "The Sonics Keep Their Garde Up," *Sports Illustrated*, November 13, 1978.

40. Greg Heberlein, "D.J. Discounts Motta's 0-for-14 Pressure Tactic," *Seattle Times*, June 1, 1979, 29.

41. Halberstam, *Breaks of the Game*, 180.

42. NBA attendance statistics sourced from the Association for Professional Basketball Research, "NBA/ABA Home Attendance Totals," https://tinyurl.com/2jvt2rt3.

43. Carol Perkins, "Sonic Fever: A Throwback to Ancient Rituals," *Seattle Post-Intelligencer*, June 5, 1979, 4.

44. "Super Gift the SuperSonics Pendant," *Seattle Times*, June 4, 1979; 15; "The Bon," *Seattle Times*, June 14, 1979; Laura Parker, "Here It Comes—A Flood of Sonics Souvenirs," *Seattle Post-Intelligencer*, June 5, 1979, 15; Craig Smith, "Suburban Sonics? Pro Athletes Live out of City's Core," *Seattle Times*, June 13, 1979, 97.

45. Mehrsa Baradaran, *The Color of Money: Black Banks and the Racial Wealth Gap* (Cambridge, MA: Harvard University Press, 2017), 177.

46. Alexis Petridis, "Disco Demolition: The Night They Tried to Crush Black Music," *The Guardian,* July 19, 2019, https://tinyurl.com/yppeb782.

47. Gillian Frank, "Discophobia: Antigay Prejudice and the 1979 Backlash against Disco," *Journal of the History of Sexuality* 16, no. 2 (May 2007): 276–306.

48. "Median inflation adjusted weekly earnings of African American wage and salary workers in the U.S. from 1979 to 2020," statistics furnished by Statista, https://tinyurl.com/53em435t (accessed December 31, 2022); "Money Income of Households in the United States: 1979," US Census Bureau, https://tinyurl.com/3wxtynsp (accessed December 31, 2022).

49. Malcolm X, *Two Speeches by Malcolm X* (New York: Merit, 1965), 5, 14, emphasis mine.

50. Gus Brown, "To the Hoop," *Seattle Medium,* January 24, 1979, 4A.

51. Smith, "Suburban Sonics?," 97.

52. Michael Sweeney and Don Tewkesbury, "Playoffs Score $350,000 for City," *Seattle Post-Intelligencer*, June 9, 1978, 8; Don Tewkesbury, "Seventh Game in Playoff to Profit Bars," *Seattle Post-Intelligencer*, June 5, 1978, 1.

53. Frederick Douglass, *Narrative of the Life of Frederick Douglass* (Boston: Anti-Slavery Office, 1849), 74. Excerpt at https://tinyurl.com/4tn38hxw (accessed December 31, 2022).

54. Cecile Andrews, "Sonics Playoffs Get to the Root of Her Discontent," *Seattle Times*, June 3, 1979, 181.

55. Frank Olito, "How the Divorce Rate Has Changed over the Last 150 Years," *Insider*, January 30, 2019, https://www.insider.com/divorce-rate-changes-over-time-2019-1.

56. Arlie Hochschild, *The Second Shift: Working Families and the Revolution at Home* (New York: Penguin Books, 1989), 12.

57. Lou Corasletti, "Growth Management," *Seattle Times*, June 13, 1979, 121; Royal Brougham, "Interesting People," *Seattle Post-Intelligencer*, June 13, 1978, 20.

58. "Sonics Energy," *Seattle Times*, Sunday, June 10, 1979, 139.

8th Inning

1. Art Thiel, "Seahawk Unity Survives while Owners Prove Point," *Seattle Post-Intelligencer*, October 5, 1987, 12.

2. "Scabs Can Never Build Airplanes," *Aero Mechanic,* May 20, 1948, 1.

3. Clare Farnsworth, "By Hook or by Crook, Hawks Give Everyone Shot to Make Sub Team," *Seattle Post-Intelligencer*, September 26, 1987, 12.

4. "NFL Strike Chronology," *Seattle Times*, October 16, 1987, G2.

5. Thiel, "Seahawk Unity Survives while Owners Prove Point."

6. Clare Farnsworth, "Seahawks' Subs Rated Weakest in NFL West," *Seattle Post-Intelligencer*, September 28, 1987, 12; Gil Lyons, "Hawks Strike Up with On-Leave Subs," *Seattle Times*, September 29, 1987, E1.

7. Clare Farnsworth, "Seahawks Beef Up Their Ground Game by Adding Parros, Two Other Backs," *Seattle Post-Intelligencer*, October 1, 1987, 18.

8. Farnsworth, "Seahawks' Subs Rated Weakest in NFL West," 12.

9. Clare Farnsworth, "3 'Subs' Quit; 2 Call Hawks Subpar," *Seattle Post-Intelligencer*, September 25, 1987, 20.

10. Bud Withers, "Replacement Seahawks Will Put Out the Effort, but What about Ability," *Seattle Post-Intelligencer*, October 3, 1987, 2.

11. Gil Lyons, "Trouble Erupts at Seahawk Strike Site," *Seattle Times*, September 30, 1987, F1.

12. "NFL Strike Talks Last into Night," *Seattle Post-Intelligencer*, September 24, 1987, 32.

13. Jill Lieber, "It's Our Strike," *Sports Illustrated*, October 12, 1987.

14. Joseph Anthony McCartin, *Collision Course: Ronald Reagan, the Air Traffic Controllers, and the Strike That Changed America* (New York: Oxford University Press, 2011), 348.

15. Cited in McCartin, *Collision Course,* 349.

16. "Seahawks: From Playbooks to Pickets," *Seattle Post-Intelligencer*, September 22, 1987, 12.

17. Barry T. Hirsch, David A. MacPherson, and Wayne G. Vroman, "Estimates of Union Density by State," *Monthly Labor Review* 124, no. 7 (July 2001): 51–55.

18. "Distortions in Claims of NFL Owners," *Scanner/King County Labor News*, October/November 1987, 1.

19. Details about each of these labor actions are compiled from a variety of sources, many of which come with extensive citations themselves. Most of the Progressive Era strikes were cited from the *Washington State Bureau of Labor Eleventh Biennial Report of 1917–1918* (Olympia, WA: Frank M. Lamborn, Public Printer, 1918), 159. Information about the Ballard strikes of 1893 and IWW radicalism leading to workman's comp in 1911 comes from Robert E. Ficken and Charles P. LeWarne, *Washington: A Centennial History* (Seattle: University of Washington Press, 1988), 40, 46; Greg Lange, "Streetcar Employees of Seattle Strike on September 9, 1903," HistoryLink, May 5, 1999, https://www.history

link.org/File/1072; "Streetcar Employees in Seattle Strike on July 16, 1917," HistoryLink, May 9, 1999, https://www.historylink.org/File/1110; Greg Lange, "Taxicab Drivers Strike Seattle Taxicab Company on May 23, 1917," HistoryLink, May 9, 1999, https://www .historylink.org/File/1117; Greg Lange, "Seattle Iron Workers Strike on April 11, 1917," HistoryLink, May 9, 1999, https://historylink.org/File/1115; Greg Lange, "Coal Packers in Seattle Strike on May 16, 1917," HistoryLink, May 9, 1999, https://www.historylink.org /File/1116; Greg Lange, "Candy Makers in Seattle Strike on August 27, 1917," HistoryLink, May 9, 1999, https://www.historylink.org/File/1119; Greg Lange, "Telephone Operators in Seattle Strike for Union Recognition on October 31, 1917," HistoryLink, May 9, 1999, https://www.historylink.org/File/1120; Jeff Stevens, "July 18, 1934: The Battle of Smith Cove," *Seattle Star*, July 18, 2014, https://tinyurl.com/y882vrtp; David Wilma, "Seattle City Light Electricians Strike on October 17, 1975," HistoryLink, October 16, 2001, https://tinyurl.com/7d86462k; "One Nurses' Strike Ends, Another Goes on in Seattle," *New York Times*, September 2, 1976; Aaron Brenner, Robert Brenner, and Cal Winslow, eds., *Rebel Rank and File: Labor Militancy and Revolt from Below during the Long 1970s* (New York: Verso Books, 2010), 23–24.

20. Richard Seven, "Labor Groups Urged to Boycott Games, Demand Ticket," *Seattle Times*, September 23, 1987, F2.

21. Joe Haberstroh, "1,000 Fans Rally to Bring Back Striking Seahawks," *Seattle Times*, September 27, 1987, 1.

22. Haberstroh, "1,000 Fans Rally."

23. Fred Moody, *Seattle and the Demons of Ambition: A Love Story* (New York: St. Martin's Press, 2003), 67–68.

24. Costas Lapavitsas, *Profiting without Producing: How Finance Exploits Us All* (New York: Verso Books, 2013), loc. 4546, 4623, Kindle.

25. Moody, *Seattle and the Demons of Ambition*, 65.

26. "Nordstroms Profit Even with No NFL," *Seattle Post-Intelligencer*, September 28, 1987, 12.

27. Moody, *Seattle and the Demons of Ambition*, 65–66.

28. Mike Davis, *City of Quartz: Excavating the Future in Los Angeles* (New York: Verso Books, 1990), 201–4.

29. Taha Ebrahimi, "Cal Anderson Park's Surprising Past," *Capitol Hill Past*, September 17, 2020, https://tinyurl.com/2brspr6s; Sally Gene Mahoney, "East Precinct Opens Here," *Seattle Times*, January 25, 1986.

30. "County Council Shortsightedness," *Seattle Post-Intelligencer*, December 5, 1986, A12; Bob Lane, "Jail-Suit Settlement Puts Squeeze on County Budget," *Seattle Times*, December 23, 1986, B2; Dick Lilly and Ronald W. Powell, "County Jail Unsafe, Say Guards, Union," *Seattle Times*, December 3, 1986, D1; Dave Birkland, "Jail Guards Call Fire Alarm System Unsafe," *Seattle Times*, December 11, 1986, B2.

31. David R. Farber, *Crack: Rock Cocaine, Street Capitalism, and the Decade of Greed* (New York: Cambridge University Press, 2019), 179.

32. Adjusted for inflation, the figure would be $24 million. "Bosworth Agrees to $11-million Contract," *Los Angeles Times*, August 15, 1987.

33. Bud Withers, "Striking Seahawks Striving to Maintain a 'Team' Essence," *Seattle Post-Intelligencer*, September 26, 1987, 11; Haberstroh, "1,000 Fans Rally."

34. Jeremy Snyder, "Veterans Who Crossed the Picket Line, 1987 NFL Strike," *Quirky Research*, September 22, 2017, https://tinyurl.com/mrxv6snu.

35. Clare Farnsworth, "Few Will Stay as Subs Learn Fates Today," *Seattle Post-Intelligencer*, October 20, 1987, 38.

36. Bob Condotta, "How the 1987 NFL Strike Divided Seahawks Kenny Easley and Steve Largent," *Seattle Times*, October 13, 2017.

37. Blaine Newnham, "Subs Only Heroes in This Strike," *Seattle Times*, October 6, 1987, C1.

38. "Substitute Seahawks Were a Joy to Watch," *Seattle Times*, October 11, 1987, 43.

39. Quoted in Richard M. Bernard and Bradley Robert Rice, eds., *Sunbelt Cities: Politics and Growth since World War II*, 1st ed. (Austin: University of Texas Press, 1983), 26.

40. Stephen L. Klineberg with Amy Hertz, *Prophetic City: Houston on the Cusp of a Changing America* (New York: Avid Reader Press, 2020), 31.

41. Tovia Smith, "Boston Changes 'Yawkey Way' to 'Jersey Street,'" NPR, April 26, 2018, https://tinyurl.com/3mwdds5h; Chris Yuscavage, "An Ugly History of Boston Being the Most Racist Sports City in America," *Complex*, May 2, 2017, https://tinyurl.com/2dds3fu9; Howard Bryant, "Magic, Bird Were More Than Rivals," *ESPN*, March 11, 2020, https://tinyurl.com/3rynwueb.

42. Warren Moon and Don Yaeger, *Never Give Up on Your Dream* (Boston: Da Capo Press, 2009), 104.

43. Bud Withers, "Houston Sees Rising Moon," *Seattle Post-Intelligencer*, December 31, 1987, 29.

44. John Owen, "Oilers Scratch the Seahawks from Playoffs," *Seattle Post-Intelligencer*, January 4, 1988, 1.

45. Bernard and Rice, *Sunbelt Cities*, 196, for "buckle of the Sunbelt."

46. Matthew D. Lassiter, *The Silent Majority: Suburban Politics in the Sunbelt South* (Princeton, NJ: Princeton University Press, 2006).

47. "1947 Taft-Hartley Substantive Provisions," National Labor Relations Board, https://tinyurl.com/2s369vrd (accessed June 26, 2022); Colin Gordon, "The Legacy of Taft-Hartley," *Jacobin*, December 19, 2017, https://tinyurl.com/ymevbxt6.

48. "Aero Mechanic Members Urged to Write Senators Demanding Repeal of Taft-Hartley Law," *Aero Mechanic*, March 31, 1949; Bernard and Rice, *Sunbelt Cities*, 1.

49. Lassiter, *Silent Majority*, 327.

50. Sarah Pileggi, "Seattle: City Life at Its Best," *Sports Illustrated*, July 19, 1982, https://vault.si.com/vault/1982/07/19/seattle-city-life-at-its-best.

9th Inning

1. George Monbiot, "Neoliberalism—The Ideology at the Root of All Our Problems," *The Guardian*, April 15, 2016, https://tinyurl.com/mr482e9d.

2. Dave Jamieson, "Howard Schultz and Starbucks' Long History of Fending Off

Unions," *Huffington Post,* January 31, 2019, https://tinyurl.com/cwbp9y8a; Merrill Goozner and John McCarron, "'80s Saw Chicago Area Gain 350,000 New Jobs," *Chicago Tribune,* August 18, 1990; "Starbucks Company Timeline," https://tinyurl.com/4fsh9h3j (accessed June 27, 2022).

3. Jerry Adler, "Seattle Reigns," *Newsweek,* May 19, 1996, https://www.newsweek.com /seattle-reigns-178212.

4. David Halberstam, *Playing for Keeps: Michael Jordan and the World He Made* (New York: Crown, 2000), 118.

5. Walt Evans, "Playoff Money Was Split Less Habegger," *Seattle Times,* June 30, 1978, 10.

6. Halberstam, *Playing for Keeps,* 118.

7. Halberstam, *Playing for Keeps,* 177.

8. Mehrsa Baradaran, *The Color of Money: Black Banks and the Racial Wealth Gap* (Cambridge, MA: Harvard University Press, 2017), 177.

9. Jay-Z shout-out in "Hova Song (Intro)," *Vol. 3 . . . Life and Times of S. Carter,* 1999; LL Cool J shout-out in "4,3,2,1," *Phenomenon,* 1997.

10. Brent Stecker, "Why the Mariners' Old Inverted Trident Logo Is Bad Luck and May Be Cursing Them Again," mynorthwest.com, May 24, 2021, https://tinyurl.com/46exh9kb.

11. "Edgar Martinez (b. 1963)," HistoryLink, https://www.historylink.org/file/21157 (accessed June 27, 2020).

12. From the January 26, 1995, episode of *Seinfeld* titled "The Caddy."

13. Max Goodman, "Ken Griffey Jr. Reveals the Source of His Hatred for the New York Yankees," *Sports Illustrated,* June 22, 2020, https://tinyurl.com/mtpm3x2p.

14. Quote from MLB Network documentary *Junior,* first aired 2020, https://www .youtube.com/watch?v=RPtrlkid-xU (accessed June 27, 2022). Other biographical information compiled from Tom Verducci, "Hitting His Prime, Ken Griffey Jr.'s Game Has Matured," *Sports Illustrated,* May 12, 1997; Tom Verducci, "Joltin' Junior," *Sports Illustrated,* May 17, 1999; Hank Hersch, "Born to Be a Big Leaguer," *Sports Illustrated,* May 16, 1988; Steve Rushin, "Don't Rain on His Charade," *Sports Illustrated,* November 15, 1999; Alan Shipnuck, "Junior Comes of Age," *Sports Illustrated,* August 8, 1994.

15. "The Negro Family: The Case for National Action," Office of Policy Planning and Research, US Department of Labor, March 1965, https://tinyurl.com/y69fuku6 (accessed June 27, 2022).

16. Quote from documentary *Sports Illustrated: 1994 the Year in Sports.*

17. Marla Williams, "M's Games in Dome Canceled—County Closes Stadium," *Seattle Times,* July 20, 1994, A1.

18. Jim Street, "Mariners Ready with 2 Plans," *Seattle Post-Intelligencer,* January 26, 1995, 47; Steve Kelley, "It's Dream Time for Baseball," *Seattle Post-Intelligencer,* February 5, 1995, 38; "M's Will Proceed with Replacement Players," *Seattle Post-Intelligencer,* February 10, 1995, 68.

19. Michael Paulson, "Griffey and Buhner Ask for Help," *Seattle Post-Intelligencer,* February 21, 1995, 11.

20. Quoted in Greg Grandin, *The End of the Myth: From the Frontier to the Border Wall in the Mind of America* (New York: Metropolitan Books, 2019), 217.

21. Jerry Adler, "Seattle Reigns," *Newsweek*, May 19, 1996, https://www.newsweek.com/seattle-reigns-178212.

22. Andrea Bauer, "Revolution and Counterrevolution Rock the Soviet Union," *Freedom Socialist,* January–March 1992, 1.

23. "Yolanda Alaniz," *Freedom Socialist*, September–November 1991, 6.

24. Bill Clinton, "Remarks on Arrival in Seattle," American President Project, UC Santa Barbara, https://tinyurl.com/748jwyzn (accessed June 27, 2022).

25. Jack Broom, Linda Keene, and Joni Balter, "Sharing the Moment—The Legacy of the Games," *Seattle Times*, August 5, 1990, A1.

26. Julia Wilson-Goldstein, "Soviets Puzzle over U.S. Poverty," August 1, 1990, *Seattle Times*, A1.

27. Shaun Scott, "Seattle Police Had a Chance to Prove Abolitionists Wrong," *Crosscut*, May 25, 2021, https://tinyurl.com/2d5e76r2.

28. "Black Churches Burned in Seattle since 1982," *Seattle Medium*, July 13, 1996; John Findlay as quoted in James Lyons, *Selling Seattle: Representing Contemporary Urban America* (New York: Wallflower Press, 2004), 66.

29. David Shields, *Black Planet: Facing Race during an NBA Season* (New York: Three Rivers Press, 1999), loc. 266, Kindle.

30. "Scorecard," *Sports Illustrated*, November 7, 1994, https://vault.si.com/vault/1994/11/07/scorecard.

31. Michael Angeli, "The Joy of Yap," *Esquire*, April 1, 1994, 108.

32. Shields, *Black Planet*, loc. 313, Kindle, for "depression"; loc. 2127, Kindle, for "white him out."

33. "Stuff in here" quoted in Angelo Bruscas, "Sampling the Nike Experience," *Seattle Post-Intelligencer*, July 13, 1996, 13; Roger Sale, *Seattle, Past to Present* (Seattle: University of Washington Press, 1976), 290.

34. Alex Nader, Deborah Nelson, and Alex Tizon, "From Deregulation to Disgrace," *Seattle Post-Intelligencer*, December 1, 1996, 1.

35. Stephanie Strom, "A Sweetheart Becomes Suspect; Looking behind Those Kathie Lee Labels," *New York Times*, June 27, 1996, D1; Barry Bearak, "Kathie Lee and the Sweatshop Crusade," *Los Angeles Times*, June 14, 1996; Samir Mehdi, "'Why Should I Speak Out against Nike?': When Michael Jordan Controversially Denied to Call Out Jordan Brand's Parent Company over Allegations on Sweat Shop Labor," *The SportsRush*, November 5, 2021, https://tinyurl.com/kd55zw4w.

36. Gary Payton quoted in Michael Jordan documentary *The Last Dance*, originally aired April 2020 on ESPN.

37. Henry Louis Gates Jr., "Net Worth," *New Yorker*, May 25, 1998, https://www.newyorker.com/magazine/1998/06/01/michael-jordans-advertising-empire.

38. Details about Sonics defense on Jordan in *The Last Dance,* and also in George Matthew Karl and Don Yaeger, *This Game's the Best! (So Why Don't They Quit Screwing with It?)*, 1st ed. (New York: St. Martin's Press, 1997), 16.

39. Phil Jackson and Hugh Delehanty, *Sacred Hoops: Spiritual Lessons as a Hardwood Warrior* (New York: Hachette Books, 1995): "The Sonics had some experienced role

players. But their key players, Payton and Kemp, were great athletes who played on the edge of fury and had never been to the finals."

40. Chloe Johnson, "The Jordan Effect," https://www.linkedin.com/pulse/jordan-effect-chloe-johnson (accessed June 27, 2022).

41. Cobain quoted in a 1992 edition of *Flipside*: "There are bands moving from L.A. and all over to Seattle and then claim they've lived there all their life so they can get record deals. It really offends me" (Al and Cake, "An Interview with Kurt Cobain," *Flipside,* May–June 1992, https://tinyurl.com/mvfa45ez).

42. David Whitson and Donald Macintosh, "The Global Circus: International Sport, Tourism, and the Marketing of Cities," *Journal of Sport & Social Issues*, August 1995.

43. Thomas W. Haines, Neil Gonzales, and Daryl Strickland, "Bruins Roar, 89–78, City's Businesses Join," *Seattle Times*, April 4, 1995, A1.

44. Paul Sullivan, "Griffey's Injury a Result of Hustle," *Chicago Tribune*, June 3, 1995.

45. "Mariner Log," *Seattle Times*, April 27, 1995, C6: "I asked for the change. Now we can make those leaping catches to top guys of homers."

46. Tim Kurkjian, "A Splendid Nest," *Sports Illustrated*, April 13, 1992.

47. David Schaefer, "Tale of 4 Cities, and Their Ballparks," *Seattle Times*, July 22, 1994, A1; "Who's on First Now? The Politics of Baseball," *Seattle Times*, September 26, 1995, B4.

48. Bob Sherwin, "Forgotten Era of Black Baseball Returns to Life," *Seattle Times*, September 9, 1995, B1.

49. Bob Finnigan, "Griffey Seeks Support in Final Homestead," *Seattle Times*, September 18, 1995.

50. "Stadium Leads by 4,000 Votes," *Seattle Times*, September 20, 1995, A1; "Vote on Stadium Was a Vote about Our Happiness," *Seattle Times*, September 25, 1995, B3; "Who's on First Now?," *Seattle Times,* September 26, 1995, B4; David Postman and Kery Murakami, "A Grand Time in Texas," *Seattle Times*, September 29, 1995, A1.

51. David Postman, "Lawmakers to Be Asked for Bonds," *Seattle Times*, October 7, 1995, A1; Michelle Malkin, "Vote No on a Monument to Corporate Welfare Fraud," *Seattle Times,* June 3, 1997, B4; David Postman, "New Stadium Pitch to GOP," *Seattle Times*, October 4, 1995, A19.

52. John White, "Lowry Calls Special Session on Ballpark Lawmakers Meet Today," *The Spokesman-Review*, October 12, 1995, https://tinyurl.com/2p9xue3w.

53. Quoted in *Madison Capital Times*, October 7, 1995, from *The Battle for Seattle* documentary, https://www.youtube.com/watch?v=zEGq465jXHo&t=983s (accessed June 27, 2022).

54. Peter Schmuck, "Candidate Griffey Still Hasn't Taken a Stand," *Baltimore Sun*, May 17, 1996, https://tinyurl.com/v8bw8c29; Griffey tirade in *George* magazine, August 1996; "Griffey Drops Presidential Race," *Anniston Star*, September 13, 1996.

55. "Griffey for President" ads viewed on YouTube, https://tinyurl.com/yz56b4w4 and https://tinyurl.com/mry6yrna (accessed June 27, 2022).

56. Segment about Arizona voters aired on KSTW in early 1996, https://vimeo.com/32654617 (accessed June 27, 2022).

57. Lily Geismer, "Atari Democrats," *Jacobin*, February 8, 2016, https://tinyurl.com/bdzckbmp.

58. Premilla Nadasen, "How a Democrat Killed Welfare," *Jacobin*, February 9, 2016, https://tinyurl.com/4z3m7cnu.

59. Steve Kelley, "Biggest Challenge Lies Ahead for Paralyzed Utley," *Seattle Times*, November 22, 1991, https://tinyurl.com/w9hhj557.

60. Linda Keene, "Bowling Loses Its Grip—Where Have all the Alleys Gone?," *Seattle Times*, February 5, 1995, https://tinyurl.com/2pk4fe9y.

61. Robert Putnam, "Bowling Alone: America's Declining Social Capital," *Journal of Democracy*, January 1995, 65–78.

62. Letter to the editor, "Stadium Vote—'Father Knows Best,'" *Seattle Times*, October 1, 1995, B7.

63. "Dan Savage's Open Letter to Paul Allen on Lidding I-5, Righting a Wrong, and Leaving a Legacy," *The Stranger*, December 6, 2016, https://tinyurl.com/yrw28fcn.

64. David Wilma and Kit Oldham, "Washington Voters Elect Democrats Bill Clinton for President and Gary Locke for Governor," HistoryLink, March 22, 2006, https://www.historylink.org/File/7707.

65. Sarah Pileggi, "Seattle: City Life at Its Best," *Sports Illustrated*, July 19, 1982, https://vault.si.com/vault/1982/07/19/seattle-city-life-at-its-best.

66. Jaqui James, "Then and Now: U-PASS a Great Value since 1991 Debut," *UW News*, January 24, 2008, https://tinyurl.com/5cskcwth.

67. "Seahawks Stadium—A No Vote Means No Teams," *Seattle Times*, June 1, 1997, B4; David Schaefer, Barbara A. Serrano, and Lynne K. Varner, "Stadium Won Big in Suburbs," *Seattle Times,* June 19, 1997, A1; "Seahawks Stadium—Voters Need to Know the Facts," *Seattle Times*, June 1, 1997, B7; "Allen Profits, Public Just Pays," *Seattle Times,* June 1, 1997, B7; David Schaefer, "Paul Allen Stars in New Ad for Stadium," *Seattle Times*, June 1, 1997, B3; Elliott Almond, "Stadium Plan Here Not Best or Worst," *Seattle Times*, June 4, 1997, A1.

68. Noah Smith, "The Dark Side of Globalization: Why Seattle's 1999 Protesters Were Right," *The Atlantic*, January 6, 2014, https://tinyurl.com/28zzrkf4; David Moberg, "How the Battle in Seattle Changed Everything," *In These Times,* November 30, 2020, https://tinyurl.com/yeb6sjpy; Carolyn Adolph, "'Smoke in the Street,' Unions Grapple with the Complicated Legacy of the Battle in Seattle," KUOW, November 19, 2019, https://www.kuow.org/stories/battle-in-seattle-is-with-us-still.

69. Schultz clip appears in the 2007 feature film *Battle in Seattle*.

Pitching Change

1. James Lyons, *Selling Seattle: Representing Contemporary Urban America* (New York: Wallflower Press, 2004), 166.

2. Quoted in Lyons, *Selling Seattle*.

3. Kim Murphy, "The Decline and Fall of Seattle," *Los Angeles Times*, August 4, 2002.

4. Tom Verducci, "Joltin' Junior," *Sports Illustrated*, May 17, 1999: "'They asked us,' Griffey says about the ballpark design, 'but I don't know if they listened. They did what they wanted to.'"

5. "Decade after 9/11, 'God Bless America' Still Part of Baseball Experience," Associated

Press, August 11, 2011; "America's Song," *Washington Post*, September 9, 2021, https://tinyurl.com/3ekjf75u.

6. David Shields, "Being Ichiro," *New York Times Magazine,* September 16, 2001, https://tinyurl.com/29ndunt8.

7. S. L. Price, "The Ichiro Paradox," *Sports Illustrated,* July 8, 2002, https://tinyurl.com/ym5cyf32.

8. Glenn Nelson, "Race and Ichiro's Muddled Mariners Legacy," *The Buzz: Glenn Nelson*, July 24, 2012, https://tinyurl.com/2p96p82t.

Extra Innings

1. Sports records compiled from the sports-reference.com constellation of websites; "Memorable Moments Inside the Kingdome," *Seattle Post-Intelligencer*, March 27, 2000, 46; stats pulled from Phil Loubere, "Defying Gravity," *Seattle Times*, March 19, 2000, https://tinyurl.com/yeyvjjet.

2. "Dome's Final Roar—Crowd Raises Last Cheer," *Seattle Times*, March 27, 2000, A1; Lewis Kamb and Aliya Saperstein, "After the Blast, Treasure the Treasure Hunt," *Seattle Post-Intelligencer,* March 27, 2000, 15.

3. Janet Burkitt, Caitlin Cleary, and Ferdinand M. de Leon, "As Walls Tumble, Seattle Parties," *Seattle Times*, March 27, 2000, A7; Vanessa Ho, "By Land and by Sea, Far-Flung Crowds Take in the View," *Seattle Post-Intelligencer*, March 27, 2000, 1.

4. Ron C. Judd, "Dome's Demise Filled Local Airwaves," *Seattle Times*, March 27, 2000, D1.

5. Burkitt, Cleary, and de Leon, "As Walls Tumble, Seattle Parties."

6. Nicole Brodeur, "Kingdome Blast Will Push Some Out," *Seattle Times*, March 19, 2000, B1

7. Aliya Saperstein and Robert L. Jamieson Jr., "Down and Dirty," *Seattle Post-Intelligencer*, March 27, 2000, 1; "The Big Tumble Makes a Rumble," *Seattle Post-Intelligencer,* March 27, 2000, A13.

8. Kim Murphy, "The Decline and Fall of Seattle," *Los Angeles Times,* August 4, 2002, https://tinyurl.com/2cdv2dkj.

9. "Dome's Final Roar—Crowd Raises Last Cheer," *Seattle Times*, March 27, 2000, A1.

10. "Seattle's Dome, Age 24, Relic of a Bygone Day," *Seattle Times*, March 26, 2000, B6.

11. James Lyons, *Selling Seattle: Representing Contemporary Urban America* (New York: Wallflower Press, 2004), 5–23.

12. David Brooks, "The Rise of the Latte Town," *Washington Examiner*, September 15, 1997, https://www.washingtonexaminer.com/weekly-standard/the-rise-of-the-latte-town.

13. Brooks, "Rise of the Latte Town."

14. Geoffrey Nunberg, *Talking Right* (New York: PublicAffairs, 2007); Jon Kelly, "Why Are Lattes Associated with Liberals," *BBC News,* October 6, 2014.

15. Jean Godden, "It'll Cost Us to Get into Name Game," *Seattle Times*, August 1, 1999, B1; "Surfers to Slammers, Naming Our WNBA Team," *Seattle Times*, June 13, 1999, B2.

16. Janet Bunyan, "The Modern Woman," *Seattle Post-Intelligencer*, November 28, 1915, 46.

17. "Hockeyettes Show Skill at Pastime," *Seattle Times*, February 11, 1917, 29.

18. Pamela Grundy and Susan Shackelford, *Shattering the Glass: The Remarkable History of Women's Basketball* (New York: New Press, 2005), 125.

19. "The Black Gender Gap in Educational Attainment: Historical Trends and Racial Comparisons," *Demography*, 2011, cited in https://journalistsresource.org/economics /black-gender-gap-college/ (accessed June 27, 2022).

20. Kimberlé Crenshaw, "Demarginalizing the Intersection of Race and Sex," *University of Chicago Legal Forum* 1 (1989): 163.

21. Jayda Evans, "To Threatt, It's Not Too Late," *Seattle Times*, May 14, 2000, C14.

22. Evans, "To Threatt, It's Not Too Late."

23. Sheldon Spencer, "Team U.S.A. Takes U.W. to School," *Seattle Post-Intelligencer*, November 29, 1995, C1; Dick Rockney, "Simply the Best," *Seattle Times*, November 28, 1995, D1.

24. Steve Kelley, "Storm Has Cause for Celebration," *Seattle Times*, June 2, 2000, D1.

25. Kelley, "Storm Has Cause for Celebration."

26. Jayda Evans, "Storm Is One of First with Gay Pride Night," *Seattle Times*, June 23, 2000, D1.

27. Exley quoted in David Remnick, "Passions Run Deep for Devoted Giants Fans," *Washington Post*, October 26, 1991, https://tinyurl.com/49msd54n.

28. Sean Gregory, "The Science of Sound: How Seattle Got So Darn Loud," *Time*, September 27, 2013; Elliott Almond, "Stadium Plan Here Not Best or Worst," *Seattle Times*, June 4, 1997, A1.

29. Chris Serb, *War Football: World War I and the Birth of the NFL* (Washington, DC: Rowman & Littlefield, 2019), 73.

30. Jesse Berrett, *Pigskin Nation: How the NFL Remade American Politics* (Champaign: University of Illinois Press, 2018), 208.

31. Erik Lacitis, "On Lawns and on Street Corners, This Is the Sign," *Seattle Times*, January 14, 2003, E1.

32. Shaun Scott, "Remembering 9/11: The Inextricable Link between Football, War," *Sports Illustrated*, September 9, 2016.

33. José Miguel Romero, "Made in Washington," *Seattle Times*, January 21, 2006, D1; Greg Bishop, "His Commitment Goes beyond Field," *Seattle Times*, February 4, 2006, D8; "Seahawks' Fisher Finds Military Tour Sobering," espn.com, April 7, 2006; "Seahawks Defensive End Fisher Charged with Assault," espn.com, June 1, 2006.

34. Fisher quoted in "Seahawk End Takes Oath," Associated Press, November 3, 2005, https://tinyurl.com/yc7r4jxt; "USO," nfl.com, https://tinyurl.com/3z34czux (accessed June 27, 2022).

35. "Air Guardsman Soars into Super Bowl XL," *Air Force News*, January 25, 2006, https://tinyurl.com/yfexycmk; "Seahawks Defensive End Fisher Charged with Assault," espn.com, June 1, 2006; Danny O'Neil, "Assault Charge Dropped against Seahawks Defensive End Fisher," *Seattle Times*, February 22, 2007.

36. Steve Bisheff, "Bettis Is the Story of Super Bowl Week," *Orange County Register*, https://tinyurl.com/ysk4ny9v (accessed June 27, 2020).

37. Joshua Hayes, "Steelers vs. Seahawks: Examining the Controversial Calls of Super Bowl XL," *Bleacher Report*, September 27, 2011, https://tinyurl.com/fu75psyu.

38. "Pulse: Bad Calls!," espn.com, February 6, 2006, https://tinyurl.com/ycktrpfu.

39. John Thorn, "Forget What You Know about the Black Sox Scandal," *New York Times*, October 9, 2019.

40. Dan E. Moldea, *Interference: How Organized Crime Influences Professional Football* (New York: William Morrow, 1989); the first chapter of this book is available at www.moldea.com/nfl.html (accessed December 30, 2022).

41. Lance Pugmire, "Donaghy Pleads Guilty in Scheme," *Los Angeles Times*, August 26, 2007, https://tinyurl.com/42vr6v7b.

42. "Condoleezza Is Super Bowl Bound," Associated Press, February 1, 2006, https://tinyurl.com/muewbpnb.

43. Jayda Evans, "Dunn Has Eye on Bird as First Pick in Draft," *Seattle Times*, April 18, 2002, D1.

44. Jeff Goldberg, *Bird at the Buzzer: UConn, Notre Dame, and a Women's Basketball Classic* (Lincoln: University of Nebraska Press, 2013), loc. 149, Kindle.

45. Rocker as quoted in Jeff Pearlman, "At Full Blast," *Sports Illustrated*, December 27, 1999, https://tinyurl.com/5dcyvs93.

46. Bush quoted in Associated Press, "President Calls Abortion Fight a 'Noble Cause,'" NBC News, January 23, 2006, https://tinyurl.com/mt7kw8z6.

47. Steve Kelley, "Punishment Is the Crime in Sue's Bet with Mitch," *Seattle Times*, July 20, 2003, D1.

48. Kelley, "Punishment Is the Crime."

49. Associated Press, "Bird Changed Mind Following Senator's Response," espn.com, July 22, 2002, https://tinyurl.com/3v9x7nju.

50. Levy as quoted in Associated Press, "Bird Changed Mind Following Senator's Response."

51. Jayda Evans, "Artistic Photos of Jackson May Stir Up a Storm of Controversy," *Seattle Times*, June 18, 2004, E1.

52. "Report: Japan publication offered $1m for naked photo," espn.com, April 15, 2001, https://tinyurl.com/2t86mz4a; David Shields, *New York Times Magazine*, September 16, 2001, https://tinyurl.com/2t86mz4a.

53. Les Carpenter, "Storm Title Would Give Seattle . . . ," *Seattle Times*, October 12, 2004, D1.

54. Kristen Lappas's 2022 documentary *Dream On* deals somewhat with racism and privilege in the coverage of women's basketball, with many Black players feeling as if Rebecca Lobo was retained on the 1996 USA women's basketball team at least in part because of her marketability to white fans.

55. Jayda Evans, "Globetrotters: WNBA Players Spending Offseason Overseas," *Seattle Times*, May 19, 2005, https://tinyurl.com/yxdbrc49; Jayda Evans, "Westlake Crowd Salutes Storm," *Seattle Times*, October 16, 2004, D3.

56. Blaine Newnham, "Storm Title Blurred by Reality of WNBA Economics," *Seattle Times*, October 20, 2004, C2.

57. Jayda Evans, "Westlake Crowd Salutes Storm," *Seattle Times*, October 16, 2004, D3.

58. Dave Zirin, *Bad Sports: How Owners Are Ruining the Games We Love* (New York: New Press, 2010), 65.

59. Dave Zirin, "Economics, Race, and the N.B.A. Lockout," *New Yorker*, October 24, 2011, https://tinyurl.com/5xj2c7hw.

60. Zirin, *Bad Sports*, 63.

61. Jordan Ritter Conn, "How the Hornets and Hurricane Katrina Paved the Way for the OKC Thunder," *The Ringer*, October 24, 2019, https://tinyurl.com/muabyz6a.

62. Schoenfeld as quoted in Zirin, *Bad Sports*, 62.

63. Molly Yanity, "Storm Deal 'Driven by the Enthusiasm of the Fans," *Seattle Post-Intelligencer*, January 9, 2008, A1.

64. Paul Waldman, "Gay Rights Opponents' Last Argument," CNN, March 29, 2013, https://tinyurl.com/bdevfw9a; "Leaders: Nickles, Largent," *The Oklahoman*, July 16, 1996, https://tinyurl.com/y9uvb54e.

65. Jon Finkel, *Hoops Heist: Seattle, the Sonics, and How a Stolen Team's Legacy Gave Rise to the NBA's Secret Empire* (Seattle: Slow Grind Media, 2020), 190–92.

66. Kevin Durant quoted in Jon Finkel, *Hoops Heist*, 192.

67. Greg Johns, "Licata Regrets His 'Flip Remark' about Cultural Value of Sonics," *Seattle Post-Intelligencer*, March 23, 2011, https://tinyurl.com/ybf8zyed; "What's the Matter with Washington Athletics," *Washington Alumnus*, October 1908, 10.

68. Bill Simmons, "Ready for a Sub-.500 Playoff Team?," espn.com, September 24, 2010, https://tinyurl.com/5actrne2.

69. Kirsten Grind, *The Lost Bank: The Story of Washington Mutual—The Biggest Bank Failure in American History* (New York: Simon and Schuster, 2012).

70. Roth quoted in "Sounders FC by Fans' Acclamation," *Seattle Post-Intelligencer*, April 8, 2008, 17.

71. Beck quoted in Dave Zirin, "Glenn Beck's Blues: Why the Far Right Hates the World Cup," *The Nation*, June 14, 2010, https://tinyurl.com/2p98jwpb.

72. Chuck Klosterman, *Sex, Drugs, and Cocoa Puffs: A Low Culture Manifesto* (New York: Scribner, 2003), 94.

73. See the ESPN special *Beautiful Game Turned Ugly: Racism in Europe's Soccer Arenas*, https://www.youtube.com/watch?v=W-iRLmaZf4A (accessed June 27, 2022); Jay Caspian Kang, "The Dark Side of American Soccer Culture," *New York Times*, July 17, 2016, https://tinyurl.com/mujjd8ax.

74. Thomas Frank, *What's the Matter with Kansas? How Conservatives Won the Heart of America* (New York: Henry Holt, 2005), 16.

75. Brooks, "Rise of the Latte Town"; David Brooks, "One Nation, Slightly Divisible," *The Atlantic*, December 2001, https://tinyurl.com/yambp4s4.

Rally

1. "Remarks by the President Honoring the Super Bowl Champion Seattle Seahawks," whitehouse.gov, May 21, 2014, https://tinyurl.com/bduf4m6p.

2. "Remarks by the President Honoring the Super Bowl Champion Seattle Seahawks."

3. Jerry Brewer, *Pass Judgment: Inside the Settle Seahawks' Super Bowl XLIX Season and the Play That Dashed a Dream,* loc. 92, 60, Kindle.

4. Allen quoted in Pete Carroll, *Win Forever: Live, Work, and Play Like a Champion* (Portfolio, 2014), loc. 12, 445, Kindle.

5. Quoted in Chris Tomasson, "Seahawks Coach Pete Carroll Came Close to Being the Vikings' QB for 1987 Strike Replacement Games," twincities.com, October 7, 2020, https://tinyurl.com/2tnxnuzd.

6. Alyssa Roenigk, "NFL: Seahawks' New Practice Techniques." espn.com, August 21, 2013, https://tinyurl.com/5yte4s39.

7. Brewer, *Pass Judgment*, loc. 92, Kindle.

8. Robin Wright, "The Mask That Inspired the Seahawks Logo," burkemuseum.org, January 28, 2014, https://tinyurl.com/bdzhfrk9.

9. Stephen Mihm, "How the Department of Defense Bankrolled Silicon Valley," *New York Times*, July 9, 2019; Charles Piller, "'Evil Empire' Is Unlikely to Fall, but Competition Is at the Gates," *Los Angeles Times*, April 5, 1999; Mike Ricciuti, "Can Sun-Microsoft Cease-fire Halt the War?," cnet.com, April 6, 2004, https://tinyurl.com/mrtvftmc; "America's 50 Best Cities," *Bloomberg*, September 28, 2012, https://tinyurl.com/45rhja7w.

10. John Breech, "49ers Fans Not Happy That New SF Transit Seats Are Seahawks Colors," CBS Sports, April 18, 2014, https://tinyurl.com/mrxt2759.

11. Love Bettina L. and Brandelyn Tosoly, "Reality or Rhetoric? Barack Obama and Post-Racial America," *Race, Gender & Class Journal* 17, nos. 3–4 (2010): 19–37.

12. Cindy Boren, "Richard Sherman Frustrated by Reaction, Equates 'Thug' with Racial Slur," *Washington Post*, January 23, 2014, https://tinyurl.com/3y3hup62; Stephen A. Crockett Jr., "Column: Stop Calling Richard Sherman a Thug," *Denver Post*, January 22, 2014, https://tinyurl.com/bdzus82k.

13. Josh Katzowitz, "Time Names Richard Sherman One of the Most 100 Influential People," CBS Sports, https://tinyurl.com/335b47r7 (accessed June 29, 2022).

14. Steve Phillips, *Brown Is the New White: How the Demographic Revolution Has Created a New American Majority*, revised and updated ed. (New York: New Press, 2018), loc. 127, Kindle.

15. Kate Rogers and Nick Well, "Seattle Passed a $15 Minimum Wage Law in 2014. Here's How It's Turned Out So Far," CNBC, January 2, 2020, https://tinyurl.com /29m5hnxp.

16. David Steele, "The Truth about Marshawn Lynch from the 1-Yard Line," *Sporting News*, February 4, 2015, https://tinyurl.com/3mwdmsf7.

17. Scott Davis, "Bombshell ESPN Report Says Patriots' 'Spygate' Scandal Was Way Worse Than People Realized," *Business Insider*, September 2015, https://www.business insider.com/espn-report-patriots-spygate-scandal-2015-9.

18. "Super Bowl XLIX: New England Patriots vs Seattle Seahawks Odds—NFL—February 1, 2015," gambletron2000.com, https://www.gambletron2000.com/nfl/11502/super -bowl-xlix-new-england-patriots-vs-seattle-seahawks (accessed June 29, 2022).

19. Brewer, *Pass Judgment*, loc. 68, Kindle.

20. Tom Pelissero, "Oakland Roots Created Marshawn Lynch's 'Beast Mode,'" *USA Today*, January 15, 2014, https://tinyurl.com/mphvf82f.

21. Dave Zirin, "The Conspiracy Theory Surrounding the Seahawks' Last Play," *The Nation*, https://tinyurl.com/ycxa7w5f (accessed December 31, 2022).

22. Luke Whelan, "Kayaktavists Take Over Seattle's Port to Protest Shell Oil's Arctic Drilling Rig," *Mother Jones*, May 17, 2015, https://tinyurl.com/2dvv3e92.

23. "Seattle City Council Votes against Area for Arena," *Sports Illustrated*, https://tinyurl.com/ym9r9vc6 (accessed June 29, 2022); Kshama Sawant, "My Remarks on the Occidental Street Vacation," https://tinyurl.com/4err28jy (accessed June 29, 2022); Doug Trumm, "City Council Rejects Hansen's Street Vacation Request," *The Urbanist*, May 3, 2016, https://tinyurl.com/d8pp4vmu.

24. "This Is Clearly Not about Basketball," *Seattlish*, May 3, 2016, https://tinyurl.com/3byptkj7.

25. Rob Ketcherside, "True Story: Trump's Family Roots in Seattle," *Crosscut*, July 20, 2016, https://tinyurl.com/smnhrw5p; Jaclyn Anglis, "Donald Trump's Illegal Emigrant Grandfather Was Banished from Germany for Dodging the Draft," *All That's Interesting*, December 28, 2021, https://tinyurl.com/2a53m6bf; Bryan Armen Graham, "Donald Trump Wanted a Fight with Athletes. They May Well Have Doomed Him," *The Guardian*, November 9, 2020, https://tinyurl.com/58f8anth.

26. Samuel Stein, *Capital City: Gentrification and the Real Estate State* (New York: Verso Books, 2019), 118–23.

27. "Remembering . . . STICKBALL!" Tenement Museum, April 16, 2020, https://tinyurl.com/yc8xe48c.

28. Glenn Kessler, "Robert Moses and the Saga of the Racist Parkway Bridges," *Washington Post*, November 10, 2021, https://tinyurl.com/3xzt6ewn; James C. McKinley Jr., "Officers Rally and Dinkins Is Their Target," *New York Times*, September 17, 1992; Laura Nahmias, "The Forgotten City Hall Riot," *New York Magazine*, October 4, 2021.

29. Jeff Pearman, "At Full Blast," *Sports Illustrated*, December 27, 1999, https://tinyurl.com/5dcyvs93; Michael Cooper, "Giuliani Announces a Program to Reduce Illegal Drug Use," *New York Times*, October 2, 1997, https://tinyurl.com/5wjnebfv.

30. "Executive Order: Enhancing Public Safety in the Interior of the United States—The White House," https://tinyurl.com/yck55z8w (accessed June 29, 2022).

31. Loren Collingwood and Benjamin Gonzalez O'Brien, *Sanctuary Cities: The Politics of Refuge* (Oxford, UK: Oxford University Press, 2019), 28; Thomas Fuller, "San Francisco Sues Trump over 'Sanctuary Cities' Order, *New York Times*, January 31, 2017; Daniel Beekman, "Seattle Sues Trump Administration over 'Sanctuary Cities' Order," *Seattle Times*, March 29, 2017.

32. Latria Graham, "Michael Bennett's NFL Black Power Salute Could Change Sports Protest," *The Guardian*, September 19, 2017, https://tinyurl.com/2xhctp9h; Dave Zirin, *The Kaepernick Effect: Taking a Knee, Changing the World* (New York: New Press, 2021).

33. Tricia Romano, "Seahawks So Woke," *Rolling Stone*, December 14, 2017, https://tinyurl.com/e2sb8yn3; Les Carpenter, "How the Seattle Seahawks Became the NFL's Most Outspoken Team," *The Guardian*, December 15, 2016, https://tinyurl.com/muw6cbnz.

34. "No, Michael Bennett Did Not Burn an American Flag in Seahawks Locker Room," Q13 News, September 29, 2017, https://tinyurl.com/trb4jzjm.

35. "Megan Rapinoe Refuses to Back Down over Donald Trump and White House," *The Guardian*, June 27, 2019, https://tinyurl.com/5a7spphu; Bryan Armen Graham, "Donald

Trump Wanted a Fight with Athletes. They May Well Have Doomed Him," *The Guardian*, November 9, 2020, https://tinyurl.com/58f8anth; Tyler Tynes, "The Minnesota Lynx's Day of Service Didn't Need the White House," sbnation.com, June 6, 2018, https://tinyurl.com/yz9n9hn6; Ben Church and Don Riddell, "Bird Remembers When Trump Targeted Girlfriend Rapinoe," CNN, https://tinyurl.com/5n8mztcm (accessed June 29, 2022).

36. Facts about US presidents, athletics, and ableism compiled from a number of sources. Dean Knetter, "How Theordore Roosevelt Helped Create America's Sports Culture," wpr.org, August 20, 2019, https://tinyurl.com/ybwsru8a; Tom Porter, "How FDR kept his partial paralysis a secret," *Business Insider*, May 10, 2019, https://tinyurl.com/5n7uvdu2; Howard Markel, "John F. Kennedy Kept These Medical Struggles Private," PBS, November 22, 2019, https://tinyurl.com/3ke7p98b; Richard L. Berke, "Politicians Find Jogging with Clinton Is No Stroll in the Park," *New York Times*, July 26, 1993, https://tinyurl.com/5yzdaf4t; Leander Schaerlaeckens, "Was Donald Trump Good at Baseball," *Slate*, May 5, 2020, https://tinyurl.com/bden7bcv.

37. Lisa Donavan, "President Trump Calls Chicago, New York 'Stupidly Run' When Fox News Host Asked about Violent Crime in Both Cities," *Chicago Tribune*, July 17, 2020, https://tinyurl.com/msr78u76.

38. Daniel Beekman and Justin Mayor, "Jenny Durkan Topped Cary Moon in Most Seattle Precincts," *Seattle Times*, November 11, 2017.

39. Quoted in Brian Robinson, "Mayor Jenny Durkan Is a Sports Fan Who Prioritizes Bringing the Sonics Back," *Sonics Rising*, January 18, 2018, https://tinyurl.com/2862m2pw.

40. Geoff Baker, "The Closer: How Mayor Durkan Helped Convince NHL Execs to Recommend Seattle Expansion," *The Spokesman-Review*, October 3, 2018, https://tinyurl.com/aajvuzcy.

41. Ashley Stewart, "Amazon, Vulcan, and CenturyLink Top List of Donors," *Business Journal*, November 2, 2017, https://tinyurl.com/4papyd6w.

42. "Teresa Mosqueda Archives," *PubliCola*, https://tinyurl.com/4jbukvt9 (accessed June 29, 2022): "It should also be noted that were it not for JumpStart in 2020, we would have faced an austerity budget. In 2022 and beyond, funding is dedicated to the areas noted in the codified spend plan which will create a more resilient and equitable economy."

43. "This Is the First Time in Three Years Anybody Has Asked Me about Pickleball," *Seattle Metro Pickleball*, October 25, 2020, https://tinyurl.com/4rhtmczc.

44. Benjamin Maritz and Dilip Wagle, "Homelessness in Seattle and Surrounds: Why Does King County Face a Crisis?," https://tinyurl.com/dvx4m5f7 (accessed June 29, 2022); "Homeless in Seattle: 'Each Year, the Numbers Keep Rising,'" *Real Change News*, https://tinyurl.com/2t24v4wv (accessed June 29, 2022).

45. Emma Prestwich, "Badass Runner Fights Off Attacker in Public Washroom." *HuffPost*, March 13, 2017, https://tinyurl.com/5n6b6mkd; Nicole Jennings, "Woman Attacked while Running at Green Lake Warns Other Joggers," mynorthwest.com, October 2, 2018, https://tinyurl.com/4nv6zmad.

46. Mike Rosenberg, "King County Council Approves $135 Million in Taxpayer Funds," *Seattle Times,* September 5, 2018, https://tinyurl.com/bfd5sh4e; Menola Secaira, "Despite Criticism, King County Council Gives Mariners $135M," *Crosscut*, September 17, 2018, https://tinyurl.com/24h8u93h.

47. Geoff Baker and Mike Baker, "Mariners Execs Faced Workplace Complaints," *Seattle Times*, July 25, 2018, https://tinyurl.com/yjusz7eh.

48. Daniel Beekman and Lewis Kamb, "Texts by Seattle Mayor, Council Member Shed Light on Head-Tax Repeal," *The Spokesman-Review*, https://tinyurl.com/msyk4mb4 (accessed June 29, 2022); Lewis Kamb, "Seattle Agrees to Pay $35,000 to Settle Lawsuit Alleging City Council Broke Open Meetings Law over Head Tax Repeal," *Seattle Times*, October 19, 2020, https://tinyurl.com/2p845nyh.

49. Tara Law, "Seattle Mayor Responds to President Trump: My City 'Isn't Afraid of Immigrants,'" *Time*, April 13, 2019, https://tinyurl.com/2c5h3myy.

50. Lisa Edge, "Despite the Data, the 'Freeattle' Myth Persists," *Real Change News*, December 27, 2017, https://tinyurl.com/2y2wzpj8; David Kroman, "Survey Says Seattle Is Not 'Freeattle,'" *Crosscut*, March 2, 2017, https://tinyurl.com/ytjzkzyd.

51. Edge, "Despite the Data, the 'Freeattle' Myth Persists."

52. Matt Watson, "How Conservative Anti-Homeless Groups Are Rebranding to Recruit New Members," *Medium*, April 20, 2019, https://tinyurl.com/4syshamw; the *Seattle Times* Editorial Board, "Seattle Should Reject Head Tax on Jobs," *Seattle Times*, April 20, 2018, https://tinyurl.com/32325629.

53. Paul Kiernan, "Conservative Activist Grabbed Trump's Eye on Diversity Training," *Wall Street Journal*, October 9, 2020; Benjamin Wallace-Wells, "How a Conservative Activist Invented the Conflict over Critical Race Theory," *New Yorker*, June 18, 2021.

54. "The Undoing of Our Public Lands and National Parks," National Parks Conservation Association, January 21, 2021, https://tinyurl.com/4x4arzaj; Emily Holden, Jimmy Tobias, and Alvin Chang, "Revealed: The Full Extent of Trump's 'Meat Cleaver' Assault on US Wilderness," *The Guardian,* October 26, 2020, https://tinyurl.com/5n6thpmj; Wes Siler, "The Trump Presidency Is the Worst Ever for Public Lands," outsideonline.com, May 29, 2020, https://tinyurl.com/3dceu77t.

55. Dae Shik Kim Hawkins Jr. and Guy Oron, "Seattle Spent over $10 Million on Homeless Sweeps in 2017," *South Seattle Emerald*, May 15, 2018, https://tinyurl.com/2m6csz7k; Benjamin Maritz and Dilip Wagle, "Homelessness in Seattle and Surrounds: Why Does King County Face a Crisis?," https://tinyurl.com/mrwp4njr (accessed June 29, 2022).

56. Manifesto in Henri Lefebvre, *Writings on Cities* (Hoboken, NJ: Blackwell Publishers, 1996).

57. Daniel Beekman, "Yard Sign for Seattle City Council Candidate Spray-Painted with Racial Slur, Drawing Condemnation," *Seattle Times*, October 30, 2019, https://tinyurl.com/25y7n9up.

58. Per data from the Seattle Ethics & Elections Commission (SEEC), Mariners CEO Kevin Mather and team partner Christopher Larson contributed a combined $7,000 to the corporate political action committee "People for Seattle"—see donation data at the following links: https://tinyurl.com/2unwufp2 (accessed December 29, 2022); https://tinyurl.com/hz8pdb7f (accessed December 29, 2022). Full list of donors for election cycle is searchable at SEEC website, https://tinyurl.com/4ss32frh (accessed December 29, 2022).

59. Daniel Beekman, "What Are the Political Lines in Your Seattle Neighborhood?," *Seattle Times*, December 4, 2019, https://tinyurl.com/yzwjsnr6.

60. Christopher Rufo, "The Dangerous New Idea Inspiring Criminal-Justice Activists," *New York Post,* December 28, 2019, https://tinyurl.com/9f4cdnf7.

61. Sandra Haarsager, *Bertha Knight Landes of Seattle: Big-City Mayor* (Norman: University of Oklahoma Press, 1994), 110–15.

62. Jane Jacobs, *Vital Little Plans: The Short Works of Jane Jacobs*, edited by Samuel Zipp and Nathan Storring (New York: Random House, 2016), 133.

63. Norm Stamper, *Breaking Rank: A Top Cop's Exposé of the Dark Side of American Policing* (New York: Bold Type Books, 2005), 33.

64. Research compiled at Shaun Scott for D4 Twitter thread, April 17, 2019, https://tinyurl.com/29dh595v (accessed December 31, 2022). Data comes from King County Assessor's public database, linked at Shaun Scott for D4 Twitter thread, April 17, 2019; Scott Hanson, "Seattle Considering What to Do with 4 Public Golf Courses," *Seattle Times*, June 6, 2019.

65. Katherine Anne Long, "Are Seattle's Exclusive Private Golf Courses Getting a Huge Tax Break?," *Seattle Times*, June 20, 2020, https://tinyurl.com/2jy42ykb.

66. Jon Marmor, "Progress Spelled Doom for Old University Golf Course," *UW Magazine*, March 1, 1999, https://tinyurl.com/y2487rdm.

67. Mike Davis, *Old Gods, New Enigmas: Marx's Lost Theory* (New York: Verso Books, 2018), loc. 3559, Kindle.

68. "What's the Matter with Washington Athletics," *Washington Alumnus*, October 1908, 10; "History of Voter-Approved Plans," Sound Transit, https://tinyurl.com/ma3aupme (accessed June 29, 2022).

69. Davarian L. Baldwin, *In the Shadow of the Ivory Tower: How Universities Are Plundering Our Cities* (New York: Bold Type Books, 2021), 7.

70. "The Economic Contribution of the University of Washington to the Statewide and Local Economies," University of Washington, November 2019, http://tinyurl.com/yc558ppc.

71. For more on biopolitics and the blood industry, see Kathleen McLaughlin, *Blood Money: The Story of Life, Death, and Profit Inside America's Blood Industry* (New York: Atria/One Signal Publishers, 2023).

72. Paige Browning, "Pay Student Athletes, WA Lawmaker Says. The NCAA Makes Millions off Them," KUOW, January 24, 2019, https://tinyurl.com/2zdkyauc; HB 1084 2019-20: Concerning Unfair Practices Involving Compensation of Athletes in Higher Education, Washington State Legislature, https://tinyurl.com/4kax4h9x (accessed June 29, 2022).

73. Browning, "Pay Student Athletes, WA Lawmaker Says."

18th Inning

1. "Astros Top Mariners," Associated Press, October 15, 2022, https://tinyurl.com/ynsmuj6t.

2. Tony Schick and Jes Burns, "Despite What the Logging Industry Says, Cutting Down Trees Isn't Stopping Catastrophic Wildfires," Oregon Public Broadcasting, October 31, 2020, https://tinyurl.com/5ycd93wt.

3. Chris Priest, "Mayor Durkan Cancels 35th Ave NE Bike Lanes," *The Urbanist,* March 26, 2019, https://tinyurl.com/2w2efnvu.

4. Mike Lindblom, "West Seattle Bridge Reopened Saturday Night," *Seattle Times*, September 18, 2022, https://tinyurl.com/sawmnnun.

5. Jed Kolko, "U.S. Population Density Went Up in the 2010s," *New York Times*, September 5, 2021, 16.

6. Kristen Gowdy, "Mariners to Appear on 'Sunday Night Baseball' for First Time since 2004," *Seattle Times*, July 15, 2016, https://tinyurl.com/4bu9yp8d.

7. "Neighbors to Get Acquainted, Seattleites Urged to 'Thaw,'" *Seattle Daily Times*, March 26, 1920, 1.

8. This happened; I was there, in attendance, at the Game 3 overtime thriller on September 4, 2022.

9. Baseball payroll statistics compiled from "Fueled by Sports," https://tinyurl.com /2a5h72rk (accessed December 29, 2022); stats corroborated at "MLB Payrolls," http:// www.stevetheump.com/Payrolls.htm (accessed December 29, 2022).

10. "A Timeline of COVID-19 Developments in 2020," *AJMC*, January 1, 2021, https:// tinyurl.com/33dd96mb.

11. Sande LaMotte, "No Need to Wipe Down Groceries or Takeout, Experts Say, but Do Wash Your Hands," CNN, April 26, 2020, https://tinyurl.com/mpm2afv6.

12. "COVID Incidence, Mortality Rates Remain Much Higher in Rural Areas," University of Iowa College of Public Health, December 8, 2021, https://tinyurl.com/4kuybs4z.

13. "Visual Timeline of the Day That Changed Everything: March 11," espn.com, March 11, 2021, https://tinyurl.com/5b8n6rv2.

14. Labor statistics pulled from a variety of sources, chiefly the Bureau of Labor Statistics and others. All websites accessed on June 25, 2022. On 2.7 million grocery workers in September 2019, see "2.7 million grocery store workers in September 2019," https://tinyurl .com/ytmjrem4; on 1.7 million rideshare drivers in 2022, see "1.7 million rideshare drivers," https://tinyurl.com/y3bb43ns; on 5.3 million nurses, see "5.3 million nurses," https:// tinyurl.com/mry67sh6; on 16.7 million leisure and hospitality workers and 24.3 million in education and health services, see "10 facts about workers," https://tinyurl.com/mrjsu6dx.

15. April Berthene, "Coronavirus Pandemic Adds $219 Billion to US Ecommerce Sales in 2020–2021," *Digital Commerce 360*, https://tinyurl.com/bcdujfd9 (accessed June 26, 2022).

16. Edward L. Glaeser and David M. Cutler, *The Survival of the City: Human Flourishing in an Age of Isolation* (New York: Penguin Press, 2021), 4.

17. Juliana Kaplan, "The Year Workers Said 'No,'" *Business Insider*, https://tinyurl.com /yyxtwvhu (accessed June 26, 2022).

18. Starbucks workers rallied at a picket I attended on August 23, 2022, where the Super-Sonics sign was seen; Shaun Scott, Twitter, August 23, 2022, https://tinyurl.com/55266kxj.

19. Gérard Duménil and Dominique Lévy, *Managerial Capitalism: Ownership, Management and the Coming New Mode of Production* (London: Pluto Press, 2018), 221.

20. William J. Nass, "Sick's Stadium: The Other Days of Summer by William J. Nass," HistoryLink, May 10, 2012, https://www.historylink.org/file/10108.

21. Tom Warren, "The NBA Is Using Microsoft Teams to Bring Basketball Fans Courtside," *The Verge*, July 24, 2020, https://www.theverge.com/2020/7/24/21337326/nba -microsoft-teams-together-mode-basketball-virtual-experience-fans.

22. Mirin Fader, *Giannis: The Improbable Rise of an NBA MVP* (New York: Hachette Books, 2021).

23. Molly Hensley-Clancy, "Parenting in the Bubble: 'This Is Mom's Job. You Have to Work with Me,'" *New York Times*, July 16, 2020, https://tinyurl.com/5n8yhmnz.

24. Orlando Silva, "Sue Bird vs. LeBron James Comparison: $215K vs. $37.44M Salary, $11K vs. $370K Bonus for 2020 Championship" *Fadeaway World*, https://tinyurl.com/2mtfza7b (accessed June 26, 2022).

25. Christopher T. Bayley, *Seattle Justice: The Rise and Fall of the Police Payoff System in Seattle* (Seattle: Sasquatch Books, 2015), 27.

26. Alfred Holman, "Seattle Ably Run by Woman Mayor," *New York Times*, July 4, 1926.

27. See Washington State ACLU's "Timeline about Police Accountability" in Seattle, https://tinyurl.com/5f3chw62 (accessed June 26, 2022).

28. "Seattle Mayor, 2 Councilmembers Share Unified Approach in Efforts to Pass Hiring Incentives for SPD," FOX 13 Seattle, May 9, 2022, https://tinyurl.com/56f8mj9t; Andrew Jeong, "Seattle Elects Republican as City Attorney, Rejecting Police Abolitionist Who Celebrated Property Destruction," *Washington Post*, November 6, 2021, https://tinyurl.com/4xuxftc9.

29. Roger Sale, *Seattle, Past to Present* (Seattle: University of Washington Press, 2019), 125.

30. Daniel Beekman, "What Are the Political Lines in Your Seattle Neighborhood?," *Seattle Times*, December 4, 2019, https://tinyurl.com/yzwjsnr6.

31. Editorial Board, "Vote no on Seattle Initiative 135 for 'social housing,'" *Seattle Times*, January 20, 2023, https://tinyurl.com/22pytdp6.

32. Reported on by Erica C. Barnett, Twitter, October 12, 2022, https://tinyurl.com/ycy8r73n.

33. Joan Wallach Scott, *On the Judgment of History* (New York: Columbia University Press, 2020), xi.

34. Scott, *On the Judgment of History*, 82.

35. James Longhurst, *Bike Battles: A History of Sharing the American Road* (Seattle: University of Washington Press, 2015), 59–67.

36. "An Object in Social Reform," *Appleton's Popular Science Monthly* 50 (January 1897): 306–9.

37. Randal Gravelle, *Hooverville and the Unemployed: Seattle during the Great Depression* (self-published, 2015), 80.

38. Bradley W. Wart, *Hitler's American Friends: The Third Reich's Supporters in the United States* (New York: St. Martin's Press, 2018), 57.

39. David Kroman, "Cities, Counties Push for New Bike and Pedestrian Money," *Seattle Times*, August 29, 2022, https://tinyurl.com/yckcb7xj.

40. Jabari Simama, "The Promise and Politics of Pickleball," *Governing*, December 21, 2022, https://tinyurl.com/2v2me3he.

INDEX

Italicized page numbers indicate illustrations.

Portland Trail Blazers, 108–10, 117, 252–53n18

prejudice, 40, 53, 54, 74, 177

Price v. Evergreen Cemetery Co. of Seattle (1960), 85

Professional Air Traffic Controllers (PATCO), 126, 127

Progressive Citizen's League, 53

Progressive Era, 26, 27, 35, 42, 55, 106, 135; activism of, xviii, 34; as age of reform, 10; ballparks of, 156; baseball and, 160; Black Seattle and, 32; "City Beautiful" movement and, 185; civic spaces of, 30, 64; end of, 22, 99, 175; Gilded Age and, 14, 53, 189; inclusivity of, 54; individualism and, 30; initiation of, 42; perks of, 14; playgrounds/parks and, 202; promise of, 21; public works and, 29; Seattle police and, 12; Seattle visibility during, 45; unions/social clubs and, 155; urban America and, 13; women athletes and, 170

progressivism, 41; conservatism and, xvi; described, 11–12, 14; end of, 53, 123, 156; fake, xix, 158; flaws in, 38, 221; political framework and, xviii; postwar, 57, 91; public works and, xxii; success for, 223

Prohibition, 41, 99

propaganda, 68, 203, 204

public housing, 91, 94, 99, 116

Puget, Peter, 47

Puget Sound, xi, xiii, xiv, 5, 6, 47, 59, 88, 107, 203; pioneers of, xii

Puget Sound Argus, 4

Puget Sound Dispatch, xi–xii, xv, 4

quarantines, 21, 212, 216, 219, 224

Quast, Anne, 93; US Women's Amateur Golf Championship, 93

Queen Anne, 30, 44, 77, 144

Queen City Cycle Club, 7

Queen City Good Roads Club, 7

Qwest Field, 174, 185

racial inequity, 72, 121

racial quotas, 24, 113–14

racism, xvi, 24, 25, 33, 73, 74, 186; capitalism and, 71–72; culture of, 220; institutional, 114, 206; resistance to, 116; reverse, 115, 120; structural, 122

Rademacher, Thomas Peter, 95; Patterson and, 78–79, 80, 81–82, 83–84

radicalism, xxi, 100, 128, 255n19

railroads, xi, xii, xxii, 1, 129, 226; timber and, xxiii

Ramsay, Jack, 109

Rapinoe, Megan, 200

Ravenna, 1

Ray, Dixy Lee, 123

Ray, Robbie, 213

Reagan, Ronald, 130, 155; football and, 126, 173; Friedman and, 137; frontier imagery and, 143; PATCO strike and, 126, 127; War on Drugs and, 131; welfare and, 141

Reds, xiv, xv

Red Scare (1919–20), 29, 33, 99, 128

Red Summer (1919), 33

Rice, Constance, *145*

Rice, Norm, 144, *145*

Riswold, Jim, 138–39

Robinson, Jackie, 72, 96, 108, 119, 140

Robinson, Nate, 183

Rodriguez, Alex, 161

Roosevelt, Franklin Delano, 73, 143, 188, 196, 200; Bonneville Dam and, 45; economic recovery and, 42; election of, 41; Japanese American removal and, 54

Roosevelt, Teddy, 11, 20, 26, 154, 200; and Progressive Party, 26

Rossellini, Albert, 79

Roth, Joe, 185

rowing, xxiii, 41, 48–49

Rowland, Chris, 113

Roy, Brandon, 183

Rufo, Christopher, 204, 206, 225

running, 93, 101–3

Rupp, Adolph, 78, 82, 83, 89, 100